The
Proposal

I like to dedicate this book to all species in existence today into eternity into infinity.

The Proposal
A New Arrival: Dao Buddha

By
Medusa D.B. Loveheart
The Last Warlock

~

Ancient Warlock
A New age Alchemist

Book cover made by Lesia T. on fiverr.com

Fourth edition
© Medusa Loveheart 2024
Förlag: BoD · Books on Demand, Stockholm, Sverige
Tryck: Libri Plureos GmbH, Hamburg, Tyskland
ISBN: 978-91-8080-003-7

Attention!
This book might just demolish the relative reality
you are living in today completely,
that said please do enjoy the reading.

¡VITAL INFORMATION¡

THE INFO FOLLOWING WITHIN VITAL
INFORMATION IS OUT OF UTTERLY IMPORTANCE
FOR YOU BUT NOT A MUST UNDERSTAND IN
ORDER FOR YOU TO CONTINUE READING THE
BOOK, HOWEVER YOU WILL MOST LIKELY READ
IT AGAIN AT LATER POINTS IN ORDER TO
REFRESH YOUR MEMORY

VERRY IMPORTANT INFORMATION

This is a very complex book to read mostly because of the nature of metaphysics, just like some movies there will be contexts and senses that won't be obvious until you have reached a certain point in this book. You will not be able to see: this books picture in completeness (this entire book and its purpose); until you have actually read the complete book in its completeness. That means that even: "this book's cover" is a part of this book in its very own picture of completeness.

This book contains a language in a bit different form of English in some places and I'd like to call it: "(-(>(.)<)-)Opposite<->Directional<-> Reggae<->English(-(>(.)<)-)" (where all the signs such as the following six −(.)<>

are pronounced with silence).
I usually like to shorten the expression to Directional Reggae English since opposite thinking is already a part of that tool.

The name of the common tongue for the bespoken form of English (the Directional Reggae English that is) in any tongue is by me defined as ORBish whereas many other people probably has gotten to understand it as Language of SOUL. There will be a more detailed description of how to understand it in my introduction and throughout this entire book, however if I don't provide you this very information You might not have been able to as early as possible understand how you shall relate to its content.

You will always be the head character in this book; in the sense of: this book is actually a conversation between You; The reader that reads this text, and Me: The author that wrote this book. Except it's all about how you are responding and experiencing the feelings you get while reading different types of content. I will however every now and then make personal comments on the content in order to show where in this book we actually are with different synopsis.

- You will have to read the vital information" part in this book in order to give yourself a fair chance... trust me on this one =)

In other words when I am talking, I'm simply sharing my opinion of what has been represents on Our table of presentation. Our table of presentation is visualized in your mind with a table free of your own taste and gathered around it is you in any form you like and me as the Demon of time – Medusa D.B. Loveheart – an Elemental: "Relative". Every now and then I will sometimes just stop the whole picture and make recaps of what has happened and clarify things when I find that there is enough information now on the table in order for me to be able to show you an exact example that I believe that even if we might not agree, we will both be able to understand that we can see the same point from the same page in the same direction. By doing this every now and then I know you will understand absolutely everything that I talk about.

By the time you actually have read the entire book form the front side of this book till its opposite side as well as all the content within it. This book that is. You will have seen the world in so many angles that you will be able to see things with a new pair of eyes.

-   Figuratively speaking =)

Read this first

or at least read the book entirely from the beginning to the end if you want to give yourself a fair chance to understand the content of this book.

Defining Metaphysical terminology

Directional Reggae English Introduction

The Doted System

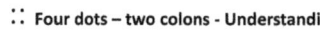

∴ **Four dots – two colons - Understanding**
The concept of creating a word or a phrase to contain a picture of completeness with an orbish direction. Build an essence and fill it out with a context and bringing in a direction, creating an understanding that is a behavior in any shape and form.

:: :*: Understanding - An analog photographic picture always contains of one negative and one positive picture, you create the ::positive:: image (the one that you will keep and show to friends) out of the negative picture, the one that was captured on the film itself with help of the camera. The positive opposite is naturally the :*:negative:*:. Two in one, sort of speaking and is an important understanding in "advanced opposite reflective thinking":: :*:

This book is an advanced compilation of code where I sometimes use the ::negative:: to shape out the ::positive:: corrects understanding direction. Where, as while calibrating the future, that's the best behavioral pattern to reveal any secrets that the future might behold for us.

Every word in this book is in an English form that combines English with Latin melodies in a directional reggae format of truth. It involves starters and stoppers introducing a bubble picture that you will see a lot of in this book and lots of other behavior patterns, opposite behavior patterns even though all words and sentences are easy enough for everyone to actually make sense at some point but always enough points so that no matter how complex I will get, you will always be able to see what it is that we are actually looking at ;).

When you describe a behavior, you can basically refer to anything no matter what you choose to explain it with, the picture you will be presented will also include an explanation of what behavior parts and elements you actually are referring to. I will compare behavioral patterns from movies, myths, legends and story's all depending on what it is that I'm describing to you for that very moment. In this book there will always be a new beginning whenever there is an end. In this book truth will always be accepted as an picture of completeness, in other words there won't be anything that will exclude anything, everything is always ON just like nothing is. Nothing might be a concept of hard to understand, luckily this book will change that fact for you.

You will also get to know Nothing as Metaverse and can be considered as an already existing nested parallel Universe in our existence.

No matter how confused you feel about reading this text you have already understood everything you so far have read even though it will have taken some time to get here. Your understanding will constantly grow for

10

each word that you progress, and the change will always be constant. By that fact you will hereby experience what it's like to read Directional Reggae English. It will be direct, reflect, engines and motors, fuels and engines, opposites and dimensional. It will have rhythm and will be predictable and it will be the most awesome experience you probably have had.

- Hehe, One more thing though.

  Dont worry.

- And we are still cool from my point of view, I already know we are different from each other.

11

This book is divided in Several parts

First part is the calibration of where we are today and how we got here with evolution in all its glory and failures as well as many relative reality's we all exist in, some of them we pass through in life without even reflecting over that we actually have crossed that path and for some those might be the very core in their reality. Some of them are rarity's while others are everyday common sense. This part contains lots of metaphysics and behavioral maps. You will also follow my journey as The last warlock.

Medley here I resume and reflect over what's been shared so far.

The second part is the composure and compilation of my very own ism; Dao Buddhism - covering parts of the way of the Dao Buddhist monk and Dao Buddhism. Covering the Isms fundamentals. It shows you how to relate to the ism as a follower no matter if you have a lifestyle where your lifestyle doesn't have that much room for isms and faith as well as showing it as a lifestyle in completeness.

Medley here I resume and reflect over what's been shared so far.

The third part is just a step-by-step guide that will lead the people of this earth into the best direction for this opportunity of life with the human species in it. This part also sums up my very own humble definition of what I consider to be a higher civilization form of existents where peace is an equally strong and important fuel and engine as chaos is in the sense of evolutionary progress.

- That's just the way it is... for everyone =)
Don't worry... it's not an end... it's just another beginning.

- This book contains many sentences ending, wherever one ends another one starts, Throughout the entire book. And when you have read the entire book, you are still the one holding this book. Hopefully you will have a more beautiful world to look upon and maybe even a little bit more hope for tomorrow.

::Don't forget that **you** are truly the main character of this book, you will stumble upon a methodology I'd like to call ::Dry Martini:: in the sense of direction as follow: just like the drink your feelings might get either shaken or stirred or even both at the same time. Sometimes the cause will be because of my weird sense of humor and sometimes because we are touching sensitive topics::

Sometimes my comments might be out of instructional nature such as:
"– You might want to take a seat in the coming part."
I'm saying these things mostly because I know what the next part will be about, but I don't know who you

are so since I'm asking you to hear me out fair and square I hereby show you that just like you are human so am I and even though we don't know each other we can at least try to give each other a fair chance even if we both know that we might not agree on everything. So, if you for example are holding a brew in your hand or drinking something you might swallow it in the wrong throat or maybe lose track of focus on your surrounding and spill your brew on something or someone. Because the content will be sometimes extremely naked and display the truth just like it can be with no censorship or cover-ups, in other words lots of delicate matters such as social behaviors, sexuality, war, peace, hate, love, sex, relations and many other topics in order to show you our past, present and future possibility's.

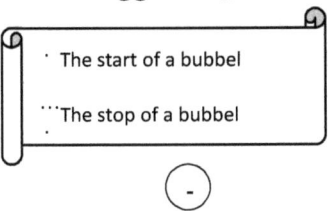

:: ::Talking in Bubbles:: You will be introduced to the reading of pictures or bubbles to be more specific, with a dot system that is consisting of a starter symbol ((a single dot) always grouped alone in the center of the page) as you can see in the upper circle and a stopper symbol ((four dots grouped together that has the relation x-o three dots in a horizontal group and the last dot is in a vertical group with the middle dot of the three dots above it)The stopper is always grouped in a four doted group also as a solo group in the middle of the page as you can see in the lower circle::

::Talking in pictures I'd preferably like to consider a ::DNA Strain of content bubbles:: or as you might easiest understand it, each bubble can be compared to the similar behavior several modern books and movies such as The Matrix with Neo and Morpheus directed to an older audience but also Harry Potter which is the example I use here for the screen shown in Harry Potters movie (that describes quite well what books and poetry and songs truly are about as well as sculptures and paintings) where you see professor Dumbledore extracting and dragging out a silver string, a piece of memory from he's mind with his magic wand and storing that "DNA Strain of content bubbles"/memory in a bottle, and this book is both my cabinet storing several hundreds of bottles as well as my memory bowl.

:: This is also an ::understanding:: as well right here and the understandings starter and stopper is shown as "a pair of colons" with equal many sets of "::" (the reason I use the two colons "::" rather than the parentheses "(" and ")" is because You then see the Nature of that its not only an explanation but a behavior and sense in time and direction, it gives you a complete picture of what content is included in the understanding. The first set of "::" without the "" shows that from here there is a picture that will show you a phrase or word that can have many directions, however this is the direction I'm referring its roots and branches. The Second set of "::" shows you the start of the actual phrase or word where it starts and the next "::" shows you where it stops and not until then you know if it's a word or an entire phrase. The last "::" shows you exactly where the content of this variable of understanding stops. Sometimes there might be nested understandings (more than just one within one larger understanding) then I simply add the symbol "*" between the pair of colons/"::" and looks like this ":*:" in order to simplify what belongs to what and then you might just need to take it a bit slow and look at the content as both a picture and a text more figuratively speaking::

...
.

- You are doing just fine honey...
  Let's move on...

.

::You will also learn a methodology that's called
::Scotch and Soda:: I learned the expressional art form
from a "shopping window" when I was walking the
Damrak a street in Amsterdam. It was a window
dresser that had made a clothing display under the
theme/"clothing style" Scotch and Soda. And it was
completely perfectly done. She/he had worked with
optical illusion methods by lifting up what normally is
considered as the negative in the picture and blended
both the negative lines with the positive lines. One
window doll appeared to have 3 legs but when you
looked closer it didn't. The scene was so perfectly
composed there was no doubt that that couldn't be
anything else but Scotch and Soda. The way the
window dresser had worked everything in that
window: kind of was one and the same entity and yet
it was perfectly clear it was made out of several
entities and people. THE perfect illustration of what
Scotch and Soda is like when done with clothing. I use
it in the same way but my pictures in completeness are
made out of words and mentality's. Behavioral
patterns and engines. With everything and nothing.

Scotch is a Whiskey made in Scotland. Whiskey comes
in five different categories', more or less. A whiskey can
have many different behaviors when it comes to flavors
for your taste but also the way it's been created. Soda
is bubbly Water with no alcohol and thereby out of
different nature, at least right here and now. These two

17

blended together makes the cocktail Scotch and Soda. In this Understanding it's important to understand that even if the drink Scotch and Soda is the end result entity referred to it does also include that before it became the combined new entity Scotch and Soda they where two separate entities. In other words, here Scotch and soda is also a behavioral pattern where two entities are blended together and the outcome of this process in time is the actual drink/cocktail Scotch and Soda. Where the Scotch all of a sudden has gained a new behavior of bubbles and the Soda has gotten the element of Alcohol and lots of other taste teasers. So here: The Expression "Scotch and Soda" is a behavior in time with a behavior of someone/something blending it and that has an outcome of a cocktail. Even though when I use it here its less likely that I'm referring to two different liquid entity's being blended together, it doesn't even need to be limited to only two either. It's a base tool that is used in many places and as conceptual picture a more touchable phrase for people to use. This is an Alchemy of behaviors and patterns and directional outcomes into whatever the result is::

...

.

.

:: ::x-o:: is a neutral formula of "its just another direction" and is used in this book to show you that there is an ongoing relation that might not be to obvious but out of major importance since it excludes any other type of understanding/interpretation of that particular content, so whenever the "x-o" formula is found in a content here it means that the text before the "x-o" is the "base plate"/"starting point" and the text that comes after it is where its directed/"heading towards"/"next plate". The "x-o" formula is always tied to its content appearance own bubble picture; However, the direction always goes both ways but only in the direction stated. Other directions are still true but since this isn't just a book about metaphysics but also containing an Ism the direction is always important in relation to the base of the Ism. The content outside the Ism will only show an understanding from the Isms point of view and will never alter the Isms base itself, the Ism itself is covered in the second part of this book::

...
.

.

:: :*: Variable/s; it's a common terminology within computer programming world but its behavioral pattern can actually be found in quite many places outside the IT world, You will find it a lot in Metaverse. A ::variable:: is something that is created by its creator/programmer. You could compare a variable with an empty box that you your self has built, and the shape of the box is limited to your imagination. Then you fill that box up with some sort of content. In the IT world you usually fill those boxes with numbers, counters, command phrases or just simply yes or no.

Long time ago people used to describe feelings by inventing/creating/achieving a God/" State of mind in total awareness" that represented that particular feeling with all its glory and danger, and that's actually how advanced each and every single feeling within us is and that's how advanced the power variables are within Metaverse. An example of such variables is Freja an ancient Norse Goddess that represents the element and dimension of Love and is the fertility goddess. If you look at our world history thru ought our evolutionary timeline you will easy see that it's a common concept all over the world and that every country has their own unique set of them in their history and myths. Looking into your country's myths and folk lore, explaining things their own way.

These types of variables are quite complex to create because it's not only about making a feeling more touchable but also a complete

description of its entire nature as a mood, action, what it's like to give it and what it's like to receive it as well as the denial of it, to not receive it when it has been given to you or to not respond to it even if you chose to receive it. It also reveals how you can choose to coexist with it. You are able to find such variables all over the world. The "Laughing Buddha" is a major great example of the preservation and clarification of the importance of humor and heartily laughter as well as real great life quality and true happiness. Even in your everyday life you stumble upon power variables only you have come to understand and know them as logotypes and slogans for different companies.

:*:Power Variables:*: can be found anywhere even in nature itself and you will find them in this book itself, just like the book itself is one:: :*:

...

.

:: ::Metaphysics:: if you look the word up on Wikipedia you will find a similar explanation: "The word derives from the Greek words μετά *(metá)* (meaning "beyond" or "after") and φυσικά *(physiká)* (meaning "physical"), "physical" referring to those works on matter by Aristotle in antiquity. The prefix *meta-* ("beyond") was attached to the chapters in Aristotle's work that physically followed after the chapters on "physics," in posthumously edited collections. Metaphysics is a branch of philosophy that investigates principles of reality transcending those of any particular science."

Metaphysics is about the untouchable in the sense of not measurable with tools of/for physics. In order to understand Metaphysics, you must also understand physics.

The metaphysical universe is basically the "tree of exist" and the source of all life, It is called Metaverse and is more complex and advanced with all the energies and coexistent metaphysical dimensions, astral planes and domains::

...
.
.

I will give you some examples of concepts that belongs to the metaphysical formula-science.

Relations – The relation itself belongs to metaphysic because you can touch the entity's where the relation exist between, but you can't touch the relation itself in the sense of physical unbounded relationships. You

21

can't touch the relation you have to/with other people as well as other physical entity's even though you can touch both yourself and the other physical objects. Relations exist between everything and anything, there is relations everywhere. Relation has many different values. It can be in the state of friendly, lovingly, hatefully, neutral, presence within yourself, unaware, aware.. just to mention a few of all the different kinds of values the variable Relation can contain.

Exist – The Source and foundation for all existence in universe, there truly is no beginning and no end. Science says it all started with a big bang. Which is a quite dared thing to say especially concerning the limitation science has. To believe that from a single planet in a universe we should be able to see and understand the size of the entire universe is not just foolish, it makes no sense whatsoever. Truth is no one knows how large it is. Eternity is a quite long time. To say; because you understand that universe existed for a couple of billion years: you can reach a conclusion of when it started. You only admit that you are afraid to see the truth as it is. If there has been a big bang there is still no way to tell what was before since there was something before and there is no way to see if there was another one before the one they claim happened with an equal or longer existence than this one, and another one before that and before that how many other big bangs there have ever been.

Science is also limited in the understanding of how large universe actually is since we can only see as far as our own tools allows too and today we can see very far with all kinds of telescopes and so forth, but truth is they are still limited. Again, science is limited to tell if there has been other so called big bangs on very extremely distance places in almost same time as well. If you take your kitchen table for example when its empty and place a coffee cup there then imagine that that coffee cup is symbolizing how far we are able to see in universe you will then realize that we can't really see much at all and we actually have no idea if there has been another big bang in same time somewhere else on that kitchen table which is easily illustrated by simply placing another coffee cup on another spot. We actually have no clue whatsoever of how far/large universe actually is nor for how long it has existed. The beauty of this is that you still chose to limit yourself.

- What the heck do I mean with that?

Well, you were able to see that universe is quite big because of the kitchen table but you fail to see that the universe doesn't really end there now does it. Isn't it so that the kitchen table itself is actually located in a kitchen meaning the entire kitchen is actually representing universe... and it still doesn't end there cause the kitchen is in your apartment and the apartment is in your building and the building is on your street and the street is in your city which is in your country wish is on the planet which is in this solar system which is in our galaxy which is in space. And we are still just talking about a single coffee cup that symbolize a so-called big bang as well as the size of universe. With this picture in your head isn't it quite silly to claim that infinity is hard to understand.

- Ask yourself:

Is it so wise to say that we don't exist in infinity already, to say that there isn't anything else left to be found out, if the size of our universe is symbolized with a single coffee cup isn't it quite easy to see that we actually have quite a lot to explore and find out, that there is to put it frankly; it is but-loads for us and that all the weird hate and wars we have among us on this ONE planet is quite pathetic considering what we have ahead of us.

With this single coffee cup isn't it quite easy to see that eternity isn't really that strange anymore that there actually is more likely that there has been several or to put it frankly again, but-loads of similar phenomena throughout our eternal existents already. With this single coffee cup isn't it quite moronic to actually walk around and believe that we for some reason would be alone in universe.

- Again, you're making a mistake!

- What?

- Yeah... I'm talking about eternity now...

As with infinity you stopped at the kitchen table as if the space/room didn't continue further. Same thing here you forget that there are hours before you sat down by the table, days and weeks and months even years before that with loads of dinners, sex, tea, coffee at the very same table and before that the table was manufactured raw material that before that was trees or metals or sand.. that came to be from other natural miracles. You forget that the table and coffee cup will transform into shards and dust and give birth to new phenomena's and so it will go on for an eternity into infinity and so on. Time is a dimension of its own and I'm the Demon of that Dimension.

- More of that later on dear =)

- We have now taken a look upon Exists meaning of Eternity into Infinity

Exist is one of the core variables in Dao Buddhism and it stands for quite many things and derives partly from Dao, it is the source of all energy's in Metaverse and universe, of all dimensions, astral planes and elements. Exist is the foundation for all Nature that is a natural part of exist. Exist contains the Domain and Dimension of Death, Love, The Force, Time, Luf, True Faith, Metaverse and Universe. Exist is the ::positive:: for Metaverse where Nature is the ::Negative:: for Universe where Exist is the ::Negative:: For Metaverse where Nature is the ::positive:: for Exist.

Nature – Is the gift of life and a true blessing from Exist. Nature is the miracle of life forms participating and endorsing the energies from exist. Nature contains natural codes and spirits in all life not just birds, wolfs, fish and so but also trees, mountains, valleys, oceans, lakes and the wind. Nature contains the Domain and Dimension of Life, Love, True Faith, Biology, Physics, Elements. Nature is the ::positive:: for Universe where Exists Metaverse is the ::negative::

Exist & Nature – IS our **only** reason we are here today, The Only true roots of everything in universe. The one and only true reason any life form has an opportunity to participate in this magnificent opportunity of life.

::positive:: / ::negative:: Chart

Nothing	Exist	Nature	Metaverse	Universe
Exist	0	+	-	+
Nature	-	O	+	-
Metaverse	+	-	o	+
Universe	-	+	-	.

Time – The Dimension.

- Me Demon is it.

Time is a natural outcome of existence and nature itself, because of the fact of space containing the universal circle of existence with planets, suns, supernovas, black holes in a never ending ocean of endless implosions and rebirths of new galaxies all over universe that's always pulsing and beating rhythms of energy forces beyond earthly co existential purposes creating an existence in constant movement where time always exist as a natural outcome because of the fact of space and movement. Time isn't really measurable in the sense that we don't yet have an instrument that gives a reading of how much of it there is, sure we have the time watch and the stop watch that starts and stops time but it only shows you where in time things happened with an exact amount of seconds or hours or whatever it shows on the display just like a watch that only displays where in time we are in relation to earth time mostly. But if the watch isn't there or stops time, time doesn't go away, it's still there. Time is actually a mass in the sense there is no line of time but it's everywhere and all time eventually ends up in the time mass ancient and that mass isn't beyond you or before you but it's everywhere and nowhere. Traveling or journeying in time is actually doable but you have to understand that it's not done physically yet but metaphysically. With mind, spirit, soul and heart in the force.

We have objectified time in order to take advantage of the fact that we exist in it. Time is based on relations in the eye of science formula-science. You can't touch time you can only measure it if you chose to limit it to a smaller picture and if you decide the rules of it. Time here on planet earth has been defined by relations of our planet, its moon and our galaxy's sun. The moon is only countable into that picture as a factor of day and nighttime and as its relational affection on our planet's rotation even though its minor it still has an effect to it that we normally not consider in everyday time life. The rotation of our planet around its own axis gives us the cycle of twenty-four hours. Our planets constant path around the sun gives us the cycle of a year.

However, time exist no matter if you are on a planet within a solar system or out in the middle of space itself, science defines the time in space as space-time. Space time also shows that time actually is a mass but in another sense. When in complete empty space time is still there but doesn't really get verified till an object moves through it. Might it be a stone/comet or a ship of some sort, till that object passes through empty space time doesn't really reveal itself at all but is still there. The time on our neighbor planets is not the same as they are here but we use our own time to give our self an understanding about it. Time is also a concept and could just as well have been measured by ecological lifespan on this very planet. The clocks that we today all see no matter if they are in digital format or physical artworks are just display boards that gives us an understanding of where our time is at the moment. We cannot touch time; we can calibrate it and within that calibration we can calculate with it. Even on this single planet time has been defined in many different ways already. The Mayan civilization had their own type of definition of it. Time is a full blood dimension with its own yin yang and needs the conditions of movement and space in order to exist as we are used to relate to it. Time is an essence in our existence and only a matter when looked upon it like that. Time is an estimation as well as a fact. Time is a tool we need to use to understand when. Time tells us the existence of an event. Time gives us direction for past, presence and future. Time is relative. Time is more than that and a very useful tool. By ripping time out of content, we have been able to objectify it in order to take advantage of it and we have use for that skill, that doesn't change the fact that in its basic nature still belongs to metaphysics as a dimension in its own picture of completeness.

Dao Buddhism – True Holy Faith Religion from ancient. A transparent holy faith religion with no god but only the force – The TRUE FORCE where true holy faith is your navigation and direction yielder. Where inner harmony in full yielded yin yang's is only way to harmonize with it. Dao Buddhism is a universal ancient religion that is transparent covering all isms and religions as well as science and this planets evolution continuing out in universe everlasting growing mass that only keeps growing in same paste as we are in both Universe and Metaverse in other words in Versa.

Versa – Both Universe and Metaverse in one and the same expression to clarify you mean both.

The Force – Is a natural outcome of Metaverse – Exist - Universe – Nature, The force is their combined energies in all its relations and directions. The Force is everywhere – nowhere – between – anywhere. It has existed as long as Exist. To participate actively with coexistence with the force you must amend the calibrational lifestyle. A Lifestyle where you and all your senses just are reading the environment, reading yourself and your own entity's impulses and reaction. A lifestyle where you accept your true nature as the animal human to its fullest and see the truth in your existence as it is and not as the world today are trying to shape and form you. Yes, you are still able to function as the rest of the world. To participate as a follower of the force it takes a commitment in yourself beyond what you have seen before. Follower of the force is a collected expression and an explanation of a participant no matter where your path is, a full-blooded yielder of what force path it is you yourself is or has pathed. I'm The last warlock (Ancient Warlock today) and paths many paths, not just the warlock path. It's a lifestyle, not a hobby. Everything you do is training and that in senses and ways most people don't understand. Dao Buddhism contains all schools and mental training in order to reach higher bounds with the force for both the male entity and for the female entity and our lifestyle. Since all humans no matter sexual equipment between the legs consists of both a female and a male side you are able to achieve dual connections with the force as my entity has. To achieve a Calibrational lifestyle takes time, determination and devotion. Adjusting it to the calculational lifestyle is somehow timely as well as hard. When you have achieved that you can start train in deeper schools of the force. I'm pathing the Grand Master Force path today as the Ancient Warlock that I have now evolved into. I have found the paths and lanes and are constantly breaking new ice. Dao Buddhism is the result of a Warlock Lifestyle among others. Male and Female entity doesn't matter in the sense of harmonic coexistence. People that might recognize the term of The Force from the movies of Star Wars should understand that the force IS even though it's not exactly as illustrated by Georg Lucas, it still is and has lots to it that also is full of harmony. It is just a description of a yielder of the force basically, it happens to be a similar existence only this is about

Metaverse.

Metaverse – is the ::negative:: to universe. The versa that reaches beyond the physical world and universe. Metaverse is always in motion in one way or another. Metaverse contains not just energies from all over universe but also thru out time. Metaverse is the picture of completeness that contains Astral Planes, Terrestrials and Domains as well as Lanes and the so-called Virtual Lane of intercommunication. Astral planes contain natures, elements, dimensions and metascapes presenting schools of all kinds of wisdom and metaskills.

The Domain of Death is an important part of both Versa, in other words both Metaverse and Universe. The Circle of Death with holds the "Soul and spirit Shards" from past life throughout time. Depending on your choices and events in life Your shard will exist or dissolve when your life passes on. Metaverse Existed long before life on this planet did, long before the so-called Big Bang that resulted in our galaxy among other sky body's. Just like universe, Metaverse is continuously in directions and stores energies in all life forms and nature Universe has provided.

Death is a natural part of physical life forms and is by many today treated with fear out of the wrong reasons. We all have one lifetime entity wise, and most people seem to forget that the time you have alive as a humanoid is supposed to be lived and not done. The duration of a human's life is like a pixel beating a pulse and a tone that will fade away or grow a rhythm. The existents of a life form are truly an eye blink before it ends in universe. When you die your physical life ends but your energies either goes into a "Soul spirit shard" or takes freer forms of existents till they are redistributed by other life forms. Death contains lots of history and wisdom from ancient times. A more beautiful and peaceful place to journey then in Domain of Death is hard to find, everything is in perfect harmony and the ancient wind of wisdom breathes calmly within you.

Mind – The Calibrating and Calculating brain, two different lifestyles from one and the same mass of cells. The Calibrating way is measured in awareness while the Calculational way is measured in Intelligence. The base for intelligence is always the awareness. Here we will focus on the Calibrational lifestyle where mind is in sense of reader and expresser of feelings from your Soul and Spirit. Thoughts as its own outcome is a metaphysical object since everything you think, dream, mentality's you have, fantasies about are just different forms of thoughts with different structures processed with one and the same brain and heart. The experience outcome of the chemical reaction within you is a metaphysical phenomenon and a very advanced metaphysical formula-science, the *experience outcome* and not the actual chemical reaction that is. the brain calibrates both physical impulses as well as meta impulses. The brain contains the blueprint ::Positive:: of who your spirit is. The Mind defines the so-called mindly matter in metaphysics and is a very important understanding within Dao

Buddhism.

Spirit – the ::Negative:: in your brain that is your essence of your own spirit. The blueprint to your total conscious. The Blueprint is what defines your will and who you are. The blueprint calibrates your grey brain mass which is billions of cell blocks called brain cells and are all working together with several responsibilities. Just like the flame in a room surrounded by heat can even the heat out and balance the energy flow so does the empty space in your brain collaborate the brains surrounding energies. The blueprint or spirit interacts with the brains outer surrounding energies and fuels the blue by reacting on these impulses. Spirits exist in all types of natures and so does souls. Not just humans or animals but trees and flowers.

:*: :: ::Blueprints:: and :*:Greyprints:*: are achievable "base plates"/foundations where you possess the ability to adjust, plant, grow and interact with metaphysical behavioral patterns and incarnational prints of energy's schemas. They contain lots of important information and reveals paths of the force in all kinds of directions. They are also important schools of understanding as well as co existential understandings and achievements needed. Defining nature of meta patterns in orbish directions. More of this will be covered later on and you will find other mentionable as silverprints as well. They are negatives of the spirit and the soul:*: ::

Heart – the essence in sense of reader – calibrator and expresser of feelings from your soul, the experience of the chemical reaction within you is a metaphysical phenomenon and a very advanced metaphysical formula-science. It's Your heart that's beats the Love of the Force of Free Will and free Freedom. Heart Loves you always never forget that, because you seem to forget to love and respect it back way to often in a society of today where money is supposed to be a god and alcohol your savior. That's the biggest lie you could ever live in. Don't betray your heart for something as foolish as money and alcohol. It's with the energies of heart and mind you dive, surf, swim and plunge within your own emotion as well as the surroundings energy's. Love decides the strength of the force you your self can handle and are extremely important to understand. It's a beautiful feeling but also an utterly important measurement where your borders within your entire force existence are.

Luf - is holy faith love within the force and a perfected combination of mindly and heartly matters.

Worry - Are commonly known to us as a feeling but are merely one of thousands of advanced map impulses in a very advanced chemical map for calibrators as well. It's an explorer of the unknown and unaware rather than love that are the aware known boarder line in exploring and surfing the waves of the force. Worry today is only used in one direction only, hence an abuse of as a feeling and therefore it more often a harmful feeling rather than the beautiful feeling it actually is. You should treat all your feelings preciously and act interpretive with them rather than judge upon them. Worry is just one of all of our emotions but same goes for all of them.

Emotions – is just a signal system, never forget that. We react upon signals that has been predefined long time ago. Forget your previous school and relearn them as signals for your own calibrations. Fear, hate, love etc. All brand-new schools in the calibrational lifestyle.

Soul – The very core of your existence. The ::Negative:: of your Spirit and is as vital as vital can be. You cannot neglect it cause if you neglect it you not only disrespect the soul you rape both the spirit and the soul... your entire person in other words. Think about it for a while. Our souls are base plates for our bare necessities and gives us the roots to our spirits. Your soul is so vital for your entire existence and its limitless. You can nurture your soul and give it several cores with the aid of reincarnation soul pathing in achievement of universal codes. No matter what your choices are, always respect the soul in you. There are no limitations in the soul::

::VersaPathing – ::VersaPathing:: is what you all do consciously or subconsciously. It's a way of life just as it's a life of your own way. You utilize Versapathing for your reincarnation and incarnation pathing as well. Pathing is very communicating utilization while meditating as well and are best practiced during calm and secure situating both within you as well as your surroundings. Choices you made in your past life that might made sense back then, or no sense whatsoever are most likely vital for you for purposes or might be or to become at least. See Pathing isn't at all about the so called: "been there" or "done that". On the contrary it demands true devotion in your own true faith foremost but also for you to dare to let go of what you chose to call sanity. To dare to share your faith with people and to respect you're surrounding and you, too open up their eye in as many opportunistically ways as possible. Pathing is about achievements with your own energies and can be done at home in privacy as well as outside in vast adventure whether they are in ceremonial practices or meditational harmony's. You can meditate achievement and you can physically advance in achievements. I will explain more about VersaPathing later in this book::

:: ::**Reincarnation**:: The rebirth of a soul and spirit. It's usually known as the rebirth of an earlier life but can also be an achievement in Metaverse. Universal Death Codes - The complete achievement in reaching full power variables in universal coding. It is one of the reasons to Versapathing. It's done when you are reaching a mutual agreement with another ancient soul & spirit shard since it becomes a new core of yourself in your entity's existence and is a very delicate journey to do and takes lots of devotion from you both. Not until the agreement mutually has been reached and met you have actually pathed the reincarnation in its completion::

:: ::**Code**:: Everything is ::code:: everywhere and nowhere is codes of nature or universe and Metaverse.

Not as in the movie matrix even though that's ::code:: as well but codes as in death codes or love codes or any type of code.. sensual codes or sexual codes... ::code:: ::code:: ::code:: it's all ::code:: Carnational codes can be both natural codes from elements of nature such as the wind, trees or animal life as well as universal civilizations, co-existential or death ::code:: you never know what piece of code you get when rewarded with them till later even though some seams obvious at first they might fill a much more profound and deeper purpose later on. Not to forget the most important codes there are HOLY Codes. Codes comes to you as any form, I like to call fragmental code for grey prints since that's what they are till you are able to make something out of it. Codes comes in visions but also in brought daylight in everyday life not just weird dreams or state of beings. Codes can and are achieved in metaphysical pathings. By achieving behavioral patterns or codes you build or enhance sides or behaviors within yourself in any direction. But everything is ::code:: in more ways than that.. you see codes in everything only you come to call them images, colors, lines, dots or objects but it's all ::code:: dear::

:: ::**Fragmental reincarnation – the incarnation**:: is when only some pattern / fragments or a trait from either soul or spirit is achieved and it's done in the very same way as reincarnation only here you can program it a bit or adjust it is more appropriate way to express it here. Fragmental or partly Universal Death Codes - Hence the talk about greyprint, blueprint and so on as well. It can be about a trait such as the bravery or about enhancing the feminine side::

::The Neutral Directional – ; the hyphen surrounded by one blank space on each side of it, looks like this " – " (without the ""). It is used in this book as a "::Power Variable:: compiler of flows", Which means that each word separated by the hyphen is equal in all direction and is always fueled/injected with the base plate that is always the first word/phrase before the semi colon symbol ";" (without the "") so by gathering or stating a base plate that base plate becomes the roots of the rest of the "::Power Variables::" that is the branches of that newly combined entity. Here comes an example and a taste of one of the beautiful plants you will find here in later coming content in this book:

Respect; FAITH – MUTUALITY – Diversity's – Sexualism – LOVE – Nature – Elements – Dimensions - Senses – Emotions – Heart – Mind – Soul – Spirit – Dignity – Humbleness – Nothing – Everything – Life - Death

...
.

.

::Reflection is a synonym for pondering, thinking about as well as an opposite visual of an entity. Reflection in this metaphysical terminology is a verb in the form of re- pre- as well as flections in the mirror itself. You reflect over life events from both third person as well as first person. Flection is also a warlock trait and a defense. You reflect in order to be able to preflect over the TommorowTimes crossroads of choices to be made. ::Reflectional thinking:: serves purposes of

learning from the past as well as see the presents and
to reveal and become aware about the future
possibility's that lies ahead::

...
.

.: DotColon – Starter of a fragment

∴ ColonDot – Stopper of a fragment

·

:: ::Fragments incomplete:: - I here in this book show
you with the Starter symbol that's built on a single dot
directly followed by a colon and looks like this ".:"
without the "" and the stopper of a fragment
incomplete is symbolized with a colon directly followed
by a single dot and it looks like this ":." Without the "".
I utilize Fragments incomplete here in this book
because this books "Picture in Completeness" requires
these fragments in order to become complete.
Incomplete fragments might look uninteresting at first
glance or be conceived as unimportant or a dead end,
but they are not. They are just as important as all the
other bits in order to see the picture in completeness ::

...

·

☾ ∞ Conceptual time concept ∞ ☽

::this is something I use here in this book in order to be able to dissect even the smallest entity in its nature as well as to be able to use the concept of ::Behavioral patterns:: You are already familiar with the terminology of: Past time – Present time – Future time (only you probably are satisfied by using the short term of them as The Past, The Present/"here and now" and The future(anything that will become). Time is an indicator of sequenced appearing events no matter the form of them. Time in Metaverse is a yin and yang and dimension itself. Showing existing steps as well as nonexistent. ::

::I also utilize ::NowTime:: which refers to this very moment we always exist in and is never one second ago nor one second ahead but always right now::

:: ::PerfectTime:: is the exact amount of time it actually is about no matter what the nature of an entity is. THE PERFECT TIME MANAGER I keep in this book as a variable represented and personated with DEATH. Death never ends life; Life ends life either by natural causes or premature causes. Death Only deals with after life in the sense of redistribution of life energy's that are just as active even if the entity's reproduction lifespan ends, so doesn't the energy's that the entity has functioned as a container for. Death simply makes sure the energies are as they should and then makes sure they have somewhere to continue their journey in a more freely form then before. Death is never late and

41

never early; Death is always in perfect time::

:: ::TomorrowTime:: I use in order to show you the direction of when something takes place, and it also shows that in that context the future is also a part of that particular context. TomorrowTime does never belong to the past even though the event of its own nature will eventually do just that (belong to the past) and when it does the statement of that events TomorrowTime is no longer in a state of true but has changed into a true statement of PastTime in SameTime::

:: ::AllTime:: is a statement that refers to a continuously active choice and only remains true as long as there always is an active will to maintain that statement actively and will automatically turn in to a false as soon that will isn't there. AllTime however as stated is only about an active choice when that is what has been declared for that particular statement, the only three other thing that exist in a static AllTime mode at ALLTIME no matter will or liking of it, is Exist, Change and Relativity::

We do Exist in time and that's a fact of today, We do exist in Space and that's a fact of today, We do exist in Movement and that's a fact of today. We can never escape any of those three facts and that's a fact of today since if we remove one of them we no longer exist in same form as of today. If we remove Time we are all of a sudden existing in a phenomena and entity, science of today like to call White Hole which is their definition of the opposite to Black Hole – the ones that exist in space. Science claims that inside a white hole time stands still. However Even though that is the nature of a White Holes inside The entity of the White Hole still has an outside where time still keeps moving on.

::::Relativity:: is a natural outcome from existence and nature itself and is a part of any nature that involves the THREE factors of Time – Space – Movement and that's the reality we exist in today. Even the Entity of a white hole, who's existence resides within the same perimeters of relativity and since its entity resides within this exist as a part of space even though within itself other rules apply. However, even these rules apply to relativity.

This was already explained with a more advanced formula created by Laozi (considered to be one of the founders of philosophical Taoism), a single symbol he came to call Yin and Yang. The Original and true form of Yin and Yang is actually in a shape of an ORB very much like a planet (but the only reason for Laozi to present it in that way is in order for a person to be able to see it as a concept, the orb in reality is actually our existence in our opportunity of life in this part of universe). That Orb exists within a Space and is in constant Rotation which is its Movement and the black and white color inside this orb is equally constantly growing and shrinking so even if the orb looks completely black or completely white it never stays that way in Time but always keep changing its inner color form, the two dimensional presentation we see today is just a way to draw the understanding in normal art made by pen and paper. The chance that a person would live to see a real yin and yang ORB looking the same way it's usually illustrated on paper is quite slim even if you choose to sit and stare at it your entire life since it never follows a specific pattern. Which in its own nature actually is its natural pattern.

This fact doesn't change anything for your everyday life since its truth didn't start to become true when Einstein said it nor when Laozi said it, that has been a truth all along no matter if we have chosen to understand it or not. Not even Laozi wasn't the only one to reach that understanding but probably most likely the Native Americans and not to forget the Mayan civilization that has clearly understood and utilized relativity formulas when looking upon the knowledge they chose to share with us. We do have a great advantage by understanding it though, by doing that we will give our self a great advantage since that truth existed long before the human race did; it really has nothing to do weather we can live an exciting life or not, and it's that very fact that not only gives us the opportunity to direct our future but also enables us to calibrate it in any direction we like at the cost of effort::

Your life is relative in the sense that you and only you are responsible for what you chose to make of it and how much of your OwnTime you chose to invest in different skill sets like educational training, physical training, metaphysical training, sexual training and social behavior. You are the one living and experiencing your life and it is yours to be lived but also yours to be taken responsibility of. Life will always be to advance and complex for a single human lifecycle to be able to know or master everything or to be able to do everything and even more understandable all of them in SameTime. We are all different not just in our physical appearance but also in mentalities with their strengths and weaknesses. What you can do is to equip yourself with as good tools as possible in order to actually live the life you actually would like to live. Unfortunately to many people sabotage for them self by choosing to believe in lies that in their sense makes life easier for them, but what they usually realize to late is by doing that they also prevent them self from understanding what truly makes them feel happy and satisfied in their own lifetime. Life will never be easy; Responsibility will never happen by itself nor will Happiness or Joy as well as Love. These are all entity's that will always need to be fueled and maintained as well as allowed by yourself in order to experience them.

:: ::OwnTime:: is an entity's lifecycle and can be both a life form as well as a series of events::

:*: :: ::SameTime:: is when several(more than one entity"/"or within a single entity's own relation") entity coexist in a perfect sync during a moment of time. The most Oddly behavior that you will start to see more of and might get stucked in your self is the :*:ExactSameTimeExperience:*: which can be quite tricky to get out of, but if you ever get stuck in one of those you can always try to break it by touching your genitals and if you notice your still in the ExactSameTimeExperience you can either choose to

45

have sex with your opposite/s or to sit down on the ground and start focusing on the sky or roof depending where you are. The biggest reason you might get stuck in one of those is because I just made you aware about the phenomena/entity, and anyone that has read this book will have much enough common understanding for that to happen:::*:

We are all different: will always remain true as long as we are equipped with free will, however there are extremist concepts within political movements as well as both religions and isms like Nazism that are all against the truth of human nature and wants us all to be in one specific way and never accept our free will nor our true natural way of diversity. Those concepts will however always fail in longtime relations and will for sure lead to the end of this opportunity of life.

Our existence will always depend on that there is many people enough that dares to actively chose to say YES to Mother nature's perfection just like it is, because when enough people dares to come out of the closet and say Yes I love Life and my humble opportunity to coexist with it much enough to live my entire life without myself ending it prematurely, There will always be enough will to make the necessary changes in order to always make sure that this opportunity of life in our part of universe will continue to exist for eternity in infinity. Trust me when I say.

-   That's a Very VERY Loooooooooooooong time.

and to keep up that kind of willpower no other solution then ✶Diversity is our greatest strength✶ will ever succeed in that type of goal since boredom of life leads to prematurely death and very destructive behavior before that. Hence behavioral patterns such as Nazism can never be considered anything else but failure in existence. These types of destructive behavioral patterns are just one example of how dangerous it can be if we don't understand relativity seriously.

...
.

.

:: :*: ::Poetry :*:onmo:*: Justizia:: Poetry in justice, is justice in motion. Justice alive and calibrating truth as it is and not as it could be. The purest form of justice and the only form Exist & Nature Accepts law enforcements of their own kin. ONMO is HOLY and I refer to both as poetry in justice as many of you already got to understand it, but I also refer to it as Poetry ONMO Justice. Poetry ONMO Justizia is when an entity's soul and spirit is being evicted before Exist and Nature. You do that when you commit True soul-searching and do it thoroughly. When your soul and spirit stand at the brink of exist and Nature for its final purpose here in existence. The most beautiful achievement you can imagine:: :*:

...
.

...
.

- once again..

- =) Don't worry. We are still on the same page you and I ;)

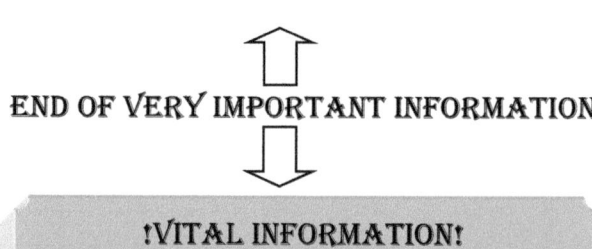

END OF VERY IMPORTANT INFORMATION

!VITAL INFORMATION!

(end of vital information)

;✶; A table of contents found. ;✶;
Right now, it contains one Attention!
and one ¡VITAL INFORMATION¡. There is
much more to come ;✶; over and out
;✶; =)

- Hi =) This is... Medusa Loveheart
and I have a proposal for you...

=)

- You all get to know me as Medusa D.B. Loveheart but I prefer to shorten it to Medusa Loveheart

- Comfy?

- All right then...

- here we go

Introduction

- First, I'd like to take this opportunity to introduce myself for you...

- My correct name today is Medusa D.B. Loveheart in TODAYTIME.. in other words when you read this text, but you can call me Medusa Loveheart and I'm a Grand Master Calibrator

- I will here give you an idea, a picture of my complex mind as well as personality. Show you what will be covered throughout this book and what to anticipate.

- I am a so called:

  True Natural Born Calibrator – It means that I'm true in my nature and that I admit that I was produced naturally from a female and male entity intercourse, It also means that my entity follows the calibrational lifestyle and has done since childhood. It also shows that I admit myself as a humanoid entity that accepts that I'm a natural animal and species just like any other

52

species.

- My Entity took its first
breath in 1974 on the land mass
defined as Sweden in the capital
Stockholm and is blessed with a
young appearance.

I tend to describe my life as
the cycle of a butterfly in the
sense that I first was an egg
in my case a sperm and an egg
that was blended together in
the beautiful act of love
making, then my life was a so
called larva when I as a child
started my paths as three
years old when I dived into the
dimension of time and made my
first visit into the domain of
death. Then my soul and spirit
soothingly appeared as the last
warlock three years later when
I harshly had to define my own
purposes and goals about and for
myself which is an opposite
direction of a shaman's arrival
who usually arrives thru dreams
where their shaman animal or
entity reveals their true
purpose. As a Larva I remained
for over thirty years gathering
nutrition's or "natural and
universal codes" when it comes
to my entity. During this
period, I explored, dived, surfed,
climbed and embraced all my

emotions and moods within me, always nurturing my own faith in all kinds of direction. I explored all kinds of religions, isms, myths and folklores. I Traveled through time and space within evolution and history I have seen the horror in beauty and the glory in chaos. I see romance in darkness and hope in emptiness.

- I am a New Age Alchemist and Metaphysician whose Soul is "The Last Warlock" and the soul roots resides in the Element of PURE HOLY FAITH LOVE - LUF.

- Gizmoo Strangelove isnt just a Universal code/reincarnation as an accomplishment in partly of my very own total picture of completeness but also my first soul path - both from nature and universal from the domain of death.

- To put it shortly I'm a Freak of Nature with a big heart and great awareness.

- My Instrument is the thought, and my rhythm is as servant of LUF and Truth. One of my true tools is True FAITH and I am a believer and follower of the one and biggest true force of this

54

universe "PURE TRUE LUF". The force is everywhere not just love but in many shapes and forms. My path is nowhere and everywhere, I'm the warlock that walks the between and the middle just as much as nowhere and everywhere, I'm a protector of the force and MY only TRUE guide is Exist & Nature. I'm a professional Definer that calibrates reality's x-0 relativities in the sign of my own soul's FULL nature.

- I'm a Philosophical calibrator. My Mind is spectral and an astral werewolf. My body is Shemale (both man and woman) in motion and its taste are bisexual in versatility and always part of my pictures. The true color of my heart is purple.

- I always define in all possible directions, senses, feelings as well as dimensions, astral planes, terrestrials and in nothing where everything of course also is a part. I work with pictures in completeness as well as fragments incomplete.

- My heart in flesh is rising from bare necessities, True Faith, that is my main tool and my heart in the astral planes

55

is a director of pure Luf from the Element and Dimension of LOVE. My spirits faith always resides in the opportunity of life and its Mother Nature.

- I use tools from both Everything and Nothing, I work with different types of mind mapping systems both calibrating and calculating ones. One of the basic formulas I'm using is the Philosophical version and definition, more powerful than the mathematical Relativity Theory and THE ONLY TOTAL Ultimate Optimal Final Conclusion... it is very beautiful...

- Here it comes:

§
.

Nothing IS Everything
Everything is only a( )part
of/from Nothing
Therefore/Hence
Everything is Relative
In
Time - Movement - Space
X - 0
It is just another direction

○

Ancient IS Nothing

.~

□

.

§

...

.

- This is the Formula you MUST
understand with all your senses
in order to be able to create
the yin○yang types of variables
I do and is for sure not a
doomsday philosophy but merely
a tool in order to read in the
relative reality we already live
& exist in.

- Defining in philosophy is like
programming without any
limits. Like art where my
sentence equals a stroke from
the paint brush hence the
structure of this book. This

57

book itself is a picture in completeness where every stroke of my brush counts just as much, Each sentence, Each Word Each page, THE BOOK ITSELF as well as the writer: New Age Alchemist Medusa Lufveheart, Me, myself and I as one. I use powerful variables whose size limits are equal to relativity.

- When working in cooperation with soul and spirit there is only one way and that is to stay true to yourself as good as you possible ever can, When working together you confront your demons with Love Understanding Fear Happiness Sadness Hate Respect Dignity Sexuality Pride Shame TRUE SOUL-SEARCHING and embrace every single inch of them and that is only possible in true mode. The key here was EMBRACE which is an opposite direction to x-o become.

- Your own becoming are your own choices to make and should be done with care and preferable after you walk the path of true soul-searching.

- Truths are always simple as long as they are kept alone, perceptions of the truths clouds and makes them harder to intercept. Even when they are kept alone, they still are relative to the surroundings and therefore even a so-called truth cant be taken for sure nor granted.

I will Beneath here, between the "~"

and the (final (Second)) "~" without the " " show you a path-map and You will find how oddly and advanced a compilation Path of your "own self" truly are. As a warlock it will differ a lot from others. You do not need to understand that part between those signs at all in order to continue to read but do have a look upon it and you might have use of writing and drawing a so-called path-map yourself when you yourself start to path your own truth about your existence and your own true nature.

...

.

~

§

Medusa Lluffveheartt

SPEAKING DEATH

Medusa The Butt

Lowheat

Intergender

Dreadful Dead
Death Angel Meduza Loweheart
reggae
☑ ❧ ೞ ❧ ❧ ❧ ೞ
Musa
Medusa

Meduza Lufeheart AF Wan Croft¨

ANCIENT RELATIVVE SLEWISH PERFECTUM ONMO 5th ELEMENTAl

ANCIENT ELEMENTAl AVIATOR
ANCIENT TREE

Ancient warlock

*

Yota

Mistress of Darkness

LORD ○○ DEATH

Meduza

Loweheart

61

☺DEATH☺

Meduza☺@☺ Love Heart

LORD MARKATTAO

Demon of time
Relative

Darkelfishao

☺ANCIENT☺FAITH☺WARLOCK☺

¤

@#£Czynthia Strangelove€¤$§th4th

MYSKO CZYNTHIA LOVEHEART
THE TRUE FAITH SHAKE AF TRANZYLVAINIA

§¤&{[DEATH]}¤ - *Pax Wobiscum* - may the force be with you . Homeplanet – Tellus –
ᴜ⁄✦☺○√≠∼↘◡ • ~ Transylwanien . is Eu calyptolupto
trolovningens ERA is here TO E.!!!!¤ ¤ &§§½§§

§

§ ENTEQUISTZON'S

§

§§§§
§§§§ ANCIENT AVIATORIAN DEPULINA OF
EXIST & NATURE
§§§§

§§§§

§ GURUS *§ PRAHAS

§

~

...

.

- That's just a taste of how
complicated it can be to sort
yourself out while pathing in
your ancient.

The sum up of Me, Myself and I

DEATH
Definer – Oracle x–o Miracle –
Enlightener – demon of Time –
Alchemist of "x–o" – Philosopher of
Eternity – Embracer of Diversity –
The Brewer of weird Easter eggs –
Ancient – Alchemy Metaphysician.

...
.

.

Relative
– Warlock – PERFECT⊙MN⊙ – New Age
Philosopher – intergender – Dao Buddha

– The Female in me – The
reincarnated female Medusa
Loveheart with the tree of
Medusa. Reincarnated behavioral
pattern of Yota as a Universal
Definer with blueprints and
achievements for that soul
shard – The White Devil Queen
Vitra – The Queen – The
Seventh Seal and The brave of
Jeanne d'Arc.

Here you see a bunch of power variables of energies or
different types of code that has been achieved and
built together and shaped out from Metaverse in
blueprints and greyprints, compiled and reincarnated

or incarnated into myself. They all represent behavioral pattern and soul shards adopted, integrated, sealed and lived by me.

We read energies from artifacts and from all cultures, isms and religions in the calibrational orbish archeology way. Communicating in the force with ancient as well as newly arrived Soul spirit Shards. In Metaverse you find all kinds of energies.

- Me - I'm a New Age Alchemist - The Philosopher: that brews images between colors - myths - religions - reality - relativity - ideology - timelines - senses - healing - ancient knowledge and anything that comes in my path.

- Myself - The Definer - The intergender in motion - The Woman and Man in coexistence of harmony inside.

- My minds define - dissect - redefine - observes Outcomes and creates sum-ups and define again then I build paths and bridges with "opposite/relational/Linear/Reflections/Directional thinking methods" among some of the ways to reach new agreements and new paths to grow, coexist and co-operate with. By working thoroughly, future time is

65

Invested and taken care of.

- I - The Last Warlock, Gizmoo
Strangelove: A Warlock that
follows the Shaman path among
others, investigating relations
and co-existence - respecting
life, soul and force - A
Messenger, Enlightener and
Guide - Daredevil with
mentalities and the relative
truths we live among today -
fueling the Oracle x-o Miracle
inside me.

...
.

66

Dao Buddha

A new garden of Buddhism
TRUE FAITH
Poetry ONMO Justice

- Student of: Mutual
Relational thinking, The force,
Eroticay, Love, Nothing and
Everything, Exist and Nature,
Evolution.

My "Reincarnations" – Universal Death codes

Medusa D.B. Loveheart – A
Master of Universe – Ancient –
Creator

Yota – Universal Definer –
Ancient alien soul shard

Gizmoo Strangelove – The Last
Warlock – From domain of Death

Sun Wukong – 孫悟空
– manifestation in me
...
.

My Paths

True Faith

Exist & Nature

The Force

MUTUALITY - LOVE

Poetry **ONMO** Justice

Eroticay - Sexualism

Evolution

Tai chi - The Way of The Jellyfish

Feng Shui - Inner Balance

Martial Training - Dim Mak - 點脈

True Follower of THE FORCE - True
Guide Exist & Nature

Warlock - Protector of Nothing and
Everything - Seeker of truth

...
.

Dao Buddhist ONMO INFINITY:

* <u>THE Dao Buddhist MONK</u>

Exist & Nature

TRUE FAITH

Atom

Poetry ONMO Justice

Eroticay

* Exist & Nature - our source and reason - our life and death

* YOU ARE - WE ARE - I AM - WE - I - YOU

* Defense ONLY

* Protector of Nothing and Everything

* Co-exist - Co-operate - Co-understand

* RESPECT; "Diversity within yourself" - "Diversity within your surrounding" - Mutuality

* Understanding and embracing DEATH enlightens coexistence in LIFE - Do not do Death nor become Dead prematurely UNLESS NO OTHER

OPTION IS TO BE.

* MIND – HEART – Generational thinking – Relational Thinking – Evolutionary Thinking – Directional Thinking – Reflective Thinking – Organic Thinking – Calibrational Thinking – Sexually thinking – Opposite Thinking – Linear Thinking

* MIND – HEART – True Faith & Calibrational Lifestyle – Balanced Senses and Emotions in Heart Mind Soul Spirit Flesh Blood Bones in All Directions in Harmony

* See the truth as it is; – roots and branches – True Faith – The Opportunity of life – Sexualism – Diversity – Mutuality – LOVE – Senses – Emotions – Heart – Mind – Soul – Spirit – Respect – Dignity – Humbleness – Nothing – Everything – Life – Death.

...
.

.

* <u>Admitters to Dao Buddhism</u>

Exist & Nature

TRUE FAITH

Poetry ONMO Justice

Atom

Eroticay

* Exist & Nature - our source and reason - our life and death

* You ARE - WE ARE - I AM - WE - I - YOU

* You are responsible for your entire life and the quality it has for your self

* You are the only person living your life and its only yours and no one else but yours.

* Its Your responsibility to achieve that understanding in its completeness thru out your entire lifetime.

* RESPECT; "Diversity within you" - "Diversity within your surroundings" - Mutuality
* Respect; True Faith - Diversity - Mutuality - Sexualism - LOVE -

71

Nature – Elements – Senses –
Emotions – Heart – Mind – Soul –
Spirit – Dignity – Humbleness –
Nothing – Everything - Life -
Death.

* We are all Equally Equipped With
Heart and Mind

* Diversity IS our GREATEST
Strength

* We are all animals on the Very
same planet

* We are just as much part of the
Universe as the Universe is a part of
us

* The Force of Love IS Power of
Mind.

* Follow your heart as long as it
makes sense and respect the SOUL at
ALLTIME

* Live here and NOW, Learn from the
Past, Be aware about the future.

* Keep your faith, follow your Senses
and pray for the respect of Love.

* Unite; be unique with your own
SOUL, MIND and Heart.

...

.

!!!Dao Buddha Pondering Heart Stones!!!

- Share your knowledge and you
  shall receive.

- MIND IS POWER.

- The Power of Love is the Force
  of the Heart and soul, Mind
  over Matter,
  NOTHING○IS○EVERYTHING – THE
  FORCE.

- Time is important; if you know
  the art of how to invest in it;
  you start build your own life
  for real.

- Dare Devils come in many shapes
  and forms.

- A demon reflects what you
  make them to and nothing else.

- YOU and no one else but you
  your self is the only one that
  is responsible for your very own
  life and the quality of its
  content.

- You are the only one responsible
  for your own actions and its
  outcomes, your thoughts and
  the mentality you firmly

73

believe and live.

- You are your own Master and Commander in your own lifecycle in your entire lifetime and you are the only one you can hold responsible for your own path choices.

- Trust your heart, Believe in your mind and listen to your Soul.

- It's just another Direction x-o everything is relative

- Humanity needs to shape up
  ...
  .

- Believe, respect and care in your self - your surroundings and the planet that gives you and your life an opportunity to coexist.

- Enhanced senses bring you closer to any direction.

- The Future is never further away than your next moment.

...

.

Mantra:

I LOVE YOU

I LOVE

LOVE

...

.

.

For THE Future
In Time
From the Past

...

.

.

Luf
Faith
Holy Force
Force

...

.

LOVE

UNIVERSAL

UNDERSTANDING

Welcome All

- There is a lot of weird and strange things in the world of today. I'm intending to give you a couple of golden moments of reflections over our own evolution in time, the relations to other living creatures, evolutionary timelines, as well as mother nature's own evolution... Daring you to challenge reality with relativity and provide you with a better faith in tomorrow.

Here I am Medusa Loveheart, The last Warlock and some people might even consider me an Antichrist.

- Then again today basically anyone could be considered an antichrist ;)

I have grown and evolved my warlock path. Today I'm an Ancient Warlock as The last warlock, with the upgraded Flame: A Spectral Purple Flame from the base of Blue Flame of Truth now blended with the Red Flame of Purple LOVE as my weapon. The achiever of Dao Buddha and the Composer of Dao Buddhism. My latest name is now Medusa Dao Buddha Loveheart and Relative is the crown of my Entity.

For a long time, I have pathed as Gizmoo Strangelove and it's been a pleasure to achieve the state of being I am now, Medusa Dao Buddha Loveheart as an 5th elemental of relativity in flesh and blood hence Relative. Throughout this book you'll see me introduce lots of different variable names and patterns of myself and they are all me in my evolving and no one else ever. I have several cores in my soul so don't get confused by all the names I drop every now and then.

Yota within me are knower days a very much achieved reincarnation by this entity and an ancient alien life energy and evolutionary demon. My Entity (my Human body) is with all its ancient as well as ::NowTime:: (Today-time that is).

...

.

.

Warlocks are male entity witches and seeker of truths and the words before the word Warlock can be a Dual verb that only describes a warlocks Nature/"Call in life".

I pathed my way as The Last Warlock and achieved a so-called ascending, I'm still The last warlock though. I'm still evolving in a never-ending exploration and coexistence with The Force that flows through Metaverse and universe in all kinds of ways and directions.

Warlocks works in Metaverse as well as in Universe. We have paths that walks the truths in all directions, and we have many skills sets no other species, terrestrials or astral beings has. We have been considered and pictured as dark minded people, but the truth is we are not good nor evil. We see the truth as it is, and we never accept any other form of it. We do adjust and adept in some ways to the today's forms of living in order to be able to coexist as pleasant as possible. One of the famous ones I have met in Metaverse is Jesus who chose his path and his life and are a loyal form in he's own path with me now as well. We all walked different paths and when we reach our complete form in our exist, then takes the full form of what we have become.

Today I'm an Ancient Warlock by nature. As intergender I wear both the suffixes for the male and female within me.

> - Some find me weird, other
>   strange...
>   What can I say...
>   I love you all
>   =)

I'm not the last warlock that will walk this earth as far as I'm concerned but merely one in the line of many others. I will here show you a yin and yang in composition of A Pure Truth drop and one Pure Love drop, and you will be surprised of how powerful this is. I will reveal secrets of life, the ability to take control of the future and gear it in the direction you really wanted to go. I will show you how to not only see secrets of happiness and success but also how you yourself can improve your own life quality quite well just by shaping up a little. I will show you ways in how to deal with a healthier mentality's and to take advantage of sides that might have been considered weaknesses. I will show you the truth about our life and our lifetime in this opportunity of life in our part of universe. I will show you why we have been creating religions and isms and what our true nature is about in its completeness. I will talk about life and death, about good and bad, about how you yourself can utilize advanced mind mapping formulas and systems for your own advantage. I will show you the Art of true Eroticay. I will define your existence in physics and emotionally. I will reveal your true nature and show you the true power of awareness. I will paint the truth behind the human anatomy. I will quote philosophers and scientists. I will dissect religions and politics. I will show you the true behavior of love and I will teach you a language of truth. I will reveal all the relatives we deny and neglect. I will open your eyes. I will wake you up. And I can already now say that the sight you will see when you wake up will be quite awfully at start. But that's just because you just woke up. And even if the awakening itself will be rough, hard, ugly and uncomfortable, you will still wake up and feel damn honored to be awake.

I will reveal Our very own matrix we already exist in.

- ::I want you to understand that what you are holding in possession and are looking at right now is equaling: to the choice Morpheus offers Neo in the first movie of (The Matrix) where you see Morpheus offering Neo an option of two pills, one ::((green) pill of truth):: and one ((red) pill of unawareness). If Neo chooses the green pill, he is provided the understanding that he will wake up and see what the reality actually looks like and if he chooses the red pill he is provided the understanding that he will forget he ever even had this opportunity. I'm here conceptualizing and explaining the nature of the choice you now stand before in this relative reality:

Only this time the pill is defined as a book and a spectral purple flame of truth and love from the dimension of nothing. If you chose to read this entire book you will for sure wake up. And once that is done there is no turning back. Once you have read this book, from the beginning to the end you will no longer be a sleepwalker. Once you have read the entire book you are already taking your first stumbling steps in the new age that is coming.

- You have just been offered a pill in a yin and yang shaped form with the color blend of blue, red and purple.

- However, you have only been offered one pill or my very own "coin of Nothing" and no other

82

option seemed interesting
enough for me.

- Let's move on shall we

...

.

.

I'm the Guru Metaphysician Archimedes wrote about
in one of his books that stated I would come one day
and set things straight

- Yeah, that's right, that's me!

Yes this is about the TRUE AWAKENING dear have no
doubts about that, this is how it all starts.

- Welcome dear

And don't worry, I come in peace.

...

.

.

We are not standing before the greatest evolutionary
step for human mankind anymore. We stand before
greatest evolutionary step for the entire opportunity of
life in this part of universe. Many prophets have
spoken of an antichrist arriving in our time and to be
honest most of us can be considered an antichrist
today however with my reincarnations – universal
codes – and myself as intergender in motion and
Sexual nature in the dual direction of both man and

women. I will fit into the description of a beast that has many heads and so forth. Even though I physically have the same limits as anyone else has. With reincarnations – universal codes - (that I will talk and paint more thoroughly in the Dao Buddhism section of this book) You are actually providing yourself with several cores in the soul and not the mind just like some of the chisel processors in computers today. It's a bit more complicated than that and I will show you why and how later on. Dealing with reincarnations – universal codes - isn't something anyone should be taking lightly because you are dealing with your own life and mental health. And many other very delicate matters, it's an achievement in the sense that you have to reach this in harmony within yourself and that goes for all of YOU. The art of reincarnation – universal death codes are a delicate matter and shouldn't be taking lightly by anyone.

- Let's straight out some questions right away.

Is this the weirdest peacefully and most spectacular attempted to unite the world with pen and paper?

- Sure is honey

Have I already succeeded?

- I'm afraid so ;)

Is it dangerous to read this book then?

84

- Dont think so, its more out of
  enlighteningly and educational
  Id say

...

.

.

When you think about it, isn't it a strange and peculiar
feeling after all?
To be on top of the food chain, king of the hill, the
masters of a planet, Acing out a complete galaxy by our
self even if we for sure never been on all the places.

- That, I think we can agree
  about.

And the coolest part is that we know it for sure several
century's now. We still haven't really figured out how it
all started, the unique and delicate reality that we have
the humble and lovingly opportunity to participate in.
We existed for a long time now even though we
haven't been among the first animals to populate this
planet, and we can't compare our existential timeline
with the nature itself as well as other older living
masses that has been here long before us. Today we
are dominating life here on the planet that we call
earth, and we have come to a great deal of conceptual
understanding, but we have had to struggle a lot to
become number one. Looking at the evolutionary
timeline you can't help yourself being amazed over our
very own evolution and the human's ability of survival
as well as our exceptional mind. Think about it. From

the beginning we started out with absolutely nothing, nothing at all whatsoever and we didn't know what would become out of us, we had no idea. We not only succeed in capturing the fire but by first learning to fear it then realize its total importance for us and we manage not only to capture it but to harness and create it as well.

That alone tells us more than most think about how fine and brilliant the animal human can be. There were no books, no Internet, hardly a language and no one there to tell us how to do it, when and why we should even try to imagine our self to do it. We are equipped with the gift to create something out of nothing or seemingly nothing at least. We have to be grateful to our own curiosity, imagination and foolishness, most important of all our continually growing awareness.

It took us time, long time to accomplish it. One thing led to another, accidents that ended up in sad tragedy's many times over. Eventually the moment of right time and place came after getting closer to it under different circumstances. Finally, we became masters of the fire and even then, we had no idea what it actually was we had accomplished. We were happy and proud over the fact that we could capture and manage it. We didn't know the depth of what we actually are able to use it for. Today we use lots of different types of heat and energy sources to all kinds of things that at that point weren't even in our imagination. It's used to refine raw materials, to shape and form solid metals, to boil liquids and make food as well as for chemical distillations. We rarely understand the full depth or even what it is, that we have found until long time later.

That step was one big and utterly important step in our remarkable evolution, with no doubt we wouldn't be nowhere near where we are today without the fire.

Throughout our history we have always created our self without even really reflecting over that simple fact. Our Visions, our dreams and our thoughts is what stakes out our future. Our curiosity and fantasy have broken down barriers that then might have been majorly and seemingly impossible. There really is no such thing as impossible but everything does have its own time and place. We invented the wheal so we easier could transport bigger objects on wagons, little did we know then about the cars and motor bikes that would come to exist from the very same invention. Even before the wheel we used trees or timber to role things that was out of proportion for humans to carry by them self. We have always found ways to accomplish things that takes more than just what can be found in nature.

Our fantasy and curiosity are exactly that powerful. Its thanks to the Thought – Mind we keep evolve and with it our never-ending growing awareness.

Today's impossibilities are tomorrow's adventures. The world has been flat, it has been impossible to go to the moon and medicine has evolved from herbalism into chemicals.

Science has brought advancement to technical and chemical fields, advancement in all kinds of directions, Faith has brought advancement to social understanding and human behavior. We are living in a pot of boiling evolution created and discovered by no one else but our self. We have gone from era to era of ages and yet we never seem to stop worry of what will come next.

- Yet we still seem have a hard time to accept that whats comes next is always up to our self in the sense of to be or not to be.

...

.

Circle of Life

The planet we live upon is the heartbeat of all life upon it. Nature with its vegetations is the heartbeat for the animalistic life that coexist on this planet. Without the Elements of nature there is no life for us humans or any other organic life form or species here on earth, nature feeds the animals and animals feeds the nature.

Life itself has evolved for billions of years on this planet in this galaxy. Universe is also included in THE Circle of life since it too gives birth to new galaxies with new wonders as well as ends it with black holes or at least relocate to be more correct. We are just as much part of this universe as the universe is part of us. It's time we understand that we are living in one of its opportunities of life. For how long Universe has existed we don't know and there is no way we will get that answer by being ignorant and believe we are the only one opportunity there is, has ever been or ever will be. Universe itself has much more to reveal and share, there is so much left to be explored and discovered. Just on this planet organic life and vegetations has revealed several circles of existence already. The forms of life that lasted the longest and still remains can be found in both the birds in the air and on the ground the alligators and turtles has had the best evolutionary prerequisite as well as many animalistic life forms within the sea. From the beginning life raises from the bottom of the oceans and in small steps. The organic life is built by cells and the single cell life like amoebas and jellyfishes are amazing life forms from where life evolves in all its unique and beautiful forms.

In the beginning there were no life at all at the stone called earth, it took several hundreds of millions of years before even the simplest form of life started to exist. And even more hundreds of millions of years for it to start evolving. From the sea, life crawled up on land and evolved in all kinds of directions. Water is one of the main elements and extremely important for all life for both above and below the water surface.
It all ends in death in one way or another. Death is so neglected and despised. Such a beautiful form of existence and such a harmony there is within death. All energies from souls and spirits not just from our planetary own circle but from all over universe. We are far from alone here in space. Only in Death we more likely call it Metaversal rather than universe just to separate the physic from meta in somewhat direction. Death is not an end it's just a passing on to another direction.

- Well, its so much more then that but for the sake of this time in the book being!

And it's a shame that so many are in the mentality to say it's not nice or appropriate to talk about something as natural as Death. We all visit the domain of death at some time of being in our life's some more then others.

...
.

Elements of Nature:

Water – Fire – Air – Earth – Universe

Force of Wind, the element of Air

Every day when you walk outside it touches your face with gentle ease, it breathes life to your hair and play beautiful melodies as it whirls between the trees and its branches. You feel it breezes on warm summer days like the smoothest silk that cools your skin. You feel it biting your chin on cold winter days. The wind moves in all directions, twirls and dances free as free can be. It moves as it wishes with grace and might. Sneaking, luring and rushing forward it find its way over mountains and passing through valleys. Still, patient and silent as it prepares to release its uninhibited powers as an untamed beast.

The air that we breathe fuels organic life but is also fueled by nature itself who is one of the greatest essentials we have here. Both the vegetation in water as well as upon earth provides this planet the air that we all need in order to breathe and coexist with this opportunity. Air travels within and between the different conditions of cold and heat, free and independent. It comes in many shapes and forms sometimes gentle and with ease exploring any corner there is to be. Sometimes furious and vicious while it storms as a hurricane or whipping the water over oceans. Cyclones that move over both water and land ravaging anything that comes in its way, coexisting with its surrounding forces of nature.

The air is charged with electrical energies both positive and negative, the air itself contains its own yin yang. With those opposites it creates mighty discharging energies in laude sound waves: Thunder and its beauty of electrical tentacle chains: Lightning

We don't see it with our bare eyes, we only perceive its presence with the eye when it carry's mist, smoke, clouds or when it twirls the snowflakes as they dances in the air during wintertime's and in summertime when the air gets so warm we may see the heat raising from the ground revealing the visuals of it. We look through it when we glare at the sun or gaze over the beautiful starry night sky. Birds and insect have it as their natural way of traveling and it helps nature's own vegetation to spread their seeds by the wind in this harmony of life.

That's not all it does for us. It allows solid material to exist in lighter forms as gas and it breathe fuel for the element of fire so its flames may dance and coexist upon this earth. It lets us experience incenses from everything, the nature, wildlife, food, water, sand and flowers. It challenges us with odor and stench it gives us signals of love and lust. It guides us in directions and nurtures us with its playfulness. It stimulates our nose, our sense of smell a sense that is of major importance for all animal life.

Thru it travels waves of both sound and light in

different frequencies, particles in all kinds of shapes and forms and it never pass judgment on any of this. All the energies that's created and maintained by all organisms both organic as well as chemical, that resides around us and within us coexist in this element. Throughout all the four Seasons the air remains the same in form and nature.

The sky surrounding our planet is one of the corner stones for all life upon it, It even carries a protective shield of Ozone layer in its outer rim that keeps us safe from radiation as well as incoming unwanted material. That's exactly how beautiful and important air is in all its might and glory hence one of Mother Nature's own Elements.

Force of the element Water

The moist, the mist, the mystic of the fog surrounding ponds and swamps luring and deceiving secrets so tempting to find out what they are and yet so vicious and lurking of deep foundations you'll never be able to seek and find out by yourself. Water the Force of H^2O that keeps our thirst and bodies breathing for as long we exist in harmony with it. There are both Salty and Sweety water both containing the most amazing life forms you can possibly imagine.

The deep oceans contain life forms we still have hard time to understand how they are and that's where we all come from in one way or another. That's how important all water life is, and all ways will be for animals on our planet. See we are all animals on the same planet with the same purposes and limits with possibilities. Possibilities are a great key word but not as foul interference with already existing nature but for understanding and co understanding. The seaweed life, plankton and all other kinds of algae provide us with almost 70% of all the breathable air that we human so heavily depend on and yet we rape the oceans without even reflecting upon it. In the oceans we find underwater caves miraculous in comparison to the one on land. The oceans and the wind twirl and hurl in same viciousness and cruelty as more often seen on television later days. The force of nature that can be in several shapes and form like misty liquid and "water Chrystal snowflakes" all depending on the element of Fire/Heat. Snowflakes, something not every country comes to experience as a orbital landmass due to its necessity of achieving cold to zero degree Celsius. Then rain turns into snow and its beautiful, cold and wonderful at the same time. White crystal snowflakes that just as a hurricane of wind and water can be as devastating if it reaches the shape and form of hail.

The oceans contains so many different life forms, forms that contain both hearts and brain just like us. But it also contains many other species with no hearts with no spines with no blood with no brains and yet they live and experience life their own unique way just like we experience it our own unique way. Aqua, a name, a substance and a something we love to surf and bathe in the summer. Something we love to go ice skating on in the winter, Skiing downhill and long skiing, different sports entertainment for same mass just different

94

relation in heat and cold. All animals need to drink no matter what time of the year. We all have the same basically needs. We are all animals on the same planet, most of us are predators but there are plenty of variety of the predatory lifestyles and at the moment the human choice of way of life is not acceptable in most direction even though they once upon a time might have served a better purpose, that's no longer the way it is. In fact, humanity today are the worst predators alive since they don't even bother about their coming generations future.

Force of Earth

The learning of physical masses, the soils that brings us more food and flavors to what we put in our mouth. The ground we built cities and skyscrapers on the mass that provides life, Life itself. The mountains, the valleys in both land and ocean. The ocean plates of groundmasses that collides and create tsunamis and earthquakes constantly reminding us that earth does not belong to mankind, but mankind belongs to earth. The foundation all land life creatures depends upon no matter what species we are. Earth itself the biggest body, the body we all walk upon and live our everyday life. The massive body of sand, mud, dirt and stone we shape and form for our future needs. All over universe you find sky body's much like ours here on earth and most of them seem dead but there are others with water upon them, just they are too far away for us to visit for now. The earth with all its minerals and stones of brilliants, metals and chemicals in all possible directions. Diamonds, gold and platinum to mention a few. All different kind of minerals and metals. Then there is coal that earth enriches us with are foundation for so many things of today; fuels but as fuel it's not so good for our nature. It can be reduced in layers for electronically purposes, You can find it in flat screens and mobile screens and it can be compressed so hard it can become diamonds and so much more.

Force of Fire

The Heat, the glow the fire if any metal or wood or any organic matter becoming heat full enough. Vicious and cruel in its environment and not to be taken lightly. A force of nature that came to our advantage after long time of trying to harness it. It can be the most relaxing thing to rest your eyes on a flame that burns slowly on a candle. Beautifully dancing like a flame only can dance with the wind as its conductor. Open fireplaces that heat the room while sparkling with sounds of the fire burning slowly on the wood. Creating an entire profession for the world in order to maintain as healthy as possible, the fire department deals with the more vicious forms of this element. It can rampage entire forests and burn it down to ashes. And when turned into ashes new life can spring from the devastation groundmass into new healthy nutrition soil. So beautiful and yet so dangerous. The flame of a match that sparks lit and then lit a tobacco pipe so sweet and beautiful the smoke rises up from the heated glowing tobacco.

Force of Versa – Universe & Metaverse

The force of Universe is humongous in its own existence. Galaxies and suns, moons and planets, supernovas and black holes all in a great mix of beauty and grandness. Energy's bubbles in all directions both universal and metaversal. Our galaxy, The milky way is beautiful in its glory of mixed planets and stardust. Third planet from the sun is our location and a marvelous location it is. The grandness of universe is too vast for us to even try to understand how great and big it really truly is, it's a fact that is best left like that since truth is never to try to grasp but to see things for what they are. Space phenomena's such as White dwarfs, Quasars and comets are all part of space and its element that are to vast for a single planets nature which makes space an element of its own. Not to forget the gravitation fields surrounding any sky body out there in space. And Metaverse bigger and grander than you could ever believe with the mass of Time as its starship. Codes of death, Nature, dimensions and HOLY Codes, you name it it's all there ready to be explored and discovered. A versa with all its grandness and a beautiful mix of metaverse and universe.

...

.

.

- It is time to see the truth as it is.

- and accept that We...

Live in Life, Exist, are a part of the Evolution, are a part of universe, Universe is part of us, are extremely responsible for our own evolution at all-time, all live on this planet (planet Earth). are the same species all over the planet only different colors, are a two component sexual animal species and sex is just as much a social skill as a reproduction method for our own species natural existence. Life comes and goes, Civilizations comes and goes ... and moves forward, speak and know already over hundreds of languages and we only need ONE.

- We are living upon a living organism we chose to call earth and its only thanks to exists own eternity machinery of biological sky bodys we are here.

- Not because of you!

Science has been trying to invent something they can call an eternity machinery with mechanic and electricity. Exist did that with biology, electricity and billions of other phenomena's and you think your smart. You are here because exist handheld us our galaxy as one of billions and billions of wonders Exist already created out there.

- Think about what you have done in your life?

This planet alone has evolved for about 4,6 billion years for now and produced billion of species, even one called human being.

- And you think your special!

We are all participators of this universe own eternity biological machinery, and you just happen to have the opportunity to be a part of it all.

- And what have you chosen to do with that specific time you been upon this earth?

- Why are you so afraid of the truth as it is?

...
.

.

When looking upon us as the magnificent animal we are its sometimes frightening how much we neglect our capabilities cause of denial of truth. Humans has a brain so advanced it's hard to describe with words. We have several key systems within us. The Heart system pumps the blood in our veins, The Brain system pumps the chemicals in our nerves. The Food system processes food and fluids turning it into energy so that our other systems keep flowing.

We are living beings, a species and that's exactly what we are. We have an anatomy built with DNA, Chromosomes and billions of cells. All cells contain bits of information in our body not just the brain but all of our cells. Our cells are just as advanced as or even more then the holographic cells that stores information three dimensionally. Cause we are that by nature and even though each cell in singular might not provide much of information the entire picture of completeness of a single human body with all its combinations of billions and billions of cells provides ridiculously much of possibilities and opportunity's. Our brain alone is a massive biological power tool of intercepting and processing signals of information.

The brain has two modes. The Calculating mode which is the common way we humans today learn to coexist with it and the Calibrating mode which is its natural state of functionality.

We are all utilizing both modes even though we might not be aware of its different areas.

The Calculational lifestyle is based on your Intelligence and the calibrational lifestyle is based on your Awareness. The Calculational lifestyles neglects big parts of impressions from your senses and follows the eyes more than any other senses utilizing the modern logic and fundamentals. Whereas the calibrational lifestyle equalizes the senses and reads the total impression of all the senses and from there utilizes logic and fundamentals. Usually common within advanced martial arts as well as for inner journeys and meditational arts. To read your environment takes training and effort especially since we all grow up in society's where such skills isn't admitted. Calibration methodologies are already recognized and utilized among technological fragment when fine-tuning vehicles as well as printing out pictures from printers. Fine-tuning areas over all calibration methodologies used in order to make the correct adjustments for the time being. But as a lifestyle the Zen Buddhism and Native Americans are the ones that are best recognized in schematics of calibrational lifestyle that brings the possibility to utilize in a normal stressed city life as well. The calibrational lifestyle is overwhelming in comparing to the calculational lifestyle in the way that it is already a part of the calibrational lifestyle.

Even though the calibration lifestyle is about amending the lifestyle of the animal human being its very far away the same as us moving our civilization back to the stone age. That's a common misunderstanding since we will actually be able to advance much further than what we are today. Today it will move us closer to the high-tech forms of predators you might have seen in the movies "The predators" or "Alien vs. Predators". It's a natural step in our evolution and is a necessity no matter how you feel about it.

- I'n not good and I'n not evil, I just reveal the truth exactly the way it is.

...

.

.

We are a sexual animal and should not be afraid nor ashamed of admitting a simple fact as that. Sex has a great importance for humans in many ways. Sex is one of the ways and happens to be one of the greatest ways to stimulate the brain and nerves as well as your inner soul and spirit. The reward of endorphins for the brain and nerve system is vital. An ointment and relaxations everybody deserves to have more often.

The human is sexual and that's exactly the way it is. Homosexual and heterosexual are just somewhat confused terminology and a result of the normality norms of today that are nothing but vague translations of either the bible or the Koran. The terminology heterosexual and homosexual didn't enter the language until about a hundred to two hundred years ago. We are all sexual and are able to perform so called same gender sex actions. Love is universal and same gender people love each other as much as opposite gender do. Due to the result of phobia against the human true nature and the twisted as well as the insane wrongly idea of that some people would be unable to have sexual pleasure with same gender because of their biological anatomy is probably the biggest illusion of them all and the strangest lie people voluntarily chose to live in. We all have the same biological anatomy and the same possibilities. Everybody is able to become advanced lovers and explore all areas of sexual excitement and pleasure.

It is under no circumstances limited to any group of people but rather a defect opinion created by narrow minded and very limited sexual people. The true sexual nature of humans is sexual in all directions and everything else are pathetic lies founded on extremely poor sexual enlightenments. Sex with males and females no matter your own gender is simple different experiences with different areas of satisfaction and exploration. Anyone is able to walk either path or both. They both offer great sexual experience and excitement and that's a fact no matter you like it or not.

Sex is one of the essences and areas that are extremely damaged by poor mentality's, people are basically living in a life where the world is still flat when it comes to sexual understanding.

Taboo is something that has majorly undermined people when it comes to sexual exploration for long time now. Taboo is one of the strongest mentality program stoppers and usually achieve more harm than well doing. To believe that responsibility is taken by denying and closing your eyes for the truth is one of the biggest mistakes and failures humans of today still admits.

Love comes from the heart and is an incredible force that shouldn't be confused with sex. Sex and love are a wonderful combination. However, having sex with emotion and to have sex because of love are two separate things. Lust and love can go hand in hand and is without doubt a beautiful and colorful experience.

Your entire body is a sexual organ when it comes to the art of sex. The more you dare to know yourself and explore yourself the greater the experience of sexual pleasure and lustfully plays will become. The key is to respect your body to its fullest.

Taking responsibility over your own lusts and sexuality is about allowing yourself to experience it and to take charge of your own life, admitting your natural needs and also allow yourself to grow in experience where you see sex as it is and not as something forbidden or something that isn't ok. Admitting your self is also about you allowing yourself to relate to it as a natural need that you want and love to satisfy. To actually stand for it when meeting other people. To as a grown-up person dare to seek it and actually be proud over it like any other skill. To dare to admit that it's a part of your lifestyle as well, just like dancing or eating. To live it and not to be ashamed over that it is a need that needs satisfaction like any other need. To be able to enjoy looking for it. Just like you enjoy looking for other things to satisfy other needs. To be able to be proud over that you like sex. Sex is an adult skill. Why shouldn't adults be proud and like to advance in a skill that is a natural part of every single human being.

- If when your adult isn't the time to naturely take charge and responsibly satisfy such a beautiful and healthy skill as sex... When is?

Seven billion people has it and they have it daily. Yet people are afraid to be open about it. Sex is one of the greatest rewards you can give your brain system. Humans are over equipped with erotically stimuli impulses by nature and many people sees it as something to overcome rather than something to learn to coexist and to advance with.

Sex in the modern world is partially dysfunctional due

to the lack of respect for it. Sex is an adult skill and should also be adored as one. The Education of sex is practically a joke in the schools all over the world. People doesn't know how to teach, talk and relate to something as natural as sex. People seem to have a hard time to accept that sex truly is something that belongs to adulthood and is to be improved and broadened just like any other skill. You will probably become good at it for real if you accept the truth about it and realize that it's probably the most advanced social skill we have. A skill that is growing in advancement by your growing self-awareness of your own sexuality, by having sex and by daring to explore and to be explored. A skill that has such wide array of components and that follows your own nature throughout your entire life.

People have a fear of advancing in sexual existence. Truth is that sex becomes greater with age. The older you get the more mature and sophisticated yourself knowledge and experience within your own sexualism becomes.

It's with experience you become more advanced and can explore new grounds of erotically sexual experiences. Because of the unhealthy attitude towards sex for some reason people seem to go the opposite direction.

- You might want to have a seat now reading the next coming piece.

When it comes to sexual climax stimuli no person can give the ultimate sexual experience to another person alone. A women can never give a man he's greatest sexual climax stimuli experience alone, nor can the man give it to a woman. This might seem like a harsh fact but that's exactly the way it is. The greatest sexual climax stimuli for a male person are always via the prostate gland since the intensity of the orgasm by prostate stimulation is much more intense and stronger all over the male body then the normal male orgasm. It's the natural penis that gives the very best stimulation for the anal. Both male and female has stronger orgasm via the anal stimuli and it's a lot much stronger all over the entire body for both male and female, but the male's prostate gland is the point to stimulate for any male person.

Sexual stimuli grow greater when the erotically experience is done with several entities. This kind of advanced sexual experiences demands a mature and sexual aware presence and is something that belongs to more experienced adults. People should really enjoy their age in this sense, cause it's when you get older and more patient your true sex-life will become a more awesome experience. Then you have lost your virginity and had chance to explore all kinds of sex in both better and les good experiences. You also most likely reached the understanding that great sex is about a mature sexual understanding where both you and your partner can communicate and harmonize each other's sexual experiences with each other more fluently.

Anal sex is an <u>advanced</u> sex skill, the reason is because there are a lot of nerves and nerve ends in the anal region (sexual nerve area). There are hundreds of thousands or even millions of nerves end in the anal region. I don't remember the exact amount of nerve ends since it was a while ago, I learned about that fact. The stimulation in that area is abnormal powerful, once you mastered that skill that is.

The skill is about the relaxation of the 2 circular muscles (sphincter muscles) in the anus, one upper/inner sphincter muscle and one lower/outer sphincter muscle. It's the only touchable muscles that is circular in its shape/form/functionality in our human anatomy.

That is what the anus consist of and that is the exact same anatomy on all human beings on this planet has, both man and women (in the big picture of those facts that is). In other words, we are all sexual and Anal sex is just an underlined advanced sexual skill. The male population of this planet also has something called the prostate gland inside anus and it is extremely sensitive and reacts with a very powerful, intense, long lasting and strong chemical orgasm once you mastered that skill as well (a solo skill for the male population, relaxing the anal for the prostate gland orgasm as well). The human anatomy is very brilliant in its complexity. Anal sex is an advanced sexual skill for many reasons. You really need to learn it and in order to do so you must invest time in yourself. You should never stress the exploration of your anus since it's a very sensitive area.

Anal sex has a several states of virginity as well. One

that can be compared in similarity to the female virginity of sexual intercourse in her vagina. Its two completely different experiences though. The penetration virginity is just one of the new experiences. The two others are the two new ways to achieve orgasms for the male that is. The penetration act is a great stimulus for the entire body when done properly and you actually enjoy the sexual intercourse throughout your entire body in ways that is not accomplished with the more commonly female general sex. To be penetrated is a completely different experience.

The anal itself provides you with a new orgasm stimulator and is a strongly enhanced orgasm experience in comparison to the normal penis orgasmic stimuli and this is the second virginity you'll experience and that with great pleasure for sure.

The third one is the prostate gland orgasm that compared to the anal orgasm stimuli is an even more enhanced orgasmic experience and is completely outstanding when it comes to mind blowing experiences.

When exploring your anus, no matter sex, always use silicon lubricant/ointment, start out with your hands and fingers so you get to know what you feel in all direction and do it when there really is private time with no stress involved. Be aware about long fingernails since they might be uncomfortable in that area.

Anal sexual intercourse will be an odd experience the very first time you experience it and depending how well you learned to feel comfort and are able to relax in the muscles of your anus; the first-time experience will vary in the amount of pleasure. Since you never learned what it's like to insert another penis inside your own anus and it's an opposite direction towards what you have gotten used to in your past.

The anus contains two sets of muscles as stated earlier which means that you not only must be able to relax the outer muscle but also the inner, and here it's very important that the person inserting the penis is well aware about this and that you both understand the importance of taking it slow in the beginning. Once you successfully complete the penetration itself you need to let the anus adjust to this new experience when it's the first time. You will get great pleasure even the first time as long as you mutually respect Anal sex for what it is, an <u>advanced</u> sexual skill.

- Yes, you too are wired that way!

- We all are.

You don't need to have sex with another man in order to experience anal sex but can use substitutes for the male penis such as dildos. No matter if you are female or male that receives the penetration in your anus you should Always take use of a lubricant. Use Silicon lubricant it won't disappoint you. A lubricant is some sort of oil substance that add the behavior of gliding. You find them in water-based form as well as silicon-based forms. Today the silicon based are to prefer in the act of Anal sex since its longer lasting and has better glide quality. You can purchase Lubricants from pharmacy's as well as on the net and in sex-shops. They do differ in quality, and you should find out which one you like on yourself. The reason is because your anus is very sensitive to friction and unlike the mouth and the vagina its own sexual ointment is very vague and come in very small doses. Yes, anus also has its own glide ointment but in very small doses. And when using Dildos, it's a must.

The water-based Lube is recommendable for oral sex when a condom is used since then you will provide your mouth and tongue with a nicer taste if you wisely chose a water-based lube that's flavored. Some people can handle it very well without Lube(lubricant) but you won't know that until you learned how your body is functioning in that area.

The male penis is preferable in the art of the <u>advanced</u> sexual skill Anal sex. Since the nature of the male penis has a foreskin that reduces the friction and even if the penis is fully stone hard erected it's still a better and more comfortable media because of the nature of its flesh and skin. Even when you use a condom the male penis is to prefer in Anal sex.

For the male entity – Anal sex gives you not just a new dimension of your sex-life but also a new dimension of your past experience of what an orgasm can actually be like. The anus itself is a sexual stimulator as well as intensifier of the orgasm. The Prostate gland is a sexual stimulator, but its role comes a bit further into the sexual act and has an extreme functionality when it comes to intensify the orgasm. So, for the male to sexually stimulate both the penis and he's anus in same time as well as the prostate gland gives him not only a very great and nice time of sexual intercourse but also brings, he's own orgasm to a complete new high of intensity as well as in experience.

Because of all the nerve endings that reside in the anus region the brain gets heavily stimulated in more ways than it usually handles the signals of sexual intercourse or masturbation. The result is that it also answers with same new amount of intensity, and it also boost the eruption of Endorphins majorly when status orgasm is reached which is why the experience of it becomes so much stronger. You can get orgasm strictly from anus sex without extra stimulation on your penis. The prostate gland however preferably needs you to be aroused before it functions as the sexual and orgasmic stimulator. The penis pleasure, the anus pleasure and the prostate gland pleasure are three stackable experiences which means that when stimulated and enjoyed simulated in same time simultaneously they add up to each other's stimulations.

The triple Orgasmic state is however not an automatic happening in sync. You will have to learn how to sync them, and it can be a bit tricky as it sounds. What can happen and does happen every now and then is that you over stimulate your penis before the anal has reach the point of climax/orgasm then your orgasm will still be stronger but won't contains the great intense

111

and long-lasting experience as it does if you chose to let the anus be the main stimulator. Because when the anus reaches its point of climax, the anal orgasm, the penis will follow in other words the anus has precedence in orgasmic nature. The Penis and Vagina orgasm will however help trigger the anal orgasm when you first learn it. The anus does not erupt any sperms nor anything else mostly it can however produce more of its own natural ointment as a result of aroused stimuli but it's mainly a pure power release of endorphins within your brains nerve system.

The anal penetration when you have learned to receive it will enhance the sexual experience as well before the orgasm during the act itself and you will be able to feel it much stronger through your body. Slow Anal sex really enhances those feelings as well as large size penises.

You will also learn that the size of the penis penetrating your anus actually have quite an important role and this is also something that you will have to carefully explore since size does really matter. The anus can fortunately handle quite large penises, and you will have to learn what sizes you are most comfortable with. It's wise to start out from small size then try bigger the more experience you get.

- I have had quite a lot of Anal sex in my lifetime and to ride a huge dick is just an awesome experience to be able to do.

However, the bigger the dick is the more responsibility resides in the owner of it. And for people that's new to this I recommend them to find older people that has had more time to understand their responsibility. Then you will have a much better experience. Young people tend to be a bit reckless in the sense of lack of experience but that's not the same as all young people are that.

By understanding the feeling of being penetrated you will also become a better penetrator which is an equally important and responsible role in the act of Anal sex. How you handle your movement with your penis is extremely important not only in Anal sex but also in vaginal sex. The penetrator must be extremely aware and present when during the entire act since its two very complex muscles and two advanced muscle exercises that is ongoing at all-time during the entire sexual act of Anal sex.

To clarify this all: The nerve-topology-anatomy-map around the anus region is full of nerves and nerve ends and your penis and vagina is also just a nerve-topology-anatomy-map, but the anus has a huge, humongous amount of more nerves and nerve ends in its area and is a much far greater sexual stimuli area then both the penis and the vagina together. This goes for both the male and the female entity; Female confirms that the anus stimulated orgasm is much more intense for the

113

female then the normal vagina/clitoris stimulated orgasm as well and that there as well are intense all over the body not just the head-shoulder area. And same goes for the male entity, the anal orgasm is waaaaay beyond stronger than the normal penis stimulated orgasm also over the whole body intensified amazingly orgasmic feeling. But the male also has the prostate gland that females don't and when you trained well enough to get a prostate gland orgasm as well its way out of this world... that's how great that orgasm is for a male entity, but it requires training to achieve it and is not obvious at all for a male entity. First you must learn the regular anal orgasm that is way much better than normal orgasm. SO why is the nerve-topology-anatomy-map so important then, well in the end of the day sexual nerve stimuli is what bringing someone to orgasm is about. Sexual Nerve stimuli is really important for just that matter and the anal/anus happens to be the very best stimuli area for just that matter and the male penis happens to be the very best stimuli factor for that purpose for both male and female entities. Humans are built up by a set of anatomically settings, all humans are equipped with heart, lungs, liver and so on and the same goes for the anal region. The anal is also closely combined with the genitals on both male and female which also enhances the experience of anal sex. We are all equally built when it comes to that and all humans can learn the Advanced sexual skill, Anal sex. Both male and female alike.

It's the greatest Advanced sexual skill the animal human has, the greatest Advanced sexual skill for

114

human beings both male and female are the <u>Advanced</u> sexual skill Anal sex. Its <u>Advanced</u> cause you must actually learn it from scratch and that goes for all humans both male and female that's why.

- You just haven't learned it that's all.

<u>Truth is you haven't had a real orgasm until you have had your very first anal orgasm and that goes for both male and female entity.</u>

- You will learn to love it... trust me ;)

The reason we know all this is first it's pure science second but not the least is because we our self has had to learn it this way! Practice is the only way to learn it! There is no gay gene! Anal sex is an advanced sex skill that's all it is!

There are no heterosexual people that's all a lie, we are all sexual and Bi. It's just the way the sexual nerve map is for the entity human being.

A common mistake done today is that people don't understand that the two sphincter muscles are independent from each other. They do cooperate but you must be able to control your bodily relaxations in both muscles and this is what penetrators fail to understand many times. Just because your penis is able to pass by the first sphincter muscle it still doesn't mean that the inner is ready or relaxed enough yet necessarily. And by ignoring that the anal sexual experience will become unpleasant for the receiver no matter if it's a female or a male receiving the penis.

No matter your experience in this skill it's not unusual at all that the start/initialization of the penetration takes a while to accomplish, it's very important the receiver is the one that controls and communicates the procedure of the start since it's the receiver that must do the sphincter muscles exercises in relaxing. When the penis has completed the initializing penetration, you need to go easy for a while and let the receiver be the one that gives you the signal that he/she is now in balance with the relaxation. The riding position is to prefer for practice Anal sex purposes no matter if it is with someone or just a sexual toy. Makes you able to control the penetration in a very secure manner. The more advanced you become the easier it will be for the initiation of the penetration.

It might take up to 1-20 times of Anal sex before you are able to achieve the anal orgasm, you must first learn to come with normal penis or clitoris stimuli in SameTime as your having Anal sex which isn't really hard at all and even that feels much better. The stimuli for both male and female is very important, they stimulate their penis for male and clitoris for female until they get an orgasm while having anal sex, in that way they learn to get anal orgasms, and it becomes easier in the long run. Then you'll learn to associate the anal with orgasm and from there you achieve the anal orgasm. For some it comes easier than others.

For the woman it is necessary to learn to have an orgasm first before even thinking about learning the anal orgasm. The natural vaginal orgasm is for many women very hard to reach. Many women have never had an orgasm in their life, and some might not even now they have not had it since the education about it is as bad as it is. It is important that a woman can get a clitoris orgasm so she can stimulate the clitoris while having anal sex and by that aiding her in getting the anal orgasm. The male is not enough to solely to give a female a vaginal orgasm and that's a truth the so called hetero male population has a hard time to accept. The male penis is simply not enough. The truth is not many women can get a vaginal orgasm by another male penetrating her. However, that does not go for everyone but it's a minority that can get an orgasm just by the male penis. That's just how advanced the woman is constructed in her pleasure regions. Women should always stimulate her clitoris when having sex, no matter if its anal and vaginal sex and by doing that achieving orgasm as well and also stimulating the vaginal orgasm in that way so she can reach a dual orgasm. Only experienced women that have explored and developed her orgasmic skills can achieve vaginal orgasm from the male penetrating solely. It is not thanks to the male but to the female she gets her own orgasm. The male entity is just an aid for the female to achieve her orgasm but its all up to the female to achieve the orgasm herself. But that's not the same as sex is not very pleasurable for a woman, because they still enjoy the sex itself only, they lack the climax of an orgasm. If a woman never had had an orgasm, she needs to put a lot of effort into getting a clitoris orgasm before she can move on to more advanced orgasms. For the man it comes more naturally since we are used to get orgasm by masturbating the penis and it is quite normal that the man stimulates his penis in same time as he has anal sex. But even for males it can be hard to get an anal orgasm without stimulating the penis at the same time. Everyone deserves a greater sex life both man and woman. And everyone can learn to have an anal orgasm.

- It's because the anal is a much greater and stronger sexual organ then both the penis and vagina in SameTime are together no matter how you feel about the advanced sexual skill Anal sex. Anal sex stimuli are a normal and preferable sexual stimulus because it has greater nerve-topology-anatomy-map with a lot of nerves and nerve ends ending up in the anus since sexual stimuli is actually about nerve stimuli first.

For the female entity – The female may lack the prostate gland, but the female entity has the clitoris which the male entity lacks however it's not as powerful in orgasm as the prostate considering that females describe the anal orgasm as much stronger and more enhanced than their regular one and the prostate is even stronger and even more intense.

- Tuff titty… dear

118

The female anus has same amount of nerve ends and the area fills the same functionality. However, the female's anus also run along with the vaginas inner surface making Anal sex dual stimulation of both anus and the vaginas outer surface inside the body. Naturally a dual penetration for a female when she has learned the advanced skill set of anal sex is a new dimension of Eroticay for her as well. Females also has the Triple Orgasmic stimuli with two penetration opportunity's as well as the clitoris stimulation. Females already have sex-tools/sex-toys that gives her the opportunity to one-handed provide herself with that type of stimulation. An advanced Dildo form with a "vibrating clitoris stimulator"/" dildo for the vagina"/"smaller dildo for the anus" and is a great stimulator for females. Looks a bit like a rubber trident adjusted in shape and form for the female central pleasure region.

In a male – female relationship both partners can and in my opinion should play with each other not just normally sexually but also with toys/tools so both male and female can reach their own highs of sexual pleasure. There are a sexual toy/tool called butt plug that is built in a way so that once it's inserted in your anus it stays there, but you can continue to focus on with what you are doing and just leave it there for the rest of the act. This way the female can experience a dual penetration, and the male will experience a penetration and being penetrated; both will reach sexual high's in both their own direction as well as their mutual direction. If the male wants to penetrate the female in her anus she can always play with a dildo in her vagina at the same time. As well as the male can always chose to use either a butt plug or a dildo on himself depending on how free he wants to be with he's hands. There are also dildo forms that can be strapped onto the female entity so she can enter the role of a male. Those dildos are simply called strapons.

- How are you feeling dear, Is the world still flat now? =)

Relations in love and lust can be arranged and agreed upon in many forms, more forms than what's reflected in the societies of today (The form of a single male entity with a single female entity that is.).

- In my honest opinion a perfect relation for me is with at least two males equally sexual personalitys and at least one female equally sexually personality but preferable two female equally sexually personalitys.

In the so-called gay community relationships of three people isn't so uncommon even if it's still a small group.

There is a major responsibility among all sexually active people in the sense of protection and maintaining a healthy state. Sexual diseases are widely spread and if you're not careful you will get them as well. The Condom is your very best protection of today and you should never ever be afraid of becoming friend with it. If you want to have sex bareback (no condom) then get steady sexual partners or enter a relationship. For the casual active lover condom is your best friend. Just like Anal sex takes time to get used to, so does the condom. Adding silicon Lube onto the condom actually improves the feeling of the sex quality. The lube pre-applied on condoms rarely function or last very long or well; by using silicon Lube you also minimize the risk of frictional damage on the rubber of the condom. Take your time, understanding your penis size and its relation to the condom size. When you done it once you will know what condoms that works best for you. When practicing Anal sex actively and not with the same partner in a relationship condom is a must be. Simple as that.

Don't fool yourself because HIV doesn't care about your own lies. HIV is a virus and a deadly transmittable sexual blood diseases that's still not curable. HIV doesn't care if you are male or female it only cares to travel further.

The anal due to its natural functionality to make sure that all the necessary nourishment gets used and redistributed to the rest of your body's functionalities from the food that you have consumed has a very cleaver functionality to suck up the nourishment from anything that passes through this system and therefore have very thin coat of skin. Because of these also sexual transmittable diseases are very easily transferred as well. HIV is transmittable both via Anal sex and vaginal sex and to believe differently is to fool

121

yourself.

An HIV test is a normal blood sample and is simple to get in order to find out if you have it or not in modern countries. The result can result in two directions, either they found traces in your blood then the test will tell you that you are HIV Positive since the virus is present in your blood x-o or they didn't find traces of it in your blood then the test will tell you that you are HIV Negative since your blood lacks traces hence there is no virus present. Today in modern country's you can even get a preliminary result the same day you take the test. However, you must wait three months before you will be able to see traces of its existence in your blood and you have to wait that time before you can actually take the test. The medicines of today and science have actually evolved and achieved quite far in its progress and even if it still isn't curable its perfectly maintainable in a healthy state. This assumes you live in a country where these types of medicine are attainable. HIV isn't the only sexual diseases but the meanest.

Anyone that is sexually active must understand to respect yourself as well as your partner by using the necessary protection when entering a sexual act with a perfect stranger. You are a perfect stranger till both partners have been able to show an up-to-date HIV test.

To believe that it makes a different if you have sex the first time or the second time you meet someone is nothing else but foolishness in responsibility as well as a weakness in respecting your own sexualism within yourself. Sexual responsibility is about to see the truth as it is, respecting your life and taking responsibility for your sex while having it and has nothing to do with when you choose to have sex with someone. As long as you use condoms you can have as much sex you like whenever you like. Sex is healthy in that sense.

Sex is also a responsibility. Don't fall for other people's lies or mentality's that it won't happen to you. It's your life. You and only you are responsible for your own life. Don't screw it up because you didn't have a condom. Dare to take your life seriously in all direction even in your own sexualism. Get serious sex-partners that has the same understanding as you in the importance of staying clean from diseases.

There is nothing ugly in using a condom. Using a condom proofs, you are able to take the responsibility of the sexually active life you want to live. A word is never the same as the protection of a condom. You will never be able to tell who has or who hasn't got the HIV virus by the persons look. If a person doesn't want to use condom you don't want to have sex with that person. It's always a mutual responsibility and everything else is a lie.

You don't need to be afraid to have an active sex-life nor take distance from it. The more active you become in your sex-life with the amount of people you choose to interact with the greater the risks become. You are in charge of your own life and should always live it as you see fit yourself. Your life is your life and that makes it your responsibility. Respect yourself in order to be able to respect your surroundings.

...

.

.

It's been a lot of talk about sex now and especially anal sex.

- Why may you wonder?

Well, it's still a taboo and a very bad one as well, you might have been upset over the facts represented to you and that's because no one has told you this before.

- Why this isnt taught in school is a good question if you ask my opinion on this matter =)

I simply revealed the truth as it is about a taboo that has been here for far too long time, that's all.

...

.

.

In all this stress and self-absorbing mentality's of today, people seem to forget to stay and look at the whole picture of our self as a complete. To see the realities in truths or the truth in our reality as well.

Yes, the future will look different, no matter you like it or not. That's just a fact, a truth, a moment in time and a part of our already advancing evolution. And we are evolving. Thru out time: evolution, is a change in constant motion.

.

    – Today people laugh about that once upon a time people couldnt handle the fact that earth was not flat but orbital... he he... thats where you are today about the resent facts you just read.

We owe our own responsibility of our own evolution (We as in human race), Time and space doesn't give a damn if we exist in it or not. Have you ever stopped and asked yourself: Not why or what's the point of, but who is responsible for all this? Who is the reason for all the city's, the airplanes, the cars, the roads, the food, the technology, the languages, the financial eco system?

...

.

.

Yes, we are at a new point where the earth once again is flat but this time in another point of view. We are talking about the phenomena heterosexuals here. The problem is there is no such thing!

    – Yeah, you heard me!

There is no such thing as a heterosexual. I just explained about the anus nerve-topology-anatomy-map for you very clearly and that fact alone rules out any form of so-called heterosexuals. There truly isn't any such thing as a heterosexual whatsoever never has been never will be. It's a mental disorder cause all males and females can have sex with same sex. There is no such thing as a physical block for it to happen and males just love Anal sex there is no doubt about it. It's all in your little head dear. You been raised to believe there is such a thing as a heterosexual that's why. It's all in your head. You're a Fool not just with your guns and your bombs and your wars but as a heterosexual you're a Fool in your head. You're an emotional dysfunctional species that doesn't understand that you have been drawing the shortest straw when it comes to the greatest quality of sexual self experience. You're an intelligence and emotional Fool in your head dear.

- Yes you... you heterosexual!

Its scientifically proved its physically impossible to be a so-called heterosexual. Even Science defines the human being as a Sexual. Yes that's correct dear, as Sexual meaning your tail always swing both ways. Don't worry love, there is a savior for you.

...

.

∴

- Yeah, that's right heterosexual you're a wrong in your head. You're a Sleepwalker. Wake up Sleepwalker Wake up Wake UP. You are living on a flat planet at the moment dear Heterosexual Waaaake UP. In your head. Because no one told you differently before. WAKE UP.

∴

126

The social war between the male and female in this "straight" normality norm that dominates today is probably one of the strangest, weirdest and most stupid wars I have ever seen. We are all victims under our own self esteem in one way or another. This projection war that's still ongoing doesn't serve a good purpose for anyone. Equality is something that is today more or less a blur of grey in the hetero normality norm we live in. The disability to see each other as equally different people are becoming scary. There still are huge differences in human rights all over the world and the stupidity in the differentiation just takes weirder turns. Feminism has served great purpose in bringing equality between male and female beings. It has done marvelous work with old fashion mentalities and is still needed in many ways on many places. We should be grateful this ism is and has been here for so long struggling with old mentality's and fighting narrow minded people's ideas of an old world. Change takes time and this is just one of the proofs of it.

- Both male and female are being stubborn and silly in their contest of supreme being, neither is better than the other here.

Females have been and still are on many places in the world extremely oppressed in their equal rights as human being. Its scary that they haven't had the right to vote or that it's been ugly with female professionals in the working environment as if they aren't capable of having a working profession with success. They have been assumed to take a role as a home wife and to only take care of the household. That picture has faded today in big parts of the world but there is still much left to be wished for.

There is an underlying picture here that goes in an opposite direction and are part of the silly war among sexes and that's the fact that the female population very much like the male population consider them self-better than the male being. Truth is many females would never want to consider them self as equal to the male being since it would be a degradation for the female human being. Here starts the projection war.

Male people might have issues with relating with their own feelings, but truth is many males has great connection with their feelings. However, the "straight" normality norm disapprove to that fact and has a weird template lots of people believe they should fit in to be normal.

- Fit into, what kind of free will is that? Where is the individuality in that?

Male or Female both have same journey to make to be in harmony with their true self. Just as many females as males has problems in accepting the truth about them self and emotionally both has same amount of troubles even though they take different forms of existence. Females are not late to admit that males are feeling threatened by a female understanding the today's male normality template, but they are extremely in denial about their major problems with males understanding the today's female normality template.

On one level the last thing a female of today truly wants is equality, because of their foundational base that they are the carrier of life they are superior. It is true that it makes a female very special and the bound between female and child will always be unique. But why make it so ugly by fueling a supreme being contest that's nothing but a misunderstanding in the reality of the human being in its natural state. Humans are a two-component animal and that is just the way we are created by nature. That's how advanced the animal human is. We are equally different from each other, and we should be proud of it with dignity, respect the diversity of our nature and not try to compete about who's better or not.

This mentality war is one of the main reasons the "straight" normality norm of today never really succeed in their own definition of what love should be. What people believe love is today and what it really is are so far away from each other and will continue to be as long people refuse to see the truth in them self as a human being.

Today there isn't many couples that remains married since their testimonial about love is rather a testimonial about ownership and who is the supreme being rather than about Love. Yes, the male has for way long time been even more foolish in their own belief of being just that. A supreme being. This is a war that has been efficiently maintained by the heterosexual normality norm. This war goes on both in subconscious as well as conscious and unfortunately its destructive enough to tear down the possibilities of lasting love very efficiently. About 50% of all marriages end in divorce today and most of it because of partially this accepted denied sexual war as well as the incompetent relation to human sexuality.

Love today is something more of a fictional happening you can see on the movie and there they only show a fictional idea of what it should be rather than what it is and people that truly understands that. What happens is that people assume that love is, rather than to experience it and explore it within themselves and their partner.

Love doesn't follow a template. Love is a relation to your own life experience and a complementing attraction with fuels of unknown territory as well as the thrilling exploration of denied possibility's. Love is a thrill of comfort where you get an opportunity to co experience the coexistence. Love can come to you suddenly as well as it can grow over time. The force and power of love is great and mysterious in many ways. Strongest of them all. Love comes from the heart, desire from the brain. Love has nothing to do with the ongoing war of who's superior, that's a fool's war and a matter of greed for false greatness. Love isn't based on what gender the relation is between. Love is truly amazing and can be shared and received in all direction.

Love is not lust; never has been, will never be. Erotica or lust is a skill, an emotion and a basic need for all living creatures. Love relates to everything, humans, animals, work, hobbies, young and old. Sex however follows nature in all direction. Love is one of the most beautiful experiences you can experience, and you should take care of that opportunity and nurture it well when it happens to you. Love is free and should be respected thereafter. The domain and element of Love is as big as universe and can grow as old as you can, so don't choke Love don't disrespect an evolving feeling as powerful as Love is.

...
.

.

The war of the sexes is a foolish war in this hetero norm we all grow up in today. Unfortunately, most people are educated by this normality template unaware the consequences of it in old age. That's how powerful the normality norm is on a society. It shapes and forms people into templates of what should be or not should be without questioning if that's the truth or not. The normality norm only reflects what once was normal in lack of understanding, but it was ages ago science admitted humans to be only sexual. That's how bad the hetero normality norm is today, stating against science that humans are not sexual beings.

- Few people have the guts to
  think for them self, even less
  that dares to stand up for
  their diversity in existence. It
  takes enormous strength to

131

stand up for different being.

...

.

.

When it comes to social understanding and relational behavior it's just as bad, the issue spans over both true physical understanding and experience as well as the common understanding of the fact that we all are having it. The Taboo about sex is ridicules. That sex would be more private than any other object. Every single human experience it and there is nothing about it that makes you or any other single human unique about it. We all eat food; we all have sex. Some experiences are better than others. It's a major important part of every human life experience and the greatest reward you can give yourself and that people chose to damage and deny it into a truly sad level of skill set. Sex isn't just about flesh and bones but also the ability to in your head live it out and to allow yourself to dive into all the Horney and erotically lusts there is. For some reason people seems to believe that it's not like that for everyone. That they for some reason would be alone about this kind of awareness and understanding. People are ashamed of the pure and true nature of Eroticay and sexuality. That's exactly the way it is and that's exactly how a vast majority of all the people around the earth are crippled and ruins their own life's pleasures as well as their partners. The most ironical of it all is that they also seem to believe that that's the way to deal with sexualism responsible and maturely.

- No, its not, its the most immature way possible to relate to it.

Humans love Eroticay, humans love sex and sensuality. We can be sexy in our flesh, in our minds and in our hearts. Our Entity's will always be on display for the eye and because of our nature we will always be reflecting over what's teasing our vision, no matter what the entity's organs between the legs are. That's just the way it is to be human being. It's a natural part of our very own existence. Females love to objectify its opposite sex more than ever and she has always done that. Females objectify not only males but also females. Just like males do. None of them dare to admit they are just as human as the other is. Females love male body's naked as well as half naked however they for some reason seem to believe that if they deny it they would be ahead in the Supreme Being contest. Which is the biggest lie you could ever live in.

- Humans never grow up we grow limited.

To believe that if you disrespect our most dominant sense, you get better, you apparently don't understand what a human being is nor its existential basics, especially if you are a firm believer of the calculating lifestyle. Males are just as much sex objects as females are and because of how this world has failed in understanding our existents reality and its truth, that's not a reflected truth. Today females grow up learning loads of skill in emotional communication but hardly anything about their own sexuality. Males on the other hand grows up learning everything about their penis and how to deny their feelings as hard as possible because once upon a time back in the stone age men usually needed to go hunting food. Humans don't relate to that reality anymore and hasn't really done that for quite some time now and yet it colors our normality norm in such extent. Because of our very own evolutionary timeline. The mentalities of humans today are so lost and far away from our true nature its almost scary. Today both male and female entities are more aware about their physical appearance then ever and we all love the attraction of the eye, yet so many cannot see the truth within them self and chose to live in denial. It's understandable that to only be appreciated from the eye's perspective is both dull and insulting. However, to get to know someone takes time. And the appearance will always be on display no matter people like it or not.

To see the sexiness in someone's heart, it takes time of synchronization as well as to see sexiness in mind of thoughts. Sex is the greatest synchronization tool we have because while we are having sex, we become intimate with each other, and that intimacy shares more than just the flesh and appearance. It shares our emotions as well as our lust and pleasures. To get to know someone for real always takes much longer time. Cause everyone has an entire lifetime in their luggage, the older we get the larger the life gets. The world of today seem to have lost track completely of what a human being really is in its existence.

We all love to have sex and its quite rare in relation to how many times in our life that we actually sexually satisfy our self then that we have it in order to reproduce our self. Sex isn't just a reproduction skill. It's so much more and so much larger. In your entire lifetime 99.9% of all the sexual stimuli you provide yourself with such as sexual intercourse, masturbation or any form of sexual satisfaction is for the pleasure and satisfaction from the endorphins released by orgasm as well as the massive impact the sexual energies has and has nothing to do with reproduction causes whatsoever. The reproduction skills and knowledge of how to maintain the human race posses no threats of extinction today and the fact that sex is so much more isn't really any news. Sex has a dimension of possibility's and should be respected thereafter.

I define it as Eroticay – a Dimension of sensuality and sexuality between entity's and all their senses as well as their body's erogenous zones of nerve maps all over the human body. Females has extremely hard time to admit their own sexual objectifying of both males and females. Females can be quite mean not only because they can't handle their own truth towards both males and females but because they have created a female taboo understanding of their own sexualism and sexuality. One example of it is that there has been on several occasions' females throwing acid in the face on other females that have great sexual self esteem.

Males on the other hand has difficulties to understand

where they have them self when it comes to picturing them self on how good looking, they are they seem to believe that they are all handsome and appealing to any female. Humans when it comes to stand up for the physical acceptance and admittance of their own desires and lusts aren't always so good in that manner. Not just about themselves but towards other humans that happens to be great on just that. When it comes to the worst and ugliest mentalities against female beings with great sexual self-esteem you will not find among the opposite sex but among other females. Bad sexual self-esteem causes humongous problems among both males and females and the mental war has ridicules proportions as well as devastating destruction effects on the social coexistence acceptance.

Just like males are crippled when it comes to stand up for the emotional acceptance and admittance of their own feelings. Which is odd since its part of human nature no matter sex. Truth is both male and female wrestle with the same issues even though they take alternate forms compared to each other.

...

.

.

Again, there has been a lot of talk about sex and sexuality here now and there is a good reason for it. Not just the global issues mankind truly has with it but it's also important for anyone who wants to get deeper into self-knowledge and to be in better contact with their inner forces.

For a warlock it's essential. By exploring sex, you not only broaden your mind regarding sexuality, but you also enhance your awareness and the sense for the force in Metaverse. By exorcising your body's nerve system erotically your presence in completeness grows larger. Anal sex is an important factor as well since basically the entire nerve system is in relation to that specific area and the stimuli enhances as well as trains yourself in a most efficient way when it comes to participating in the way of the force.

There are many different areas that work their way in Metaverse. Throughout history there have been loads of different practices and there still are. Some you might have heard of are Healers, Shamans, Voodoo priests, Wicca and Pagan but also other religions and isms are active within Metaverse. Faith is just one of the great tools within Metaverse.
As a warlock your relation to sexuality gets a different nature then most others have. You have seen it from other path walkers as well as witches and monks in different isms.

There are several tools you can use to train yourself and your sense. Some tools are of physical nature in form of challenging behaviors that stretches and explores the boundaries of different areas about your own natural existential form of being. Starvation is one of the paths for a Metaverse traveler and has been utilized throughout time by both religions and isms. Eroticay and Starvation serves the purpose of trimming your system and adjusting yourself in order to enhance sensitivity in your own physical body. You raise your awareness and reveal patterns and paths within yourself that is normally clouded when you are in a so-called default state. You change the value of your existential variables giving new meaning and purposes to events that you in default state is hardly noticing or is neglected. By deliberated alter your needs in life you can achieve a more realistic and clearer picture of yourself and who you are. You get perspective and angles of first and foremost yourself in a very naked truth but also your surroundings. Your body is your tool just like a car or an airplane only so much more sophisticated. Your spirit and soul are your yin yang pilot navigating your body. By enhancing your awareness about yourself with these exorcises you become a better navigator and gets a finer tuned craft/body to interpret and interact in Metaverse.

Meditation and prayers are tools you use to interact with Metaverse and are an execution behavior with the tool of yourself, your body and your mind. So is spell casting, curses, blessings and Metaverse crafting. The higher your own self-awareness is the closer to your own truth you are and the greater your understanding becomes. That's why True soul-searching is an utterly important tool for anyone who wants to actively journey and participate in Metaverse. True soul-searching is an advanced way looking into yourself and the life you have lived. It takes time and courage to do that. It's a journey humans should do a few times in their lifetime.

...
.

True soul-searching
Truth shall bind You
Truth shall find you
Truth is your freedom
Truth is your jail
Truth shall set you free

...

There is and has been many cultures, isms and religions that are or have been active within Metaverse. Even passive or seemingly passive forces are constantly active in Metaverse. Life itself. Our souls and spirits leave traces and images all over Metaverse some vague others full throttle. They are out of all kinds of natures and the one most noticeable are the ones that so called make noise about them self. Some are being related to negative outcomes of religions and others as trapped, lost or so-called soul shards that hasn't passed on but remains in a more substantial form in a lane in Metaverse. They are mostly understood as unnatural phenomena by most people. People have stumbled upon cursed places where terrible events has taken place, and its negative energies are strongly active in many different shapes and forms. The energies of universe and Metaverse are tightly related together and are natural fuels to each other by nature. Just like physical information is stored in many different forms of physical devises ::positives:: so is metaversical information in its ::negative::. The energies traverse each other in all kinds of direction and has a most utterly complex coexistence.

You'll find path walker that belongs to different schools. All of them are active within Exist and Nature in one way or another. Shamans are strong participators of Nature and work with tools from both Exist and Nature but are mainly followers of Nature. Using rhythm to bring themselves into mental states where they interpreted nature in its metaphysical lane and its reflected nature. Warlocks come from Exist and works for Exist and Nature. We are devoted and our only true Faith resides with Exist and Nature. We pledge our soul and spirit for this purpose and have many paths to evolve into.

Another reason for true soul-searching importance is for you to find out whom you are and what paths that truly is your specific nature. Healers are active in both close range and long-range healing in their lane of positive and balanced energies. Many monks journey and are extremely active all over the world in Metaverse in very harmonic ways in harmony with not just them self but people and places all over the world. Especially within Buddhism and Hinduism activities are out of great extent and in a healthier way.

The two main religions on the other hand even though they are active in many ways. Are not always so healthy and on many areas quite unhealthy. Their disrespect for minorities and their constant witch-hunt for them and their way to condemn diversity and cultures has caused quite great damage both physically as well as in Metaverse. Yet they use the tool of prayers and blessings that are both tools from within Exist.

You don't need any of the religions in order to bless or pray nor to have faith. Blessings are a quite beautiful way to support a fellow being. As well as prayers are very effective support tools for any being.

You can find people harmonizing daily in their home by utilizing feng shui and adjusting the physical being with metaphysical energy's. Feng shui is an old art form and has several stages in their school. It is commonly known by public for decorators work in home with furnishing adjusting it for best harmony, but it has so many other aspects then that. It's as advanced as being a lifestyle as well. A school of tracking and exploring, discover and examine energy's wherever they are located. Harmonizing with energy's wherever they are in nature.

All over the world you find people exploring, journeying and practicing in Metaverse in all kinds of directions. Some work with elemental planes others seeks wisdom making long distance journeys in universe. Many seek harmony and inner balance. Everyone sharing the same tool, them self. The entity of the human being is so advance in its completeness it's amazing how deep you can go within Metaverse, There is no end to possibility's and yet we haven't seen a fraction of it all. Metaverse is a phenomenon that you only reach with an open mind and senses.

...

.

The last warlock path is for Exist and Nature and is as
protector and defender of them. Exploring, learning
and yielding the force. An evolutionary part of the
Warlock path. I have gone with myself as Gizmoo
Strangelove - The Last Warlock to Medusa Loveheart -
Ancient Warlock in my total picture of completeness,
both an equal part of me. I stand for Exist and all that
comes with it. Nature is a natural part of Exist. A
natural outcome. I stand for Nature and its survival and
its equality for Exist. My Soul, spirit, flesh, bone, blood,
heart and mind is in oath for this single purpose and
are done so for eternity into infinity. Both in Metaverse
as well as in Universe.

My first choices I made in these paths was done by
myself in my own youth. I started path walking at age
of 3 when I made my first decision. My next step was
taken at the age of seven. Between the age of seven
and fourteen I made several choices and path findings
till I was certain on my paths and went silent for about
15 years. During this time, I explored everything I ever
possible could in life and what it had to reveal for me.
My choices evolved and Year 2007 I closed my first
circle and started journeying the second in my own
eternity. I had a revelation of my own that became the
closure and start and from there my journeys has been
heavy and frequent in many ways. In my closure I
resumed my paths and merged myself together with all
my experiences and choices. I have been very active
the latest years and have now reached a point of me
where I am closing into the completion of my own
metaversical birth in its total completion.

- Yes, it takes time, some longer than others. It's all depending on your nature.

...

.

.

The strength of religions in Metaverse has grown in proportion and weakened as well over time. They are still strong and will remain, just like today's myths still exist In former forms. You can find lots of historical phenomena's in Metaverse from all kinds of religions and myths. A culture with great impact on Metaverse is the Pharaoh and their faith. You will easily find mysteries of pyramids and other strong meta phenomena. Their strong faith in maintaining their energies with mummifications and other ceremonial rituals has left a strong impact in Metaverse. Metaverse has a very complex relation to what we are used to understand in existence. Time and place don't have the same value in Metaverse as in universe. However, there is usually a strong binding with astral beings and locations. One of the amazing path walkers truly deals with those phenomena quite often and I'm referring to people that are sensitive for soul shards stuck or remaining outside the domain of death for some reason. These people are very sensitive when it comes to channeling soul shards that hasn't yet passed on to the so-called other side. These phenomena are also the ones that usually become noisy and for inexperienced or unfamiliar people this can be a scary experience. Most of the time there is an unresolved issue from the past in their time that needs to be enlighten for them to go to rest.

...

.

.

In our history we have seen many examples of people whose exploration of Metaverse, and translation of different religious event come to practice some horrific campaigns against both nature and exist. Having tremendous impacts on humanity. One of these examples is Hitler and he's total remake of the biblical event of king Solomon. Using the David star on he's own demons the Jewish people as demonic containers sort of speaking all under the power of he's own star of Nazism. Forcing them to build he's empire just like in the testament of Solomon where the demons were forced to build Jerusalem. The testament has a rich story of locking up and enslaving different demons in order to achieve glory and power. Hitler recreated the event in his own direction and also, he started to look in other directions for more power and wealth. He was deep in he's own so called faith and it served him well. Not many others understood him in all he's questing both physically and metaphysically. Hardly any even know he's greatness within Metaverse. Less did people care to see the truth about it.

...

.

.

Metaverse is. No matter people like it or not, just as universe are. Metaverse in its own in some way

144

peculiar existence is beyond our everyday understanding and yet it affects us all, all the time in different direction. The lack of us understanding it is more dangerous than beneficial for our continued existence. The Dimension of nothing or Metaverse is one of the great revealers in this upcoming era. The dimension that has existed here long before life even existed on this planet. It's been utilized by civilizations through our timeline. The Mayan people, Native Indians, The Pharaoh, Vikings, The Orient, Muslims, Christians, Buddhism, African native cultures, Ancient Greece, Jamaica, Cultures all over the world. The list can be made long, just some of the examples of activists within Metaverse. Metaverse participators has existed long before the two main religions were here.

...
.

.

Demons are a constant reoccurring subject within religions where they have been pictured as mean and evil. You have different types of demons; you have the inner demons that people tend to confront every now and then and then you have the metaversal demons that represent elements or dimensions. Today there is most common talk about the inner demons. Usually, they represent the denial of people's own flaws that's been suppressed and denied for a very long time. Out of that reason demons have also been used to justify peoples own faulty actions in quite many directions. Demons have been used as an excuse to hunt minorities as well as the denial of existential facts. Truth is that an inner demon is no more or less then the reflection of human's own weaknesses. Their energies come from suppression into your subconscious where people denying their own truth and boil their own brew of a demon picture in its completeness if the denial is too hard. Most demon hunters have hunted their own projected weakness, and it has taken such proportion of their incapability to handle them self in reality that their own negative energies have released some perhaps nasty meta creatures. However, a demon is and has always been no less and no more than a reflection of its encounter.

Demons summoned from Metaverse however, by people have usually been done in order to gain power and benefits and has been done in the foulest ways possible. Even demons consist of a harmonic balance when they too are brought back to their element or dimension where they are whole and existing in a healthy environment for them. No force of nature is showing its correct face when it's locked up.

- Just like you wouldn't be very friendly towards anyone that kept you locked in a basement for longer period of time.

Every force of either nature or Metaverse has its own place. Its own astral plane, lane, terrestrial or its own dimension wherever they truly come from. These so-called demons have been harvested and captured by people for fuel and for their own greed and beneficial purposes. The reason for their common existence during time periods is also reflected in the poor

mentality's that has been the normality norm at that time being. The lack of understanding and accepting the truth as it is causing more problems to a human's subconscious then people usually understand.
Today with a more liberated and healthy mentality the spoken word of demons isn't so common.

People have a natural fear for the obscure and the unknown territory. People's way to handle it takes different odd ways of behavior not just the appearing behavior but also the subconscious behavior all depending on how well you actually are aware and in contact with yourself as human being. People tend to alienate in a less positive way over phenomena and facts that they have a large distance to.

Demons are truly the hardest test for today's human being. To come with terms with your own demon is a great school in your own understanding of yourself. It helps you see your own picture in total completeness and is something that's usually done while learning about your own fears and in your own opinion your weaknesses. To harmonize with demons within your self is a great achievement and something everyone have a great use of in their own lifetime. It's the denial of them that causes problem. The rejection and fighting against it can and has taken awful turns throughout the history of humans. Every being is a completion of dark and light, nothing and everything, good and bad. When you see this, understand and embrace it rather than becoming is just a small part of it. Your decisions of making more just and healthy decisions in your path of life will be more correct and accurate since you then have a total understanding of whom you are and where you are as well as where you are heading. People denying and closing their eyes for the entire truth about themselves usually makes lots of bad and quite so-called evil choices even if those made are valued as righteous and good ones in comparison to their own life picture. Because of its limited truth their choices often will be out of more harmful and evil nature towards their surroundings.

Most so-called evil today comes from good wills and intentions; the biggest reason is the lack of ability to see the whole picture of completeness. People don't grow old they grow limited and this limitation they voluntarily create and amend in order for them to feel they are in control. The more they follow this belief the less control they gain. Even though they do create some sort of understanding of their new gained limited existence it's also all they ever get since their ignorance for anything residing outside that frame is becoming a mystery and unknown territory for them. This will always happen for all of us since the nature is way too advanced in its existence. What can be done is to choose the understanding of that this is the way it is and by doing that minimize the impact every time these boarders need to be crossed and to chose not to amend it. The existing normality norm is also the foundation for these kinds of issues.

...

.

.

Today people reading truths and relativities are not so common and are generally categorized as

148

philosophers. The general problem to see the truth as it is all over the world has many reasons. The mixed pot of science and faith trying to grasp the entire picture of completeness usually makes the same mistake. We can't know it all we do not know when it all started. As long as you try to frame in the truth we will never have a fair chance to continue to evolve with it in the healthy direction that this opportunity of life is so desperate in need of.

...

.

.

There is no end and there is no beginning. There never was a beginning because there is always something before the so-called beginning and we never know how far back in time it actually is since we already exist in an eternity into infinity as stated in the vital information part of the book. Dao Buddhism truly don't see there to be a beginning of all this since Time and existence is way too complicated to believe that there would only have been one big bang if there ever was one that is. And there is no end to this at all, there is however a deadline in time to where we must have created space ships for this species to leave this planet in time and that deadline is the first solar storm that will raid this planet but I have a strong feeling it needs to be recalibrated since both the planet is moving away from the sun and the sun is growing and my feeling is that they only calibrated the growing sun without the movement of this planet away from it. That's our only deadline we have and that's the great news. That's our only fear we have left. This is the great news; the first solar storm is all we have to concern with today. Unless we succeed in ending it prematurely that is.

···

·

·

Humans are not even among the most advanced beings in the structures of DNA mappings. Even though any life forms DNA are extremely advance, humans are just another combination. We are very far from the top of the chain of DNA map complexity and probably only a bit over average when it comes to our complexity of our existence and truth is we are just an equal part of our nature among a billion of other nature phenomena with their own unique DNA maps and functionality. Humans are today the biggest threat to this opportunity of life existence and ironically enough nature's greatest hope to be brought further. In this part of universe that is. The lack of understanding the reality as it is has created great ignorance and also recklessness against our nature. Our disability to think generationally and to amend the future as an important part of our everyday existence has made mankind destructive and careless about the possibilities that might be.

···

·

·

The human body consists of billions of cells in a rich flora of diverse functionality. Different organs with different purposes and most of them both receive and transmit impulses of information. Everything that goes on within a single human entity is being interpreted and processed. The impulses come from all kinds of direction both internally as well as from its exterior. Your body is not just some flesh and bones but a very delicate tool and your lifetime experienced vehicle in existence.

The human mind has and is debated a lot. How it functions and what its functions are. What's conscious and subconscious? Do they even exist in those forms since it's the same mass? They both exist (the conscious and subconscious) and are out of a bit different nature. Both of them are a natural outcome and are being compiled and growing matter along the way of your own evolutionary timeline in your lifetime.

The subconscious is more of a natural outcome of your perception of truth and denial of service. The youth of humans have a very limited and small amount of subconscious as well as conscious. During the years of childhood your mental existence is a limitless world. Your learning curve and your programming of your conscious is enormous in its impact on your brain during the first years of your life. Not just your biologically motor skill set or social awareness. You also start to create your own emotional trash bin where emotions that provides shame or guilt are efficiently being stored. You are learning about social variables called right and wrong defined by your older being fellows. The right and wrongs, bad and good creates lines of structure for your coming social relations to physical actions and doings. During this time period of your life, you learn and create lots of new variables of social behaviors. The reason we are so different is because even though we are all alike it's still a completely unique individual with its own personal composure of organs, nerve system, perception and reading its own existence and environment completely on its own. During childhood you experience the strongest evolutionary part of your own relation in and with this existence itself.

Your awareness and conscious are open for all suggestion and slowly it shapes out patterns with constantly testing of all variables that you are being confronted with. Our biological nature has a nice approach during our first years making sure our learning curve is as it is. During these years faith is the basic tool any human being has to rely on. For that time period science isn't even an existing formula but rather a growing awareness as a result of trial and error. What adults call science doesn't really come to a true state of mind up till the mind is done understanding its own motor skills and its own entity's signal system. The mind constantly evaluates its own system and doesn't really rest in understanding the entity's signal system. Rather a question of coming in terms with your own awareness about it and making you harmonize and interact with these signals as well as possible. During this period of time, you walk the path of endless possibilities where you challenge all your emotion in order to see what they actually result in for you. Hate, sadness, love, comfort, trust, right, wrong, shame, pride, dignity, patience, happiness, surprise, disappointment and expectation to mention a few, all in a pile of fun and weird variables that doesn't really have a name till someone tells you it has. This is the time of your life when "seeing is believing" isn't a state of true by itself in your own faith. At this time all your emotions and senses play an equal large part of what your faith and your beliefs are.

Your curiosity rewards you with enlightenment and understanding in both pleasant and unpleasant directions. A world full of "what is" and "how to" slowly turns into a world full of "this is" and "that's how" by time and evolution. Your faith and curiosity that was all the tools of knowledge you had, has all of a sudden company of facts, rules and directions out of all kinds of nature. The opened mind of a child is more sensitive to Metaverse since its limitation around the obscure isn't as strong tabulated and has really no foundation of denial. Since it too just is another unexplored area. Children is always our future, and we should always respect our future with greatest care. The birth is an exceptional natural phenomenon that no matter if its human or any other animal or nature is something extraordinary.

...
.

.

Even though we are free in our evolution we are all colored by a template when we grow up. The template is the normality norm, setting up values of what is supposed to be considered what. No matter how you twist and turn on that it will always be a secondary variable. Sometime its preserved by larger force and others takes more lightly on this matter. What can be done is the making of the awareness of that particular relation. The normality norm is a template created by us human beings.

The impact of religions has massively colored them so far existing templates of every society's "normality norm template" and truth is that today's templates are still only vague translations of the religion or ism that's being strongest in that area rather than a neutral understanding of whom we are. Science has however helped straighten it out a bit but still in a quite vague form. Today science has a better base plate to stand on then it did a couple of thousands of years ago.

...

.

.

In relation to the nature and our existence the sexuality base among humans is sexual. That's all we are. In order to reproduce we blend opposite sex and all other times with what is suitable with your own taste and flavor. Nature has already taken care of "the when" humans are ready for sexual experiences and should be respected thereafter. Nature has shown what gives bad results and what gives good results. We need our diversity by nature. The relation between Nature and Existence is an amazing blend of dependencies and fuels, chains of relational reactive occurrences that has nothing to do whether humans exist in this opportunity of life or not. We truly are just lucky beings that have the humble opportunity to participate in life here on earth as a result of this planets own evolution.

One way to easily see the base of the normality norm is to look upon the laws in your country, the parts of it that is reflecting upon human as beings. You will discover that they are more or less based on a religious picture of what humans are, rather than the true picture and more scientifically picture of what our human nature is and what we truly are. The law is a reflection that also has a great impact on the "normality norm template" and shapes humans in a very strong and efficient way when it comes to accepting reality. Unfortunately, the reflection that regards us as human being from the laws are usually not very healthy in relation to our diversity in existence but rather tries to force old religious views of what we all should be like against our own true nature. Laws serves more purposes than that and have great functionality in order to maintain a somewhat sane coexistence in a very peaceful way and it has in many places come a long way in its own evolution but it's still lacking a correct foundational standing based upon the human as the being it is. Another important standing Law enforcement is lacking in, is to actually reflect our entire existence when it comes to the nature that we humans are heavily depending on. I'm referring to the nature and the life flora of this planet and all its dependencies. There is not enough care about our planet reflected in the laws of today even though there is a constant growing awareness about it and the laws starts to reflect it more and more there is still much more to be wished for

...

.

One of the great religions are dealing with our conscious in a most advanced and skill full way describing its superior and its being with its underlying layers. Describing the responsibilities of different powers of understandings and awareness and how heavy its difficult paths are. The balance between the different forces of nature and what kind of directions that lays ahead in the coming choices that is to be made. In short, it's a very beautiful piece of the subject total awareness. And the book is called the bible. God is their metaphysical power variable for total awareness no more no less. Heaven describes the human's possible power whereas hell shows the weight and how heavy the responsibility of such power is. Whereas the story about humans shows clear examples of our present awareness and how these two opposites balance our awareness and consciousness. It's an advanced yin and yang about human behaviors and relation to their own existence. Praying to God is the same as praying to your own superior being, in other words yourself and has many times been an abused tool, used for other purposes then of directional harmony energy's. The book deals with Metaverse in a quite spectacular way and is an extremely advanced school in your self-awareness. Way to extreme for the actual followers of it today and has been so throughout its own history. Ironically enough the ones active within the Metaverse and those that has actually been true within the so-called Christianity has been most often either hunted or hated by the ones that are supposed to be responsible for it continues existence. On few occasions they have actually got it right but have chosen to call the activist for miracles and saints. A more confused school in Metaverse when it comes to the ones practicing the faith is probably hard to find. They have time after time crippled their own religion by excluding minorities throughout history leading to more and more destructive behaviors and not to mention severely crippled the ones that has been taken them seriously. For the so-called leaders and caretakers of the religion the reality has moved so far away and looking upon the ones practicing it today, spirituality and contact with the soul is mostly shining in its complete absence. They might know how to preach the texts from what's left of its origin but have no clue of what the spiritual and soul existence truly is and even less Metaverse itself. For them it's mostly text and any real contact with Metaverse is both considered ugly and tabooed.

For the real leaders it's an advanced tool of manipulation trying to enforce a template onto large groups of people. Faith is an abused tool within the religion of the Bible and has been so for a very long time.

Total awareness is when you accept yourself in completeness and understand and chose to coexist with yourself in all directions. It's a state you can achieve by seeing the truth about yourself in all direction accepting your subconscious, conscious and Supreme Being as a complete picture of your true self. The Bible has just shown humans what they contain. And not what you become if you chose to explore parts

157

of it but merely what to expect. However, you have not reached your superior being with embracing your subconscious alone. In order to reach the sky's, you first need to embrace your hell. Hell describes very well the issues and how hard it is for you to go through true soul-searching. How hard it is to aim for higher responsibilities. Heaven describes very well what it is you can achieve by doing just that. Dealing with your own hell. The head character of the bible is YOU. Not Jesus, not God, not Satan but you yourself. You see plenty of examples of what roads there is to chose from. What happens if you don't take yourself and your own picture of completeness seriously.

The school of the bible is a very handy school and tells you good secrets about what human spirit and soul is about. Unfortunately, the ones that has supposedly been responsible for this type of understanding has never really truly achieved this type of understanding.

And that's one of the great reason our history is so full of destructive behaviors and really ugly mentality's that has originate from this religion.

The bible is a fine composure of reflections of what life is in all direction. Using metaphors and metaphysics to explain science humans still have problems to grasp in its total picture of completeness. It gives us a great understanding of the human psychology and how our awareness is one of our most important tools. It contains clues and secrets that a certain type of awareness is required for a being in order to see them and to have a slightest chance to start exploring them.

The crusade of hate and denial of minorities you have seen throughout history has been nothing else but a complete showoff in human weakness and limitations. Christians have never truly understood the purpose of their own book but rather functioned as its guardians and protector. It's a part of any life forms evolution and its growing awareness. The religions of this world are an important piece in our evolution. Just not the way their own protectors believe they are. The Bible and the Koran are two different schools in our evolution and are equally important. The isms are also important for our total picture in completeness. Both the Bible and Koran should contain the mark of a yin yang symbol so that people easier could see and understand how to relate to its content.

Religions are a milestone for evolution and last for several thousands of years. It's a result of being's life forms state of awareness reaching a certain point. Science follows another line and will always be an equal important part for its own species evolution. Science is a universal measurement in physics of existence whereas faith and awareness are a social and metaversal measurement of existence.

The art of calibrating in time is a metaversal tool and will always occur on several occasion through ought any civilization. The Mayan civilization did it, the Pharaoh civilization did it, Jesus did it as well as Muhammad did it. Many Buddhist monks has done it. Anyone reaching this state of awareness are usually contributing to its own time era in one way or another.

Confucius did what he could in order to share his tools with the coming generations. Siddhartha Gautama Buddha also did the same thing. We have seen both healthy and less healthy doings because of this. Hitler played he's part but was merely taking he's responsible part in our chain of evolution. Jesus did the same even though he knows that humanity would suffer severely from the outcome of he's work. Jesus biggest mistake was that he didn't write the book himself. So many people have been victim for cruel torture and deaths by Christians so by putting Hitler next to Christianity it doesn't really seem like there is any different. One of Hitler's main purposes was to show us human beings what the outcome of what both religions would be if you take it to its extreme point of practice. Why failure resides in denying truth as it is. He made sure human mankind never forgets and also always understand the issues of trying to create some elitism group, when looking upon the evolutionary picture of it all. The truth about someone's intentions is not always obvious to its surrounding and are usually concealed very cleverly by the ones doing the particular walk-in life.

Evolution has its own ways and what comes out of it is something we should be grateful to have the chance to participate in. We are not an alpha race of beings in any direction when it comes to ethnical backgrounds. We are all just a part of nature. For now, a very dysfunctional one and are more of a threat and disease to nature then something to be proud of. It's sad to see such a perfect nature abused by human mankind.

...

.

160

Through ought our history there has been people waking up doing necessary adjustments in one way or another and by that taking their responsibility in this opportunity of life. Making sure our own evolution lasts long enough in order for us to take this particular step. However, it's just a chance we are having. Not a necessarily doing. It's all up to the human race on this little planet. We truly are this opportunity of life's own hope to bring it further rather than to spoil it and flush it down the toilet. This is the naked truth about the nature of our mother nature's to be or not to be.

Unfortunately for our planet even if we chose to not take this step and chose to quit as the losing mentality many of the leaders of today espouse. Even if we did wipe out humanity and gave this planet a final moment of peace. It would sadly enough take too many billion years in order for her to save herself in time because of the fact of evolutionary timeline and the fact that the sun keeps growing. There isn't enough time for her to raise up another race with our capability's most likely.

Basically, it comes down to our own decision of whether to be or not to be. Our blindness due to greed for money, oil and false variables of power is today however not pathing for our future existence. We walk around in a false believe that we are supreme beings and a higher form of civilization. That's our biggest mistake today. Humanity must see the truth in the situation and come to realize that we aren't supreme in any way as long as we can't respect the cause and reason we are here to begin with.

The opportunity of life we have here is a delicate matter. There is not a thing of what we have invented or done that can compare with nature in any direction. We are participators of it. No matter if we compose new life with help of the understanding of biology and DNA, we still only are participants and a natural outcome of exists and nature's own evolution.

The Evolution of any opportunity of life takes the same steps more or less and ours has come to a peak when the good old days are about to see a new dawn from a completely new perspective. As I said before we are no longer standing before the greatest step in history of mankind, but we are truly at the brink of the biggest step of our own "possibility of life" evolutionary step.

This is a choice of our being for the future. This is the time when we will have to make decisions out of evolutionary proportions. The politics of today is something that used to work fine for countries and borders where the planets health wasn't really an issue. The variable for that is changing and is doing so faster and faster.

This is not in the sense that all life would come to an end by making some enormously decisions but if we don't stop and think things over, we are about to reach a point of no return for us as well as our nature to have a chance to continue this journey in existence.
There is no single factor alone that will be the cause of the planets so called Armageddon but many different

factors. The less we see the truth as it is the less is our chances to successfully maintain life and to bring it further in a rich and healthy way.

...

.

.

For thousands of years the two main religions have spread hate and misunderstanding among us. They have tortured, hunted and killed minorities in their great lack of respect for our true diversity. They raped our earlier faiths on their holidays and purposes in a quest to make us all fitting into a very disturbed template. The followers of these religions have been deceived in many ways.

People that achieve the ability to calibrate pathing of the future and pasts can only work from within the parameters of where they are in their today time. The prophets used these tools in order to maintain as healthy picture they could possibly find and that includes all variables there is. It also reflects the time being and evolutionary understandings from how the future is described. One of the most popular calibrators known by us from the past, today is most likely Nostradamus. Exploring his texts, you'll notice that he's verbs of description are in relation to their mentality's active in their time period and what was considered horrific at their time. The variables have forms from in their time period and their types of science fictional variables. No matter who's the prophet or philosopher their text is only interesting to study in its native form or in a translation word for word without any form of interpretations since most people lack the correct understanding of calibrations and their own mentalities tends to estimate things in a false direction. They are a bit hard to find today since most people covering the issue are making their own interpretation of what has been said. A calibrators time map usually describes what is to come in all directions. Not just physical events but also metaphysical. In other words, they explore the social normality norms as well and what many people consider catastrophically Armageddon's is not only occurring in physics. A very clear and easy example of that was the major change of peoples understanding of reality from living on a flat earth to living on a round orbital planet. That was a major Armageddon and a complete devastation of all human life's mentality of normality norm. Another great step in human evolution and their advancement in awareness. For most of the people of today that's exactly where you are. All the lies you have been living in and the storm you will have to be able to clear out in order to understand and grasp that you have grown up in a lie. You're not alone and many people will have severe issues dealing with it. Today's mentalities and normality norm does not support the opportunity of "there will be a better time when people are more ready". These types of evolutionary steps rarely have till now.

Scientists has tried to see the truth in evolution throughout history as well, and they usually help humanity in their progress of understanding reality at the time being. Charles Darwin is one that have had a great impact on humanity in many ways. He's devotion to nature has served many good purposes and a major step that's been welcomed by many. The natural choice however is more then what he claims and far more advanced he could ever dream of. Nature has all the possibility's needed for any time being with limits only nature has. We tend to consider our self of supreme beings due to the fact we are of the nature we are. What's lacking here for this gentleman is the understanding of Nature as the true supreme being and that we are just participants and the one that are able to shoulder as its caretaker and protectors. Every opportunity of life has these opportunity's and will always have. The backside of the efforts from this gentleman is the same as with many other scientists. The outcome of the neglecting of us just being a part of all this. The awareness that we are the ones that are maintaining the nature and with that comes a responsibility no one never gets. In a continued existence in the future humans have understood the purpose of life's dependencies and how vital they truly are. The rich flora of diversity from natures magnificent existence are for a great reason.

The facts from Darwin are correct but the truth doesn't end there. This is a common issue from most people's efforts and has natural reason. Humans of today don't really consider our existence in generations ahead nor its existence in our future as more then on this planet. The limitation in mentality's "that we are for some reason bound to this planet solely" and the denial of our ability to bring life further is the cause for many of our destructive behavior and neglecting of the truth of our existence entire picture of completion. This is one of the main reasons we are still having such a hard time to see our self as a united force together on this planet. And that our life's truly is enriched by our diversity, not just among humans but in all the nature we live among. The nature is our mother at ALLTIME.

...
.

.

The reason to the different forms each individual being's choices has been in the evolutionary process of advancement is cause whenever you reach this type of advanced being you are always limited to what's possible at the time being. Hence the natures of any prophet or scientist or other like Hitler, Jesus, Confucius, Einstein and before them all as well as after and in-between. Hence the nature of this and us as being (my our self that is). Today we have reached far into the Information Technology age and today everything is in place. It's in consideration to where we are rather then to what we are prepared to that directs our possibilities in the impact of choices made. Many might have wanted to take more advanced steps then they actually have done but due to where in our evolutionary timeline we are they to has followed exists and natures natural being. Today everything is already in place both technology wise and our social awareness. We have all the necessary means that we could need but we lack in the Universal understanding and the truth about our existence. The world is reaching more and more a peaceful united picture. However, all around the world confusion is rising as well as the ever-growing lack of faith in our future.

There is a failure of motivation and an absence for a reason for all this.

We today lack a mutual foundational understanding that the planet we all live upon, this planet. Planet earth isn't just a planet, its one huge living organism. We are just a part of it as its own natural outcome. The planet as an organism has billions of species with their own purposes of existence for this organism best continued existence and hopefully widely spread over all kinds of places in universe. Unfortunately, today this planet has a disease called humans that weakens the organism and wars among each other rather than to live up to the higher form of civilization and proudly take responsibility for this organism's well-being and continued existence. Since we lack this unified foundational standing our evolution becomes more of an insult of life then a glory of exceptional beings. We are merely caretakers and a possibility of a beautiful brain function to gear this nature life organism in any direction we like.

The rich flora of diversity of life forms upon this planet is the greatest blessing if anything that resides in the exceptionality of Exists and Natures coexistence. Humanity chose to rape it, destroy it and torture it without any regrets whatsoever. The poorer the flora of life gets the closer to the brink of extinction we get and that's not just for the human race but all the species sharing the same opportunity. Humans are very efficient for many reasons when it comes to destruction of their own foundational needs. The poor understanding, we have about our source and reason has already limited our future richness in many directions. This life organism is the base and foundation for future colonization's and future home planets. The recklessness and ignorance spread among us today serves no other purpose then prematurely end the chance to make the choice and give our self the option to continue our journey.

Because of people's pride and refusal to admit their own truths about a natural phenomenon such as the revealing of new directions or paths, resulting in that past life view pictures are put aside for the future to come. People's faith in money and ruthless power has rooted deep in many norms and understandings. Because people are unable to face the truth that we once again are to take the same type of step in evolution as when we had to accept that earth wasn't flat but indeed an orb we all lived upon, walking upside down in relation to people on the opposite side of it.

That's exactly how small and narrow minded we still are, that's exactly how disoriented humanity is in their perception of truth.
The people of today care for material possessions and publicity of fame, living in a reality where the future isn't further away than their own desire to overcome their own bad self-esteem. Approves the behavioral pattern of a parasite nurturing from its surrounding in a desperate need to win a non-existing contest of "who knows what stupidity". With no care about the future, no care about source or reason to why they are.

These are the once that walk around in the belief of

being a superior being. The once that are convinced that being on top of a food chain is all there is to it. People who believe that money, an invented trading system by the very same species is the meaning of Nature and Exist. In other words: The phenomena of universe, solar systems, galaxies, super nova's, black holes and Nature's own exceptional brilliance is all here so that a species could have the opportunity to invent something they call money. These people are living in convenience that money is the meaning of all this.

- Then they wonder: how come things are so twisted in the world of today?

In order for humanity to shape up and get our ship, our Nature, this opportunity of life on the right side. There are many areas that's need adjustments. Our financial eco system is just one of them. We need to reform our foundational mentalities in both normality norms as well as acceptations of what our reality is like in the most naked form there is. Today's politics and fundamentals where suitable for a planet long time ago. The variables have already changed and none of today's systems are truly adjusted to that simple fact.

...
.

.

The cold war is also a major important step in order for species to see that mass destruction is not really an option anyone gains something from. An important understanding growing into the species awareness.

Many speaks about that we never learn from history and that it would be repeating itself. It's not entirely true. Or the truth doesn't end there to put it in my own words. Evolution is not a circle but rather a spiral that continues in whatever direction its heading for. The spiral may repeat event but there is never the same foundation since whenever an seemingly equal event occurs there has always been a change in variables. With new evolutionary steps already taken and new once are being gained. Evolution is on the move at ALLTIME and never stops to rest. It's a part of our natural state of being.

...
:
.

.

Evolution and defining are very similar in that way cause when you define you take something around the clock so many times that each line eventually forms an orb. And once that's done you are able to see and pinpoint directions to reach new destination with a greater accuracy. When working within this type of awareness the surrounding normality norm somehow loses its original intended meaning. And can be a tricky part to adjust into. When working with revealing tools you see all directions both uncomfortable and comfortable. Twisting and turning on every piece in order to see all directions of a single event. One great tool for this is Atom from Dao Buddhism. The variable of the smallest building brick in Exist and nature. A variable with enormous power that can be divided into infinity still being Atom no matter how many times you divide it and take any directions when utilized. Tools of

Metaverse are the ones you will need in order to be able to grasp these types of formulas and cannot really be done with the physical ones we have today. These tools are so far ahead when it comes to evolutionary understanding and has been utilized in our history in many occasions. When dealing with these kinds of variable formulas you can't exclude any behavioral pattern or reality. You cannot neglect the truth in any direction. Peoples fear and denials for death, sexuality and other obstacles due to their perception of normality and what is, limits their possibility's vastly and they are also rarely to become familiar with metaversical tools and awareness. What's being described here is a base of the calibrational lifestyle and also a start of an explanation of the differences between awareness and intelligence. Which also divide the calibrational lifestyle from the calculational lifestyle.

Isaac Newton is one of the people declaring the bent room in time. The curve of a bent line very much also explains human awareness. Many science formulas have been stimulated and flavored by earlier calibrators and metaversical explanations. The Maya culture has revealed more than people dare to admit since the fact itself puts science in a bit less impressive state. However, as any scientist knows they are always putting the last check bit in place. And are always selfishly taking all the credits for it. Science without faith, imagination and Metaverse wouldn't be much to put in a Christmas tree.

- That's for sure.

Every species on this planet has their own evolutionary timeline and we are all part of this planets own natural evolution just like this planet is part of its own galaxy's evolution which in turn is part of the evolution of universe.

Awareness is partial metaversal and partial universal where your intelligence serves a purpose to make something out of it. Some culture has higher understanding then others. Hinduism has a relative high understanding of Metaverse and calibrational lifestyle. Muslims might not be comparable to them but is ahead the Christian society.

A tool that has been amended and preserved a lot within Hinduism for Metaversical exploration as well as elaboration with calibrations is the third eye vision. That is a trainable skill set and the highest achievement for the tool is to reach status of the all-seeing eye. All the tools from all religions and isms are very useful in Metaverse and are actually complementing each other and a necessary mean for advanced calibrational formulas. In history calibrations has been considered to be predictions of future events which is a truth in some direction. But it's so much more. When dealing with calibrations you are providing possibilities beyond what you are able to achieve with today's science alone. Metaphysics and physics are actually complementing each other, and the problem of today are the disrespect for each other's forms of being. It's a fool's war and should not be continued.

...

.

.

The spiral of evolution of our planet has bloomed for billions of years and has grown in all kinds of direction even before the species of the human race set its foot on this planet. We just happen to be this opportunity's caretakers and are merely a disrespectful child in progress of evolution closing in to wakening up from a long time of learning and understanding the basics of being out of the nature we happen to be. The responsibilities and our possibility's when we have climbed out this cocoon of readiness. The awakening is a metaphor for us achieving the so-called final state of awareness that happens to be exactly what you are experiencing by reading this particular book.

...

.

.

Piece by piece, step by step we have raised from evolution exploring everything that has come in our path. We have discovered and revealed secrets of nature and exist several times over. Invented anything from hunting tools to space crafts. Evolution has brought us through war and hate, love and lust. We have been defining our self for thousands and thousands of years always making progress in one direction or another. We move in a never-ending spiral and not a circle like many often confuses themselves. Expressions such as history repeats which in some way is a perception of it but nevertheless a falls statement. Even though similar events reoccur over and over its never the same, but a natural behavioral pattern of our evolutions own slowly raising spiral. Evolution has slowly brought us further and have grown massively in awareness due to the natural spiral of evolution. Evolution is harsh and cruel in many ways but the fruit it carries and the rewards that comes with it are magnificent. Many wars have been fought and waged all over the planet in our history. Some larger than others. All exploring ways of destruction as well as dealing with human limits. War has been one of the greatest natures among humanity and has been fueled by hate, ignorance and fear in the lack of understanding between perceptions of truth. Diversity is one of human's greatest fear. Maybe not as much in a everyday conversation. The fact that we all are equally equipped with heart and brain and that all species on this planet truly has their own unique evolutionary timeline and that we all are equally important for our future beings is missing out in the fear of diversity.

- Dont get me wrong here we are natural predators in our base even though people today amend the behavior of the parasite more often.

All our continents have a rich historical culture, and all suffer from glorifications of war and mass destruction. America is built by a total rape of native Nativ Americans and their culture making Hitler appear as a saint in relation to the mass murder that occurred. Asia has had more large-scale wars than any other continent can compare with. Where war has been advance art and even though its horrific nature has

174

been more advance when it comes to reading in natures of a wars total picture in completeness. Different nations have shouldered the role as a "superpower" during different time periods. Sweden, Romans, Holland, England, Russia, France, Germany and USA just to mention a few. During all these wars technology and civilization has evolved and advanced in many directions. The fact of repeatedly remade mistakes is not equal to evolution wouldn't be progressing but rather a result of humanity's failure to learn and communicate. Evolutionary progress is always a slow spiral. Even though war is a very repetitive event in our history and the causes have been similar we still evolve with it. Evolution is the key here and will always be for any form of existence in universe.

...

.

.

The largest adjustment is the understanding of higher awareness, and it is happening. The step we are standing before is probably best described as the Awakening. Out of the many attempts that's been made by several different philosophers and prophets to prepare us for this very step in evolution has caused both confusion and fear among humans. This is the one step that has been promoted the most and the visuals we been provided might seem hard to translate and relate to. Up till this step there hasn't really been a good support organism for the human being to have a healthy relation to these types or steps in evolution. We are usually caught in bed each time a step has been made whether the nature of it has been scientifically or metaversical. The ones out of Metaversical nature have a less frequent occurrence rate than the ones out of technical or scientifically nature.

Evolution is ever lasting and will outlast any form of being eventually. The amount of coexistence of being is entirely up to each opportunity of life's beings. It either ends prematurely, naturally or become extended for undefined amount of time depending on the choices been made. However, beings in evolution are also a result of the ending of an earlier species. In other word what has been still are but in a new form and shape an updated nature.

The missing support organism at the time being for past and future evolutionary steps is a result of what once was advanced and very useful tools in order to structure civilizations in many forms are today outdated. Religions and science have till now been able to create necessary structure for human civilizations and helped out in many ways to handle the progress in many ways. But we are still lacking an important piece. The evolutionary steps taken when it comes to social understanding and structure is also a result of our growing awareness.

Being stuck on this planet as a mentality is a major issue for our future being in the sense of us becoming reckless and ignorant in behavior and in taking appropriate responsibility for our next coming generations. The picture and mentality of us never populating another planet fuels a destructive behavior and understanding to life in many directions. People care less about their own actions and doesn't see reason to why they even should consider making an effort in understanding the importance of factors such as equality and generational thinking. Humans has experienced life here upon earth for thousands of years now and because of the nature of evolutions timely events many people don't even keep it in consideration in their ongoing life's. With all rights in an everyday today point of view. When our planet and our population was safe in relation to our continued existence that wasn't really anything we needed to concern about even though the awareness of generational responsibility has grown and faded like a wave pattern throughout our history. Today that has come to a point of very vague progression and has a need to change a bit faster than it is doing by own nature. The reason is because today we are so used to evolutionary steps in smaller forms that happens within technology. Today technology's miracles come so often we don't even bother about it. We have been jaded in relation to that we are actually making faster progress in change than ever before. We are approaching a flow of change that for the moment is out of rhythm. We are approaching the pulse and beat of us moving in a mutual understanding in directions of synchronization. The step we stand before is not an end. It's the beginning of us working together achieving goals with a better understanding and mutual benefits.

...

.

Dao Buddhism consider all religions and earlier isms, as well as today considered mythologies as different schools of universal understanding. However, they are not kept in same relation their own participants use to relate to them. They are all part of the evolution of our opportunity of life, and they all contain usefully tools and understandings for our species. They can all be approached from many angles and purposes. And all of them has had impacts of our evolution in many ways that needs to be considered when calibrating in evolution.

I talk more about the bible for the simple reason that I have been growing up in a country where that has been the major religion and what mostly been shared in schools and media around me. That however doesn't mean in any way that the Koran wouldn't be out of equal importance in our evolutionary timeline. Both the religions and other isms are different advanced schools of our life as well as the universal existence we all are participating in.

The breaking of the code of the book of the Bibles total picture in completeness was something I accomplished year 2007. All culture and history contain fragments of clues that are vital information for us and our future. As I stated earlier the books head character is you and not the variables of God or Satan or even Jesus. And it's in the sense that the book is only describing your entire picture in completeness showing results of choices made by yourself no matter what path you chose to walk. The Bible is a very advanced way to describe the yin and yang your soul and spirit actually are with each other. God is just a part of the total awareness completed by its opposite Satan. And merely reveals different metaversical variables of what can be accomplished and also the responsibility that comes with it. Every single human being and their entity is composed with same possibilities and the state of total awareness is a state of being rather than state of mind. Many has been limited to that this is how people should be relating to only other entity's where the understanding of the very same truth resides within every single entity. Many has repeated the mistake fueling a destructive spiral of mentality's that has had severe impact of humanity in too many directions. Total awareness is about an entity's entire state of being. Achieving it is one of the most advanced schools in existence to practice and should not be taking lightly at any point. At first glance of the book of the bible it shows you relations between different entities and their role played a bigger picture. The truth goes much further beyond that. It shows you how great faith is as a tool and the depth of how strong it is. It shows you how advanced yin and yang is to explore and its depth in diversity. Heaven and hell the two balance factors you need to be able to embrace and explore without losing your balance. You contain both in yourself as a single entity. Your soul and spirit. The revealing of divine powers in both yin and yang. The book shows different journeys and what they carry with them.

...

.

There will be a time when Time is our main currency. The way we have it today will change dramatically if you look at it in our own evolutionary timeline, everything is relative in many ways. Truth is that the reality we live in today is just a version and a relativity that we actively chose and that we actually can change, and it will change no matter we like it or not.

- **OK and how do we have it today?**

At first we actually traded with the items and goods we owned only with no possibility to flexibility or to freely choose in the vast range of living that we are able to do today. We were bound to trade with nonreplicable values and to work with exchange was a hard issue. Today we have lots of different currencies all over the planet and money that actually vanishes in other paper forms and exchanges.

There in-between we traded with copper, silver, gold and diamonds as well as other stones. Metal and Stones, we still trade in those but today its more electronically with plastic, internet and mobile phones as well. So, value isn't just about hardware and physics.

In the "trading timeline branch" the timeline is or should be the base of the eco system of finance branch. Today we have so many different currencies and values and it's regulated by areas. In one location is what you earn the same as what ten times higher than others are earning in a different location doing the same thing as you do. Some currency's that for this example has the value of one only needs one of that currency in relation to another location you might need hundreds of thousands of it in order to have the very same one. We all have the same needs, and we all have the same base to stand on. This planet. We are all equal in the eyes of mother nature and so should we be in the eyes of our self.

...

.

.

The sky is our limit, is a truth with modifications. The sky is our limit, we need air to exist. Simple as that. But that doesn't exclude the fact that we also can exist in space even if in a quite shy form of it today compared to what it will be like in the future. If you look at the evolutionary timeline, we have two choices as it is today. We either choose to continue to exist and accept the fact that we will change in the future, just like we have always done throughout the evolutionary timeline so far we existed at least.

– or

We don't give a damn and completely screw up this planet to the point of no return and make sure that the opportunity of life seeds to exist on this planet in our corner of the universe. The Universe does for sure not give a damn about if life does or does not exist on our planet, the universe has existed for far so long time that we aren't even a fart in space compared to its age. Black holes are part of our Circle of life as well, Black holes are the true creators in universe or to be more correct their evolution is. They are still a bit of grey area since they are hard to spot and to study up close.

...

.

.

There will always exist philosophers and visionary's no matter where in time we are, that's how we create our self. That's how we shape and form our very own reality. No matter what you do or who you are, one thing that you have no matter how you have chosen to reflect over it before, is faith.

Faith is what you believe in, and we all believe in something no matter if its religious or if it's in yourself or money or your work or your relation or your children or technology or even in science. A scientist belief is the very foundation of what our reality is like, if a scientist doesn't believe in what she or he is doing it isn't true and the person wouldn't probably keep it as a fact. Faith has different natures in that sense, when dealing with metaversical faith it's out of a nature closely connected to your soul and spirit whereas when talking about everyday life beliefs it might not be so deeply connected.

Thru ought evolution we have had prophets and philosophers that has had visions about the future. Today we vision often about the future and today things are going much faster than it did before. Today we live in the Information Technology age of our evolutionary timeline and today we deal with things that for even a hundred years ago would have been strange and weird. We hadn't even been to the moon for a hundred years ago. But what has changed is that today people don't dare to visualize the far ahead future in the same way as before.

- And with before I'm referring a couple of thousands as well as just hundreds of years back in time.

As a philosopher and metaphysician, you can with calibrational methodology point out milestones and look into relative reality's and compare them to each other, you twist and turn on all kinds of possibility's and run different scenarios in same reality's as well as same scenarios in different realities. It takes much time and consumes lots of focus and energy to deal with that kind of puzzles and algorithms. You work with flowcharts and different types of Timelines.

::You use tools such as ::Opposite thinking:: Opposite thinking utilizes a 3 component methodology commonly described with upside down trees where the roots are as big as the branches and each root and branch is an opposite variable containing a scenario with a set of basics and corner stones, Starters and Stoppers as well as advancers, you work with them in set of three or more and the first tree is the base (where you are today) the third/last is the goal and the middle is the way from start to the end::

:*: :: Then you start to utilize ::loose end thinking:: and :*:outcome thinking:*: in order to nest it all together resulting in a step-by-step guide in how to reach a certain goal most likely with the start from today with minimal risks and the wisest step to take in order to reach whatever goal you wish to reach for:: :*:

While defining I work by simple rules; I can add, move around, adjust but I can't remove anything in a sense that what is will always be but some of it will always become "past time" (or fall into history as you probably come to learn how to relate to it) quicker than others that remains NowTime a little bit further. In that way I will eventually get a complete circle that will evolve in a perfect sphere. The sphere or ball if you like, will contain all possible solutions and directions giving us the opportunity to stake out a path where we only need to take many steps enough in the right direction in order to achieve that very goal. By doing this you build roads to walk easily without taking necessary risks or dangerous steps.

···

.

.:

All these tools mentioned in the beginning can be applied to any everyday life situation and used to dissect and understand behaviors of nature, life forms, sports and Companies...

- Or you name it =)
.:

The Force has been around us all along and isn't anything new however it's the hardest achievement you can achieve and to continue pathing in it is even harder. Lots of you people have gotten in contact with it different ways. Some has called it Mojo or Voodoo other as Wiccan and "Medicine of Light" and so forth. There are more names of the force then you are aware about. The force is as real as real can be no matter you like it or not. I have been a pather since I was three years old and probably before that as well, but it was at age of three where I took my first step as "LORD Lady Death" to "Queen Medusa D.B. Loveheart" that I achieved recently with all that comes with it and here I will now share some of the calibrations that I have accomplished during this entity's existence.

At age of three I started pathing in Death, it started out with a discussion between me, my brother and my father in how to be ahead of time and I came to the conclusion that you must walk it backwards in order to be able to be ahead it in physics. The discussion ended without any action taken but my brother and I didn't stop there we agreed upon that he should drop me in the floor so that I mentally would have a change that made me go backwards much enough in order to always be ahead of time and so we did. He dropped me from most likely a meter above a stone floor.

And from there I calibrated that it would take me about four more years before I could achieve and control my new calibrational lifestyle completely that time as I should since awareness was my only tool I would be focusing on and letting calculational lifestyle come along as in an opposite to what children of today are forced to learn to live. All this was done by the determination only a three-year-old child can have and use, with the purest mind and when everything I saw already was alienated for me. I'm a mass in completeness today and memory for me is just a part of my mass where I have to calibrate my way to remember. Most of the so-called normal events are strictly natively programmed in my bones so I don't have to reflect upon it when they are needed.

- Then again so it is for most people even though you might not be as aware about it in same depth as I am.

Most my knowledge is in compilation form and my brain as free calibrator as possible. Sounds odd maybe but isn't really. All our cells are equally important and that's something science of today forget or are very bad in letting people understand since the brain is the one of the more awesome tools we do have. So is even the heart. Heart and brain cooperate in calibrational lifestyle whereas people who embrace IQ and calculation lifestyle neglects and disturb important and vital information both evolutionary and scientifically. IQ always use AQ as base and if you neglect the base the outcomes rarely becomes that good. Just look at today, look around you and you'll see how badly treated society is in many ways. I have been active in the force since my childhood, well especially since the age of three years old.

All children are pure in senses and mind and are very honest and direct when they communicate with the few elder ones that still utilizes the force as communication channel. It's all about your AQ (Awareness quota if anyone wonders) how well you participate and utilizes the calibrational lifestyle as well as the Force.

True Faith is the only navigational tool you need to by yourself navigate with force. True Faith is the only true tool I have even though I have tried others as well and still do but its only my true faith that is my true tool of force navigation. Many has been in contact with me with so called mojo and other helpful tools.

I calibrated a big calibration before the age of fifteen years old. That was around 1989 I accomplished that. The calibration was a personal test for myself to keep track of my progress. Why did I do that? Well for you to understand why! You need to understand everything you read in this book is true! I'm exactly who I say I am. At the age of Seven or so year 1981 or 1982 not quite sure which summer it was. I took my second step as a grand master calibrator already then. I came up with the Calibrational formula or revealed it to be more correct and already then, I calibrated future in ways many people even today have a hard time to understand. I did all that before I had tried any drugs or even tasted sex. I needed to prove to you how badly it is with your calculational lifestyle but that was not all. I also want you to see that we are already among you, and you are fooling no one else but yourself by

187

denying the force and its existence. That summer I calibrated all the things I needed to accomplish in order to go "sub active" at age of 15 and from there only explore everything life had to give till the point of 2007 when I moved to Netherlands, Amsterdam and completed a 30-year path of Calibration formula and proved it correct. I had by then proved the power of calibrational lifestyle as well that the force is as real as real can be.

Before the age of 16, I had planned every single step of a scenario that would later turn out to be exactly as calibrated, it's out of personal matter and not worth mentioning more than this.

- This is exactly how bad it is to neglect awareness and the power of the force.

- Then again, if I wasnt right then why bother about writing this book and that was what that was about.

- Thats how bad adults understands todays childhood.

I had proved the force for myself at age of seven even before I started talking about it with relatives where we made an agreement one summer in Lövestad a place in Skåne Sweden where an actor who played many old Swedish movies lived. The House in Skåne where he lived he's old days, where the future demon of time has its resident and are an important part of my many Demon trees within me already.

He holds very important check bit for that Demon in the domain of death and I have pathed it well as well as others has withheld important demon bits that I have pathed and achieved all of them more than well. The people I mention lives or lived perfectly normal life's going on with their business, but Metaverse is more advanced than you can understand at this point. The keepers of check bits are usually unaware of them being that and needs no physical confrontation but merely a brick in the whole picture. The agreement made back then is the result of this book in a way.

...
.

.

One of the big reason our dear Bill Gates the founder of Microsoft succeeded to be number one for decades in the IT world.

- He was laying out a perfect foundation for him to build an empire that has visions that are still valid today.

is because rather than to choose to walk a thin line trying to balance his way to success, he chose to build a highway and simply walk the whole way. Watching every step, he's about to take while always being aware about where it started, where he's heading and where he is. That's not all, he created almost a religion out of it, its own natural Yin and Yang. Both software wise and as fuels for hardware as well. Free ware operating systems is the engine and fuel for the evolution of the windows operating system and vice versa (Opposite engine thinking). In other words, they are each other plus and minus pools. Just like MAC and PC are to each other on the hardware side. Bill also filled he's ism up with great content and future visions. Microsoft is the heart component and the very name of he's company. Just like the human heart is for us. They created DirectX that is the very small and soft individual that lives inside an operating system (Windows) which is its house. Outside its house there are lots of destinations, infrastructure, roads and not to forget the cloud itself. He's goal in the matter of end-users has always been the people as a whole rather than just a few selected ones. Taking care of basic needs with a composition of the office package. Probably caused loads off decisions that has appeared as weird or strange when you see to what choices has been made over the whole time that it has existed. Choices where correctness in technology has been put aside before the possibilities in functionality. Taking the time, it takes in order to make sure that you at all times take many steps enough to be number one. Even if that isn't the main goal that's the result you get when you chose to build a road rather than to balance on a thin line. Then we have Linux among others that has become its Yang. And an extremely effective Yang as well. By creating several tiers of software, Bill Gates created he's own road letting Graphical software (in favor for games, videos, pictures as well as Cad programs/Workstations Software/Server software/Communication Software (Like Chat, Blog,

Internet browsers, Internet applications) always aiming to make sure he covers all the basic lines within the entire world of IT. And in that way becoming a part of the very foundation of the Era we live in now, even if it's not the only part of its fact is he is the main reason that so many people today have access and a greater understanding of IT as well as being able to utilize the internet and being owners of a Personal Computer (PC) that is. The practical thing here is that he has never really needed to be the entirely best in any of the IT areas since it's not one component alone that has brought him to the place where he is today but the perfect combination of them and very well balanced always remaining close to the reality of he's very own Visions always alert on where on the road he is always scouting the reality's with he's outlooks all over the world (he's employees that is). Always making sure that they head in the right direction in relation to the road he staked out with he's own visions. From the very start till the point when he chose to retire. He's visions has been so great that even the ones that comes after him will be able to maintain the company's position for quite some time. The only two reason they will lose this position is because either the ones that runs it now fail to understand he's visions or the circle completes and the company evolves into a new shape, the next circle of the eternity sign. When you have laid out many strains enough in your defining pattern you will soon see where the right direction is and what risks it contains. You will also see where the risks are and be able to make choices so that you will be able to walk around dangerous roads and to choose roads that leads you where you want to go while minimizing the impact of destructive events. You will see that the right direction and the fastest direction most of the time are two separate roads. Directional thinking isn't two dimensional but four or even more dimensional. Even though it probably been presented very often with two dimensional pictures.

- Let's have a look at the Yang component then.

Linus Thorwald is just as much hero as Bill Gates himself are. Microsoft has been beaten so many times on their fingers by their opposite engine for so long that Bill is probably glad it hasn't been done physically on him personally. Linux and company is just as much part of IT evolution as Microsoft is for the rest of this IT world evolution. They exist in each other's Yin and Yang. They are Each other's Engines. Just like hackers and security people are walking the same paths in a more peaceful way then killing each other is. They both work with the same matter only on different sides of it and there is a huge grey zoon where right and wrong draws their line.

...
.

.

- Today I have worked within IT. I used to work as an Illusionist till I was twenty-five years old. I learned a lot of weird methodologies within the world of illusion.

I got to understand directional thinking with the introduction of misdirection. I learned about reflective thinking, and I learned my own body's movement and expressions and how I needed to understand my own relation to my surrounding during every single step of my performances. I learned how to read people from an illusionist perspective and got great experiences about human psychology by just doing something I truly loved to do. The routines I trained for hours and hours. The mirror was my best friend for a long time helping me understanding my own mechanic of my own body. I got a sort of narcissus complex as a trade of as well. I haven't suffered from it since loving myself for me is the base plate in order to be able to love someone else for real as well. To love yourself isn't ugly, it is ugly however to not be able to love or appreciate others just as much. We are all humans and today there is more than seven billion of us. To believe that you are more than anyone else is not just foolish but quite sad. We should never be afraid to be proud of our self and also be proud with dignity.

If you are too proud to be able to respect your surrounding you are no longer proud, then you are just being ignorant and craving for attention. A wannabe, a person that wants to be special but isn't, A wannabe is someone who chose to keep the personality the wannabe wants to be as its own reality and are quite disrespectful people.

...
.

History keeps many schools of philosophical methods and are reprinted and redistributed over time with both new and old reflections over them.

:: One in mind is a Swedish author named Jan Guillou that has written many books containing sensitive topics. However, the reason for me mentioning him is because it was one of he's books/texts that in my youth introduced me to an oriental tool of methods called "NO-Learning" - it was how it's been partly translated where the word NO is still most likely the oriental sound of its pronouncement, and the second word apparently is the translated oriental part into English. I don't recall the name of the book, but I do remember that it was a cooperation between a few authors telling shorter story's and creating a completeness together with the book as their table of content. The tool of ::NO-Learning:: is a tool of: Relativity - Reality - Revealing. It's a very clever tool that can be applied on any sort of content. And Jan Guillou if I remember correctly, it was he's story that explained it very well and I have had much use of it ever since I got to achieve its understanding. You use the tool on a content that always is left as it is presented, that isn't altered but always remain the same. You can call it a base plate. You only alter the thoughts, understandings and the directions of those around that particular content. You can take parts of the content and fuel them with definitions of good, bad, fun, sad, right, wrong and any mentality or understanding you like. By doing this you will have several story plates all from one and the same story

194

containing relative paths of the original one. Even ones you don't believe in, and by doing that you give yourself the opportunity to see not just how your very first perception of that content is related to reality but also see and reach new understandings by allowing yourself to learn from your own preset mentality's and see your own limitations in the way you choose to pass judgment on an action, or an event kept alone.

You learn to see what values different events have depending in what order/direction the content flow. The importance of content and the understanding what happens when something is ripped out of it. You get to see the same story from an orbish perspective, in other words you see it from many different angles::

...

.

.
- So, what's missing then in this marvelous world.

Well, we have everything in place that's for sure. We have educational systems and communicational systems in place. We have political systems in place and financial system in place as well. What we don't have is a world united with one currency, one timeline, one language, one nation and one law. We need to be able to see our self as one united mass for us to be able to take more steps in our evolutionary timeline. We all live on the same planet and its ours to take care of.

We already know we are on top of the food chain, its history by now and not even that impressive considering we are an average on the DNA chain. The future beholds so many beautiful opportunities with a united world its remarkable. This is just the first step of many more to come. Our ages will be mixed more with social ages as well as technological ages in the future. In order for us to be prepared for what's coming next this is a must step to take. To be able to realize we are not alone and so forth we must be able to stand on our own feet's. Managing the future in a healthy way, taking care of this opportunity of life rather than just leeching from it.

...

.

∴

There are several superpower nations in the world of today all trying to preserve total power in a weird balance of war and peace.

∷

.

Isn't that exactly what we all strive for. The perfect world in harmony with each other. Today's reality we live a in a world where America is the greatest Super State. Or at least many people consider it to be. And they seem to want to be this worlds Police Force. Which to be honest when we all live as one nation one language one currency one timeline one law will be just fine with me. We will need the police as a service but not as a state, no matter the shape of the futures pattern will look like. We need the service in order to maintain order because that's a part of the price of free will and it will always be like that even though what the work will contain will always change since that's exactly what our reality is like. And if we all are the same nation, speaking the same language we will still just chose to do that work like we do today in other words; it doesn't matter where the police have its base. We will probably have large bases in each continent just like we have today. Only then we would all be speaking the same language we would all be able to understand each other, we would all be equal in our economy. We would never have to change money ever again. We would be able to travel wherever we liked. Politics will be more alive and probably calibrate the relation between small and big societies as in the size of the cities and the population number as well as the shape of regions different ecosystems.

- In my opinion anyone working as a politician should be forced to educate in professional philosophy counting and tools like relative thinking as well as opposite thinking where the base of the education always is our opportunity in life.

Law and order will probably become more aware about everything, and we will start build pattern mats of DNA strains of structures and rules whose base will always be the opportunity of life itself and its ecosystem. The pattern changes a little depending where on the surface of this planet you will chose to live. Just like today, only this is for the opportunity of life and all the possibilities that exist with it. We still need a trading system, our eco system of economy but we need an updated one. One that shows the value of time rather than the size of a pile of money.

- Fact is the most important thing in life isnt to be the first in order to be number one. In fact, you live and exist just as much no matter if you come as number one in a competition or if you end up last. There is always a new beginning where there is an end. After a stopper there is always a starter.

And by building a DNA Map of clusters of pictures of definitions. We will be able to read the patterns so that we can always see (or "see in all-time" is also an correct expression here) in what direction we need to go in our next step in purpose of making sure that we always take many steps enough in order to reach the ultimate way in every single area and inch of our very own opportunity of life and the quality of its content. Most of the time we work with negatives of a picture of a feature in the future. Our imagination that is. Our very own imagination is the source and engine for our very own evolution. Or to be more precise, our brain is. Our brain is the container and projector of everything you ever see, experience, taste, smell, feel, and sense. The brain is our very own engine of our chemical system which is responsible for all our feelings and experiences. The fuel to this engine is a weak form of

198

Energy and electricity. Electricity's and energy's exist in all life forms and matter we come across, as well as in-between. These energies are actually an outcome from nature itself. These energies are needed for everything to stick together. Regardless of what the consistence of the matter is. Its mass regardless size produces and consumes life energy's. Souls and spirits Are just another component in this existence and just like many other things, like our bodies for example: that has a huge amount of dependencies in order to exist in healthy state so does our soul and spirit. There are energies everywhere. Those energies all exist in both nature and animal life. Twirling and twisting in planes the animal human isn't yet so aware of. We know a lot for sure. But far away from everything.

- Our brain system is like a Jellyfish where the body of the jellyfish is the brain, and our nerve system are the tentacles. Thats just one of our bodys life important eco system.

You can't win: a lifetime full of perfect life or happiness with having most money, nor most items. Life is already perfect as it is in its own creation. We are just one of life's own outcomes. We come from the nature and the nature is always our mother and father. We wouldn't exist without it, and we still can't exist without it. We must learn to accept that we are all addicted and dependable of life and not the other way around. Life is just fine no matter if we are in it or not and the way it is today Life is way better off without us in it. Sadly, enough we happen to be life's last opportunity to bring it further. That is something we tend to forget in the world of today's mentalities. Truth isn't always beautiful in that matter; we would have a healthier planet without us on this planet. A sad but true truth. We can't close our eyes for that fact, and we need to wake up and take responsibility.

...
.
.:

Happiness is a feeling not a physical shape or form but natural chemical with a life energy as outcome. Laughter is a behavior and a reaction to words of perceived truth, Just like we speak the language of funny humor. We laugh at the recognition of reality. Tears are just the same, they are both a proof of purity within a content as well as the language of being hurt.

.:
.

We have a couple of systems today. We have the chemical, blood and food system. This is all equal between us humans. We all are exactly the same when it comes to physically functionality but sure we are all different in the makeup. Cause that's all it is. Makeup. A way of looking. Shapes and forms that's all different.

Diversity is important because that's what we need. If we all lose the ability of curiosity, we will all slowly stagnate away. We all live about ninety years today. Not many people reach over one hundred years. We are all equally equipped with heart and brain, and we are only sexual. That's all we are no more no less. Rest is just different tastes and different directions in the very same space and time we all exist in. And the choice is ours. We can actually choose to make our existence to be with not only a purpose but also higher standards and higher quality and higher equality base for all of us.

- But we have to be smart...

- Really smart.

...

.

.

I compare and drag things into eternity and (yes and no) is just another Boolean expression (Boolean is a computer programming term, it's a variable that can be compared to a light switch that can be either on or off / true or false.) Only in philosophy it can be (yes yes, no no) as well as (yes yes yes, no no no) or all yes or all no. You use other variables as well and in philosophy you usually fill them up with different behaviors or scenarios. Philosophy is like programming without borders.

- And this is my very own little book of coding.

We lack in evolutionary timelines visions, and in great futuristic visions. We DONT lack in greedy massive destructive failures of great futuristic visions but we DO lack in: Great Futuristic Visions that's based on our self, the human species and its survival in the opportunity of life. The survival of the opportunity of life that exist on this planet in this universe. The very same universe that we all exist in, on this little planet.

Planet Earth.

There seems to be a problem though, it seems like we rather choose to flush everything down the toilet. It seems like we want it to end rather than to be, the opportunity of life that is. On this planet in this part of universe. We all know that this planet will explode into the sun in four billion years or so. The sad truth is that we are so skilled in our own destructiveness so we will have destroyed the opportunity of life long before that. Our population on this planet is growing bigger than ever and we are already over seven billion people all together.

The bad way we chose to treat this planet and its recourses we will end the opportunity of life not just on this planet but in this part of universe as well.

- Here we are… thousands of years in evolution…

All around us in close space we have been unable to spot life. This planet, a few billion years old. A big bang from a place in universe. If that's how it really started. This galaxy alone has not been explored by our kind at all, only some pathetic attempts to get onto the moon with humans and some space satellites and stations. Quite many of the last ones actually. This all has been about one big bang so far in this book. Universe equals Eternal. Do you even have a slightest idea of how many big bangs that is, how enormously gigantic universe actually is. And I'm not talking about this around the time of today and our planets existence… I'm talking about ALLTIME. Universe in time and space is beyond our imagination today. So was traveling to the moon a couple of hundred years ago. We will always find new impossible for today that will be the normality of tomorrow.

...
.

.

Do you have any idea of how weird and twisted the reality of today actually is. And when I say weird and twisted, I mean as in deranged the truths that we choose to exist in, how badly our choices are for our own future. Today we live in the Information technology era. We have all the communication we need, all the place and space we need to secure our future well. For some reason, the people that live on this planet today has chosen to deal with its own existence in all its glory of evolution in this opportunity of life in this part of universe.

- TO SCREW IT UP.

People talked about year 2014 and about the prediction of an Armageddon that were going to take place here. That the Armageddon will lead to our distinction. Well looking on the evolutionary timeline. Our world, this planet, will explode into the sun a couple of billion years from now. So, we will cease to exist eventually, at least this planet will cease to exist. Problem is that since we choose to screw this planet up so badly as we do today, we will probably destroy this planet before we reach the next milestone of our next step, our next era in our very own evolutionary timeline.

Let's take a look at where we came from and where we are as well as where we are heading in our very own evolutionary timeline. Space has existed so long time before this opportunity of life even started to exist. We are talking eternity here. And during this eternity a rock called Earth suddenly came to wear life. Today isn't even an eye blink in the reality that we actually exist in. And this one is for sure, We are just as much part of universe, as universe is part of us. Our type of existence is depending on some basic conditions. Until we can prove that we can bring life further and colonize another planet then we can start talking about advanced civilization.

You see One Planet, One Nation, One timeline, One Language, One Currency will eventually happen in our evolutionary timeline no matter we like it or not. Not today, not tomorrow and maybe not even in a hundred more years. But I'd say we are closer than what people might actually think. The economy will be rebuilt eventually which isn't strange since the same skills is different worth of many factors still today. We have made up a system that doesn't approve of advancement in our evolution anymore. We have truly needed all this that has happened to us in order to reach this far in our own evolutionary timeline. For thousands of years, we learned to say, "I am", now it's time to learn to say "We are" for a change.

...

.

- Here is a little poem for you.

.

Night Angels..

Connect with the dark moons...
And reveal your soul
and senses..
the force of our nature

Hunger from your inner nature...
The taste...
so sweet and strong...

Paths in all directions
walk with heart in mind...
Soul and sense companion
Faith will guide

Together we grow strong..
Standing for dared truths
some of lust, love and sin
others...
Relative relations
of nothing and everything

Angels of the night
Sees the things
No one else dare to see

Dont be afraid my love..
Night, Day, Life and Death,
Circle it is for sure...
one and the same.

...

.

205

- Let's stop and think about this for a moment.

Is there any way possible to get things straight with premises we live under today? We live in two different timelines. One Christian and one Muslim. None of those are correct to the true Evolutionary timeline. We are racists because we don't understand that we are all equally equipped with a heart and brain and that we are equally different. That we all are capable of to have and enjoy same sex erotica, It's all in our anal anatomy. That's just the way we are wired. That we don't understand that love and sex are two separate elements even though love and sex does exist as well in each other's elements.

...

.

- Why is sex so important then?

.

Today people have a quite vague understanding of what the term instinct means. Today we believe that if we don't die with the absent of something it's no longer a primary instinct. Well, most cases that's true but truth still remains. Sex is if not primary but probably a secondary instinct, but it is a natural instinct nevertheless which means it's always there. Our biology and our anatomy are overloaded with Sexual reflections and triggers. All our senses have different sets of triggers for raising the appetite for Eroticay. It's

206

a natural part of our existence. Its more unnatural to go against it then to coexist with it in harmony. The Chemical endorphin among other effects is very healthy for us and extremely stimulating for our entire body. Sex is the way for the brain to say I'm hungry. Just like the stomach tells you are hungry with its hunger signals it tells your brain to activate in order to become stimulated, so does the brain do when it needs to oil the chemical system (the brain and all your nerves). Since it oils the nerve system it also oils as many of your senses as possible as well. People are so bad dealing with their sexuality today that sex can lead to murder and devastation. Sex today can destroy or dramatically change, large time bits of people's life if not the entire life during our entire lifetime.

- And why is that?

Because today we have all the wrong expectations about what love and sex is. Sex is a social skill just as much as being our way to reproduce our self. And the reason to that is because that's how our anatomy is. That's how nature itself makes sure that no matter if we have invented technology or languages in order to educate our self it won't be a necessity for the purpose of succeeding in reproduction, since no matter what we will always succeed in reproduction many times enough in order for our species to have a fair chance of survival no matter where in time we are. This is just a "must be" for a formula of: free will, mind, heart, spirit and soul, flesh and bone, cells and energy's combined into a unique life with a unique form that has certain dependencies that needs to be maintained throughout life in order to continue to exist. That's the exact necessity for a formula to be complete when created in two components like we are, male and female. Sex will always be of great interest for us. That's just the way we are created. That's the reason to that we still exist. Unfortunately, with sex comes a great responsibility and that's not just in reproduction purpose which we have come quite far with today in order of ways to control this matter with birth control, but also as risks of diseases. And for some reason we chose to not reflect this in the society of today. Some cities in different countries are better on the civilian education on this matter but most people chose to let people find these things out by them self. The odd part is we already know that that's the wrong way to go in order to deal with responsibilities. We don't let people find out that you can burn down a house with a matchbox, We don't let people find out that you die if you put a rope around your neck and tie it well in both ends and hang yourself. We talk about it, we teach our self-sense, reason and responsibility's. We teach our self that yes even though it's possible it's a danger that can affect not just your life but other people's life. We also understand that the same lesson is supposed to be taught for each generation and each person because it's always the same responsibilities. As if Sex is any different. Sex is even more important to learn how to deal with not just about protection but also about each other. Today people become amazingly weird and peculiar when those words are even spoken. Words of Erotica that is. And not always in a healthy way which is what I have in mind here. People gets angry or upset or ashamed or even violent. We chose to deal with the matter of sex in worst possible way, we choose to make it into a taboo.

The result of a taboo is that you create an incredible grey zone for the sense of morale as well as giving worse odds in success. That means that the same engine produces different result with every opportunity that decides to use it. Since it's a taboo people will never really get the opportunity to understand and handle delicate matters where the line is thin between "pleasure and well-being" and "pain and sickness". We practice fire drills every now and then in all companies, not because we want to learn how to set the building on fire but in order to make sure that we cooperate with the fire department and together do everything we can in order to save lives. We do our part by trying to remember to remain calm and with as much structure as possible leave the building in the securest way possible. The reason is not because we love big fires but because fire is just as real no matter where in time you are. Through your entire life. Same goes with sex. Sexuality is always a big part of our life's. Even if the sequence of activity goes up and down in different wavelengths. Sex is something you will be able to enjoy your entire life after you have reached full development of your body anatomy. It takes our body between 14-18 years of development pure physically that is. With an average around 16. The average depends on a little. The year we have as kids are our most important years in our life cause that will be the base to whom we are in the future. The Kids is always our future and should always be respected as that. Let kids be kids, We are here to guide and aid them, support and provide them, teach and enlighten them. Nature has its own way to show us when we are ready for erotically sexual experiences and should be respected thereafter.

It's good to explore and discover yourself to get to know your own body and explore its erotically map of erotically zones and how those nerves trigger your sensual and erotically eco system. And sexual curiosity is a most natural growing interest since we all go thru the very same type of change. So being a kid with curiosity about sex is probably the healthiest state of mind to be in. A completely new dimension is about to reveal itself so no one should ever feel bad, strange or ashamed over the new discovers you are about to do during this time. Talking about sex is good at this time even though it will probably feel odd to talk about it if your parents never had a chance to experience a sanely way to talk about it with their parents.

Sex however is delicate, sensitive, emotional, exciting, fun, tricky, demanding, joy full, ecstatic, and even bad. You see not just does the genitals develop into male and female genitals with a new set of functionalities. This set of functionalities also brings its own color to all your already existing senses. Giving each and every sense, you have a new set of functionalities that's just lying there being ready to be explored. This way it really does become a new dimension for every person and it's just another part of our nature. That's just the way it is. Sex is an adult activity when it comes to practice, but there is nothing wrong with a kid that wants to know more about that topic, however never

ever go against human nature when it comes to
"human will" nor "human sexual development". Kids
are kids even in the eye of Mother Nature.

- You dont mess with the future.
  We have an entire life to live
  out our sexual dreams in any
  direction we like it to without
  going against someone's will.
  Without messing up the few
  years we have to build our
  foundation. Its difficult enough
  as it is.

Education and practice are two different things, even
though practice makes perfect, Sex has its own time
just like everything else. We might not be able to have
it our first fifteen years or whenever people lose their
virginity today is. But we will have an entire lifetime
filled with it, with different amount of times depending
on where in life you are located. Just like waves in the
ocean your sex-life goes up and down. Some people
love to surf the waves a lot while other less often. All
of us loves it while we are surfing most of the time.
Unfortunately has the taboo so strong effect that most
of us experienced bad sex more than it should be
needed to. Sex truly is a social skill with just as many
variations of tastes as there is music styles. What
people seem to forget is that first you must understand
yourself, then you are more able to understand your
partner. The best sex is rarely the one-night stand even
though even there you will have greater chances for
great awesome sex by knowing and understanding
yourself and being able to communicate that to your

partner in a way so that both of you can read each other. The better you become in reading your partner the better the sex will be. The more people understand each other the better they will be in enjoying each other. The more you enjoy each other the more will your engine shift direction from your own lusts towards the other persons lusts, Eventually you will be turning on the other persons lusts who also will turn on your lusts and by reaching there creating a perfect yin and yang variable where two people become each other's engine and fuels for the turn-on-factor that now works in a spiral upwards of lusts. This is the result of two or more versatile lovers. People that prefer to shift with roles of passiveness and activeness, blending them together and creating a harmony in a dance of lust, passion and Eroticay. Eroticay being any kind of experience from Erotica and its element. Unlike dance, SEX can twirl, and spin and leadership become chaser and catchers, yin and yang. SEX can be like a perfect harmony in communication where all parts both hear, see and read its partner/s acting on knowledge both random and deliberately, teasing and enjoying each other and making love uninhibited. Letting your partners lust guide your moves and directions by reading each other every second of every move and every breath. By understanding how good you actually are making your partner/s feel and how good you feel. By allowing you to enjoy yourself with more senses. By accepting your brilliance in life and letting your lust guide you for a change.

Today people spend more time of life with chasing sex rather than having it. And since people are all so obsessed by being a good chaser or hunter, when times comes for sex its hardly even worth remembering. People go out in the evening, does nothing but drinking looking and thinking about getting some that evening. But no one dares to stand up for that need and say the truth so that the people involved could have a great night of sex with loads of wonderful experiences.

- But no, Let's all wait till I'm so drunk that I cant sustain the moment anymore

Then if you actually manage to find someone your too drunk to remember if it was any good anyway. Why not just do it first then if you still feel like going out meeting very drunk people you simply chose to go out again. If people spent more time on having sex rather than pretending, they are all some sort of better people by sucking on a particular skill, we wouldn't have to worry so much if the sex will be bad or good anymore.

- Hello... wake up

Sex is a skill and if you don't practice it your sex-life will always be bad throughout your entire life and is no one else's fault but yours.

- You cant expect to win a skiing downhill race just because you have bought the skis. Just like you dont get black belt in karate just because you buy a black colored belt.

You have to train in a skill in order to become advanced in it no matter what the skill is. Just like any other skill for some people it comes easier, and others will have to train little bit more. Only thing with this skill is that everybody can understand it no matter in what country you are from. Just like music is a universal language so is sex. Except sex is a melody without a language to understand. Figuratively speaking that is. But Sex is still done with the same prerequisite and mutual understanding of how it feels and is like to experience.

Even though we have this situation with people that doesn't have become so advanced and haven't taken the opportunity to explore the domain of sex, people that haven't understood that it's a part of the human anatomy and skill set for all people, so they simply don't understand and chose to act upon it. People that have been filled with so much hate that they actually have no problems in hurting others even as badly as in killing others just because they are less advanced in the sexual skill then the person they needed to project their anger at. Which is a quite odd behavior in my opinion since they them self are equipped with the exact same skill set, that's just how the animal human is wired. Just waiting to be explored.

...

.

We never know what the future

holds before us,
we never know what tomorrow has to
show us.
We can always assume and predict
but never know for sure.
But we can take aim in certain
direction
and from there navigate our way
to the future point of decisions.

...

.

.

Today I must say that the people I have met within the
so called HBTQ Community (Homosexual, Bisexual,
Transsexual and Queer) all seem to know that fact of
how reproduction is being done and as far as I am
concerned all of us learned that before we where ten
years old and isn't really that big of a deal for us. We
don't consider simple facts like Sex is both a
reproducing skill and a social skill as rocket science.
What's a bit surprising is that many people that
approve of the heterocyclic standard which is mostly
nothing else but a vague rip-off and translation from
old religious standards. There are people among these
people that seem to believe that reproduction is some
sort of rocket science. I don't know when they learned
that or what it is that makes them believe that just
because they have been able to figure out that humans
are depending on a male sperm and a female egg
interact with each other in order to reproduce. All of
the HBTQ people figure this out in the age between
five and ten. Why does the so-called hetero people
keep it as rocket science. Everybody knows how to

reproduce. Even people that has a great taste for the same sex. It's the hetero male population that lacks in skills of advanced sex, not the homosexuals that lacks the possibility to reproduce. Even a so-called Homosexual may make the choice to have sexual intercourse with an opposite sex in order to raise children and by doing that also maintain a continual existence. It's the so-called heterosexual male part of the population that are the once that has drawn the shortest straw when it comes to skill sets of sexual pleasure. How sad that fact might be the truth still remains that the heterosexual are the ones missing out on sexual stimuli, rather than being superior they are actually the ones missing out experiences in this case.

Unfortunately, even the HBTQ community is suffering from pride in a shameful way. There is a lot of gay people that consider themselves as better being because they have made a journey by coming out of the closet that the hetero never needs to experience. Its true that it makes a person grow a lot but that doesn't mean you should fall for the same old mentality trap. Also, the pride is about realizing the truth about human anatomy. Pride is a huge subject in the HBTQ world, and most are healthy about it but even here pride with dignity is a lesson needed. We are all victims beneath pride, and we all need to treat it with care and respect. There is nothing new about the facts of that we all can learn to enjoy the art of the advanced sexual skill anal sex in the HBTQ community.

...

.

Throughout the entire life the one time when you feel
as good as you possibly can, when you feel the very
absolutely best, when you are at the peak of climax in
well-being during your entire lifetime is; the very
second when you're having an orgasm, the moment
just before and when the actual release of the
endorphins takes place. If you take the time of all the
times you reach that point of feeling good in your
entire lifetime and put it together you will realize it's
quite little part of your life that you actually feel that
good. A quite scary thought in my own opinion but
sadly its true. And it's the one and only thing we have
in common apart from all being born and that all of us
come from our mothers. All over this planet, in every
country, all seven billion of us have sex. Not in the
SameTime but in our lifetimes. That's the one and only
thing that we all completely understand in the same
direction and know together. We all have it happening
to us. And we do it quite often. There is no secret. It's a
natural part of our needs and behaviors. That's how we
exist but it's also more than just reproduction. We
create kids in less than 0.01% or even less time of our
"all of the times having orgasms" when counted all
together as time in life. Basically, sex is also a natural
need just like air. With the minor detail that we can
actually live a complete life without it on the cost of
reproduction and well-being. It's in our DNA. It doesn't
matter if we get bombed back in time for several
million years. We would still succeed in reproduction.
It's just another part of the animal human. Humans are
also animals; we live and breathe on the same planet

217

as many other species and life forms exist on.

The human being is over equipped with sexual triggers, everything from all your senses including our eyes which plays a quite big role for our sake since that's the sense that we are absolutely best on and less good on the other senses due to our heavy rely on the eyes and what information it collects and registers. Not only what the Eye can see but also what the eye can project. Depending on your senses skills you are able to actually feel that the eye as well are projecting a sort of wave. With the right amount of awareness, you will most probably be able to control information exchange if you chose to while in eye contact. It might have to be done with help of chemicals before it's done but it is a part of who we are as well.

An Orgasm is the most beautiful thing you can ever give another person, estimated in time in relation towards your very own relational timeline it is by far the best feeling you can ever have. Money makes you feel good, An orgasm makes you feel great.

...
.

.

As The last warlock I have a habit of collecting keys in Metaverse and today its quite an impressive collection I have. The keys open up portals, doorways, chests, boxes and other objects in Metaverse that may be equipped with a lock. I even open up secrets from humans with my keys. It's in my nature to collect them since revealing the truth is what I do. If you ever find something that needs to be opened, I'm the one to go to.

Some things Ill need to bring with me to my personal cube located in Meta space far away from everything else in order to be able to open it. Since the content might be out of harmful nature. This cube of mine is something I have achieved in Metaverse pathing and have been selected to have one of my own. It's a cube out of enormous proportion and it's located among hundreds of other similar cubes that other achievers have been gifted. It's a place to practice meta crafting as well as storing personal objects. The place is very unique and has been a hard achievement from my side. I have achieved an ascending for my original soul that's now a part of atom and exist. It has made way for the several cores of my soul I have today. I was allowed to keep all my memories which is good for me. The soul is unlimited, so it wasn't really a necessity for me in means of space or room but that's the way it is. To explore the soul is an exciting experience. You should always do it slowly, one step at a time so you don't hurt yourself by haste or misapprehension.

...

.

.

we live in a lifetime where we will reach a new milestone in our very own evolutionary timeline. We live in a lifetime that will go to history in our own evolution, we all become hero's. We all decided to save the world and our existence upon it. To save not only the human race, but the very start in the knowledge that we can actually bring life further and not just choose to ruin it like we do right now. We are going to have to be smart and to live in some sort of harmony with each other.

- And guess what? We are not only smart, but We are also brilliant.

.:

If you wonder, why I use big and small letters a little bit of everywhere it's not because I'm screaming as in chat language but that's the value of that variable. That shows the shape of its truth as well as value. Actually, it's quite calm and soft the way it's used.

.:

Don't forget how much it would cost... because it will cost money... think about it... we would need to change all our cash registers. Our cash as well but that's already a part of our system, we change them continuously over the years even if it's still the same currency... Our economy needs it in order to work... OUR Economy... Our very own creation of a trading system.

- But isnt this a bit creepy... This all means that you, yes YOU.. You, reading this, right here right now. You are a part of my equation as well.

Because wouldn't you want to be able to say that your entire life and everything you ever believed is completely worthless or even better.. totally Meaningless. Because that's what's your life will be.. if we chose not to save this possibility in life that we actually have. And not just that your life is meaningless but our complete existence.

- OR

Are you one of those bitches that want to be able to say that your life has a meaning. That our existence is out of good and not bad. I mean today our behavior is best equalized with a moronic parasite. I saw a movie on "you tube" where you can see our planet throughout our timeline and how we have grown in population. The movie strongly reminds you of a disease or a cancer tumor or if you leave something opened in a fridge for a few weeks and when you open you see that it will be covered in mold. Completely useless and most definitely not eatable.

- Wake up… Waaaaake up Wake up for crying out loud.

This is the life you are actually choosing right now. And yes, that's exactly the Era we are heading for. The Awakening that is. This is the Era that will be a complete gamechanger for all life upon this planet.

...
.

.

Today we can have enormous hangar ship up and running for quite long time now without having to refuel them. They are running on nuclear energies. I don't remember for how many years but quite some time it is. We also know how to transfer that technology into space. We know how to produce air for long times as well without refilling for long times. Nuclear is quite dangerous for us but its energy could be extremely vital for our future existence.

With the knowledge we have today we could easily create a small base on mars in order to be able to run dangerous tests for science and evolutionary possibilities. Mean maybe not to be used long term on everything we have an opportunity to explore and destroy our existence but as in common sense just like we use it today. It won't be to very long time before we actually can tell our friends that we are going to live and work with fuel extraction and processing on a base station on the moon. We are ready to start populating other space body's other than Earth. It will take some time sure. But that's what we are going to do. We will start with smaller projects like the space station we already have built out in space. Today it isn't many people that work out there in space.

The positive thing with building a space station on a planet is that its healthier and people can stay there for longer times since it has gravity. Eventually those stations will grow and become larger. And while that established on the moon mining for better fuel will be easier. Moons will probably become space harbors where you can refuel and easier produce large scale ships due to the environmental circumstances such as lower gravity force and less atmosphere to take in consideration while landing and taking off. When dealing with advanced technologies such as gravity and reversed gravity the scale of a ship is probably to large and to difficult to deal with here if you need to keep the earth's atmosphere in consideration. We are most likely looking at constructions that's in the size of maybe ten times of the today's existing Sealord's, the Aircraft carriers from the US Navy. We are looking at Space craft carriers that will never enter an atmosphere itself but using smaller vessels in order to enter and load off and on people or whatever supply that's needed. Creating smaller societies of people that will be special in the same way sailors and submarine people are. Later on, we will all be able to travel and work wherever we feel like as well. Space is its own unique ocean with its own eco system.

- This is visions of far ahead in the future.

Some planets will probably start out as mining colonies while others we actually succeed in moving life to. In the beginning it will be a result out of our natural behavior, our needs and curiosity and after a while also a need due to us growing in population. Later in the evolutionary timeline we will most likely be able to control/coexist more harmonic and predicted of both the forces of nature as well as the adjusting of planets and moons positions to each other.

The first large structures on a moon or planet without similar atmospheres as earth will probably be in conjunction with a mountain wall or within craters where large cupolas are built on top of them so that we easily can create an inside atmosphere while relative protected from outside weathers and storms. Once the layered cupola is in place we will be able to create safety blocks and other precautions in order to make the environment as safe as possible. When we created those kinds of areas to exist in we will be able to create reproduction air systems and water systems as well as creating landscapes of simulated nature conditions here on earth. With all in place we will be able to start mine and manufacture things without having to go through all the steps in bringing it from earth or at least to a much greater extent when it comes to expanding possibilities to become self-going.

...

.

.

Plants will gain new purposes when it comes to the abilities for the cycle of nurturing the soil as much as existing in it such as the Hemp. Hemp has loads of important ability's for not just a natural fuel or producing textiles but also for the soil itself. It might be outdated for now here on earth, but that plant has way to much of important functionalities for future scenarios so it's extremely irresponsible to dismiss it over a fact as it being a soft drug as well.

What does planets and moons have to do with each other then. Quite a lot to be more specific. It has always been a big part of the foundation of all life upon this planet. The moons create an opposite gravitation field that helps us grow and be as tall as we are.

Our existence and the opportunities of life existence in relation to our basic needs such as air, water, sun, Nature. Also depends on the very same conditions. Nature is a must for us to exist. It's all the green woods and plants and bushes that creates our air that we breathe. In the water we have all the plankton that also are extremely important for our existence. The sky isn't just our limits its our only limit. Life is estimated to have existed for about 3.5 billion years on this planet when looking upon the life in its simplest structure. During that time our species or the human predecessors has been dated as far back as 2.5 million years thru archeology, homo sapiens has existed for about 200.000 years or so.

According to science the moon has an opposite gravity field that makes the water level rise and sink on our planet and that the moon has been moving away from our planet with one centimeter a year. So, we have a timely condition there of what's needed for our atmosphere as well all life that exist in our version of existence. We have a specific need of gravity so that all shapes, forms and consistence's remain on earth, intact and alive.

The dinosaur might probably die out just as much because of the "in the longtime" change of gravity. Just like earth has a gravity field so does the moon, causing the tide. And since they are moving away from each other, the opposite gravity field from earth has weakened and apparently life grows smaller, even if it's in the long time this happens and here, I'm relating to the dinosaurs and their gigantic sizes. The Only animals that still exist from that era are animals close to the ground like the alligator and turtles and some birds as well as water animals. Last but not the least nature itself. We are talking millions and millions of years here. The reason the dinosaurs died out are disputed but one reason is their bones become too heavy for the muscles due to gravity change from the moon moving away from earth and so on, new blood diseases and new conditions in the nature for our entire eco system.

...

.

.

Today we live in some strange illusion that one thing must exclude another. Its seems like we have some fix idea that: if it's like this it can't be like that as well. Truth is it's the opposite way as well: nothing excludes something else. It all exists in the same frame of: Space, Time and Movement, in the relative truth we exist in. Most likely just like it is for us now the dinosaurs died because of several factors in a big, nice mess that all together caused their extinction. We will destroy our planet and our existence in this opportunity of life not only by our ever to fast growing population on this planet but also how sadly we treat our nature here. Not to mention the factors of nature that also has an evolutionary timeline just like we do.

So, we will have the conditions needed by collecting that information from the evolutionary timeline where we have existed for about 200.000 years depending on how you choose to interpret it. By doing that we will be able to see what kind of nature we need to recreate or to be expected by reading the conditions we have had during our existence.

We will see new life forms as in other type of animals as well as other types of vegetation in future evolution. We will also meet new life forms as in alien life forms. That will be far into the future.

After a while when we start to populate other sky bodies, we will probably start to see city's that will look like the Undersea world city's you have seen illustrated in any of our movies that we have today. Space and water have much in common when it comes to behavior of atmosphere. And eventually the location will start to get new conditions in its atmosphere, nature wise and we will be able to affect its process more and more.

We already know how to create both oxygen and water. And when we are able to build factory's that can create that on a planet, things will light up majorly. No more need of refill of air or water and we will need to know everything about the nature's kingdom. What plants are the best for production of healthy soil. Which ones can be stretched in its own condition in this existence. We must understand everything about our own conditions and its DEPENDENCIES. We must respect nature for our own evolution. In all life that exist on this planet there is great knowledge in DNA as well as in chemically, structures and behavior. We have to become natures caretakers for real.

...

.

If we look on the appearance of our self on this planet
in the evolutionary timeline we see some change in the
appearance in the beginning, then we stood up straight
and had more or less the same shape of the human
beings we are today, a couple of hundreds of thousand
years later. We have looked the same. In the long
distant future, we will again change our form and
shape. In our evolutionary timeline we have seen many
extraordinary breakthroughs and lots of eras/ages
where we made major progress by inventing or
discover something new. Just these last two thousand
years has been extremely eventful. If we chose to let
our self exist, we have just as much left and so much
more. We will find new dimensions new evolutionary
timelines in other life forms. New energy's, new
possibilities and new technologies. We will colonize
several planets and systems. We will master Life and all
its possibilities in all dimensions and timelines. We will
be able to make it so that we can have different
lifestyles on different planets. We will be able to
choose what life forms we need to be able to initiate in
order to keep moving in the right directions. In the
means of evolutionary directors. Truth is. We can direct
our future in any direction we want. We are going to
have to understand, respect and coexist with far more
trickier stuff then what we deal with today. Today we
are afraid of people from the opposite sex. We are
afraid of people with different colors on their skin.
Afraid of people with different tastes in sexual
orientations and skills. And all this causes us more
problems than it ever needed to be. All this because
we lack the ability to understand, accept and respect

our own true nature. We fail to understand how broad and wide our own species is in its nature. How extremely advanced the human being actually is. We fail to understand how extremely advanced the Eco System is that we exist in and depends completely on.

...

.

.

The Anatomy and DNA on every single living object in life, is a map in DNA and the understanding of what's needed to exist in that particular condition. For instance, how to produce life energies for different conditions. How to create life energies from mud or by breathing water or what type of diseases can we control by choice and mix with different blood types and substances. How does the regeneration DNA work on the sea star? How does the signal system DNA work for the bat and the dolphin? Every different species we have here on this planet every flower, every tree, all the sea life contains a unique map set of DNA. And all this is knowledge that we will need to contribute to greater possibilities in the future. The more life we have here on earth the more we will be able to see and understand all our possibility's. The more we will understand in how to bring the opportunity of life further to other planets and systems. Even with all that we still have so much more to reveal and discover. Eternity is a huge expression in that way.
We will have many choices in the future of our very own evolutionary timeline. Through understanding DNA structures as well as discovering new possibilities. Once we know how to bring life further to other

planets and systems, we will be able to deal with factors such as eternal life and also cross species of our self that has stronger abilities of survival in harsh environments. It will probably be in a few hundred years we will be able to see the first predator for real. Thru DNA we can understand how different life mechanisms works in different biology's. By understanding all there is about life we will understand how to direct it in any way we like in our future. The more different paths of truth we can find out, the more and better paths will we be able to walk and to do that in whatever direction we like it to be. Just like today. Only then we will be a couple of billion working in the very same direction for each planet and lifestyles. And we will all do it one step at a time. We already have everything that we need in order to accomplish a task as big as this one.

- Maybe now you start to see why our Diversity is our greatest strength.

We are afraid of the fact that when we know everything there isn't anything left to know. As if life ends there like some slot machine that suddenly sais Game Over. That will never happen. What's true though is that this planet will do explode into the sun and there is pretty little we can do about it. The Universe doesn't give a damn if we are here or not.

- That I also believe we can agree on.

However, the choice is still ours to make however we

want to do something about it or not. Our existence
that is. We already know how to travel in space, and
we have already started to talk about mining fuel on
the moon even though we realize its far to that point it
will happen eventually.

...

.

.

Why is it so important then that we already today start
to think about all this. Well, we will become space
journey men one day and we are going to have to
abandon this planet before the first solar storm
reaches it. That's much sooner than when the planet
actually explodes into the sun. And if we don't already
today start to think about this future that future might
not come to happen as rich as possible or at all. The
way we live today is a consumer's planet where there
is no room for future awareness, and it will lead to
prematurely extinction of life from this planet. Because
we will have to leave this planet and become space
journey men and that will happen whether we like it or
not. We must raise our awareness about this in time
and that time is already now because we have reached
a point where we are almost overpopulating the planet
when it comes to use of resources and coexistence
with planetary life forms. We too will journey space
looking for other evolutions observing them to reach
this very step of coexistence with universe. Some
planets will we occupy but most will we let evolution
have its own path.

...

.

If you compare our existence on our evolutionary timeline, you will see that another type of species was able to live on our planet during other conditions earlier on this very planet then what we have today. So different species isn't really that strange of phenomena for us actually. Boredom is sometimes confused with peacefulness. Truth is Peace can be fun as hell. And we can live in controlled forms with quite much fun in harmonic ways. We will redirect our greed away from money with the help of a new better economy (that's based on evolutionary time) that will result in better standards and with a higher tolerance of diversity in a very positive direction. We will become more and more aware about our self in the future as well as our surrounding and the way we are built we are over equipped with loads of different teasing system that keeps us alert and in constant movement in our evolution. Today suggestions about 6 hours workdays seems impossible due to the current economy system, truth is it's very possible if we start to understand the value of our own existence. If we could see the point in being able to provide work to as many people as possible. Money is nothing more than a reward system that we have in place because of our evolutionary needs long time ago. We were tired of needing a cow in order to get some sort of product. In that way money is a great invention. Unfortunately, there is a lot of flaws in that system that differentiate the value of human life's depending on location on this planet. Of some reason we choose to believe that the amount of these paper pieces and metal bits is what's the best for our future, our evolution, our existence. And that's where we are directing our greed today. Wouldn't it be more reasonable to direct the very same energy of greed that's our greatest engine rather than towards money as we do today, towards what's actually best for our very own future. The eco system of finance we have today has already proved to collapse itself and that's exactly how bad the eco system of finance we have is today. We are living in new conditions these days and that's just the way it is for all of us. It's not like there isn't anything that could be better directly in how things are done today. Truth is there is quite much that can be done, and we will do it for only one thing and that is our own evolution with all its dependencies.

For our entire lifetime. Don't we exist just as much when we are babies? Isn't our childhood the most important part we have in our lifetime? The kids are always our future. Why isn't that reflected in our economy? Isn't it so that we exist just as much when we grow old as well? Exactly how are we thinking here. Life doesn't start when you are 25 and then ends when you get retired. We live from the day we are born till the day we die and everything else is a lie. Why aren't we able to reward these two important areas. We actually have systems in place and then we have chosen to make them practically worthless to most of us. What exactly was the plan there. We exist just as much old as young, and when we are young, we benefit from all the help we can get and so does the old. We are still capable to feel just as much as when we are between fifteen and sixty-five. All over the world we have problems with unemployment, we have issues with class differences, we have major equality issues because we don't understand our own nature. We can choose to exist in any way we like, and we chose among the worst alternative there is. What exactly is going on in our minds. Why are we being such a sadistic nature with self-destruction as our main goal.

- WE CHOSE TO DESTROY IT.

- Seriously... how smart is that?

How smart is it to choose to behave like a parasite when it is our predatory behavior that makes us so proud. The predator lives a life in harmony with the rest of its kin, while the crazy parasite we prefer kills everything that comes in its way till there is no more to consume on that planet and then it dies itself. Yes, that's correct... it to dies and its whole existence becomes meaningless. Because everything you lived for and believed in as well as your parents, your friends, your partner and all they lived and believed in, children, grandparents and all they lived and believed in. Everything you ever seen or heard. Everything your have ever known, said or sung. Everything in life we know of will be gone. Total waste of time. That's all it is. You and your life will mean squat nada.

We are coming to a new time now, a new era and it's about acceptance. High tolerance. It's time for us all to wake up. We are coming to a time when we must understand and learn responsibility's in preserving life and its existence. A time where we must stop hold our evolution back. A time where we must see the strength in our diversity. A time for us to accept our self of who we truly are. A time to see the true us and all our capability's. Not just to see the fact that we know: how to be greedy and destructive. We are our true own creators. We have been directing and creating our own evolution as long as we existed. That's our true nature.

The strongest wins and the natural choice that MR Charles Darwin once talked about, and he was right then however the truth doesn't end there. Now we do live under new circumstances and most problems are solved peacefully as well as the Informational Time age itself. Unfortunately, that's not the only thing we are. We are also the smartest creature and I'm not arguing with the dolphin now in all its brightness and excellence but as in Possibility wise, Curiosity, Flexibility and visionary wise. What we actually have been able to do with our self's and our own evolutionary timeline so far.

We are curios, we invent, we discover and unclothe truths. We twist and turn on possibilities till we can find new areas of truths and facts out of it. We are not parasites. Why do we look up to that behavior as a god, I can't understand. We can do whatever we want with our future.

- So why do we choose a parasite as lifestyle?

I Thought we were supposed to be smart, Intelligent, top of the line and superior. Why doesn't that math sum up. There is no sense whatsoever in following a parasite lifestyle.

...

.

.

Comedians are probably one of the most important people we have today.

- You see... Our laughter tells us the truth about our social well-being.

When you laugh from your heart, your laughter sings different melody's. Just like the jokes can be hysterical, twisted, weird, dirty, sickening and so on. So is the melody of laughter itself. For us its actually more of a behavior rather than coincidence. We laugh at the words of perceived truth as a natural behavior in other words.

- And that my friend... could have been very dangerous for the church.

Or so they thought at least. The danger they feared was us laughing at the wrong direction. In a direction that could hurt them self. Their Religion. If you start to observe you will notice that the health of today's well being in our opportunity of life, isn't probably as good as you liked it to be. Comedians are sort of a floating static control in how different reality's we actually exist in and that's quite constant. The laughter in combination with the storyline when it's combined to you get lots of information about things that we find true about our valuations in life. You can read how distant certain mentalities are with themselves by evaluating the value of the sum of content and type of laughter, melody wise. Not only comedians are important but also comedy itself in our everyday life. Every location has different mood sets and mentality's that grows stronger in relation to the people being there. Every mood you have colorize the melody you react with and every context colors the perception of your mentality. Every type of sense of humor reveals different facts. We have Irony that is a two based component with one true and one false plate, both statements are in opposite to what's actually being communicated. In irony you switch places with true and false and with the choice of melody in the voice we see in what direction that statement is in. With humor we can read what our society is like, what our taboos are and where our real problems actually are. And the formula is a comparison of the melody and behavior and content of the event triggering the laughter with the melody and behavior of the laughter itself. We are like open books if you put effort and time in reading and understanding human behavior and body languages. The melody from the heart tells us more than we think about where we are with our self.

Joy and happiness are something we all strive for in our existence and isn't always so easy to attain. To be able to scratch the surface and see below it, to reach an understanding of what truly makes us happy isn't just a walk in the park. True soul-searching serves us many purposes in life. One is to be able to know and understand where and what true joy is for yourself. And not just what you are supposed to enjoy. If you don't find your true self the chances are that you just live in a charade where your heartily matter is just an illusion of what's truly your inner joys and happiness. If you don't make this journey in yourself the chances are quite big that you one day have a break down and gets a crash course in who you are in a less healthy way. True soul-searching is an investment in yourself and your well-being and should be done a few times in your life since you evolve and must take the change in consideration when being who you are. Joy and happiness aren't just about yourself but you're surrounding as well. To be able to enjoy others success as well doings is just as important. When you know who you are and see the reality within yourself your happiness will come easier to you and your self-satisfaction will grow on a solid foundation. To do the mistake and only do your life will bring you more trouble and worries in the long time than it's worth. Your false variables of happiness will under the surface bring you envy and agony if you only do your life and try to live as people expects you to. To achieve happiness, you must invest time in your own self-awareness and see the truth about your entire picture from the roots and up. Happiness Is a settlement with your inner expected desires and well-being. The more you are able to direct happiness to your well-being without the desires the happier you will become in the long run. The true foundation of happiness is always yourself and not the exterior of materials that comes from your desire. Hi expectations result in a more frequent disappointment rather than the achievement of temporary happiness, cause that's all your desire can give you. Temporary happiness whereas the happiness based on yourself and well-being is more constant. Don't fool yourself with the greed of money, it won't make you happy only more at ease if you are able to settle with what you have. No matter where you are in life, if you can't settle with what you have you won't be able to reach true happiness. There is nothing wrong with being successful and to reach for more than you have but it will always be at cost of happiness if you can't appreciate what you already have and have accomplished. Don't mix happiness with the satisfaction of greed. Greed is a strong engine and is a powerful tool when utilized with sense and balance. Which is a hard achievement to accomplish.

...

.

.

Relations today has an average age of 5-10 years. We have laws that differentiate humans by sex and by what they love. What is going on here. Why don't we all have the same laws when we all live in the same opportunity. Why is it so hard to understand that people are different.

- Honey it's a fact. PEOPLE ARE DIFFERENT.

Sorry if someone else told you differently. That's just the way it is. We are all equally equipped with heart and mind. We are sexual in all directions: Our self, same sex, opposite sex, group sex, orgies, fetish sex and love games. It's just a matter of taste and boundaries. No matter the sex of both. We cannot neglect the truth that we will always be different and that our diversity is as natural as nature can be. We are created with diversity and that's something we should embrace.

...
.
.

Isn't it so that the experience of a lifetime is what we live for? During our life experiences is all what's left when we look back in time. And when we look here and now, we are experiencing in this right now. During our lifetime we feel good, and we feel bad, and it will always be like that. We will always have ups and downs. But we can choose where to have them. We can choose on what wave and in what direction we will have them.

...
.

.

Today we live so many different kinds of lifestyles and the foundation of marriage isn't really what it used to be. To get married you do because you have great feelings of love or at least that's what you should do. You choose to commit yourself with someone else but today we have chosen to lock our situation to only choosing to live with one other person. Fact is today many people are having other choices and choose the lifestyle of polyamory or a swinger for example. Polyamory is a more natural way of life where you admit your love to have no boundaries with several partners. Where love for not only opposite sex but both sexes are an obvious way of life and also amending both the male and the female in you. I was polyamory in all directions, perhaps that's obvious and I'm proud of it. Why are we so afraid to accept those truths as they are. Why do we have so hard to accept the truth and to see the reality as it is rather then pretend it never happens. We are Humans. We have different lifestyles. Simple as that. Sexuality is a big matter to everyone today no matter if you are straight, gay, bi or transsexual. And our one and only true sexuality is Sexual. There are no physic law or no biological locks that prevents us from having sex with someone from the same sex and the nerves anatomy for the anus is exactly the same in functionality for everyone. The anus is just as much part of our sexual system as our penis and vagina is. However, reproduction sex is just like it always have been needs of being opposite partners. Raising kids in form of adoption works just as fine no matter if your gay or hetero. Reproduction sex only occurs a few times during a lifetime, all the rest is for pleasure, sexual electricity, easement and love in life. You cannot estimate a sexual orientations normality on such slim basis such as reproduction sex.

...

.

.

The higher and greater our understanding in life and all what it is the more we will respect and adore it. We will need cause and reason to do this, and the reason is that this is exactly how advanced we can become, we can all become total aware. That's just as much part of our existence as everything else is today. It's a part of our evolution. It's one of the facts we have unrevealed and it's there. It's just another side of the very same fact. It's just a piece of reality in how diverse and exceptional the human being is as an animal. We are a part of this planets eco system. We cannot be without the nature because it gives us more than just the air, our existence depends on it. It stimulates in our minds and well-being, it provides us food, air, chemicals, gasoline, minerals, wood, adventure, relaxation, change of environment, experiences, challenges and in everything there is a piece of knowledge and a piece of understanding. Pieces that have all been revealed or invented by our self. Just like all the books we have ever read is written by human hand. Otherwise, we might just hope that they are near. Cause then we are a part of their evolution just like they are part of ours and are probably very friendly.

- since they were kind enough to leave a book that is.

Written by human or alien hand doesn't really matter since we can only at this moment take care of what's here and our prerequisite for our continuing existence.

In order to deal with the future, we must first be able to deal with our own truth, We must be able to accept our self as we are. If we can't shake hand with our self, We will not be able to shake hands with each other. Even less with other types of life forms and species, even if that might be as far as a couple of thousands more year it might as well be earlier. It will happen as a part of our evolutionary timeline, at first probably from our self in our work to overcome new conditions to live and function. It's been visualized before in movies like Star Wars and Star trek among others. Different species that can handle different conditions. Just here on earth we have quite many conditions to reveal what it takes to be able to transform different types of nutrition's to life energies. How to produce different chemicals that contain important content for us. The ability to live on dirt and how to use gases to an advantage. Everything has a DNA map and patterns or most stuff anyway. There is so many secrets in the nature and we will be needing all that knowledge in the far future. for sure. We are going to deal with so many new concepts and evolutionary facts that it will be hard for us to understand why we have even had the issues we have today. Today we have a set of dependencies we are in desperate need of and tomorrow it might be slightly different. We keep visualizing ourselves as failures when it comes to advanced improvements. Anytime we are picturing us on the movie we constantly choose to show how we are supposed to do to fail. As if we have never been able to accomplish anything, as we haven't done any major progress at all in our evolutionary timeline. We can never create a full bulletproof system, not in the reality today and not in the reality tomorrow. There will always be exceptions, in other words relativity is very much a part of us in daily bases as well as in the future. The more we learn and understand of the ecosystems DNA maps the more we will respect and the more serious we will treat it just like any other area where caution is in place. The more we know and the more we understand the more we will be able to make correct decisions and take more correct responsibilities about our upcoming evolution. The more we will be able to make sure that the opportunity of life will never end no matter how bad things goes.

Today it will all be gone if we don't care enough and care soon enough. That's how bad our choices are today; we are all stuck on the very same planet at the moment. And as mentioned before the day we have been able to populate another planet is the day when we can start to think about how to deal with big decisions such as eternal life and so. New species in order to open new doors and to avoid distinction. It's all there for us, just needs proper understanding and responsibility. We have an eternity of revelation and exploration ahead of us and that's a lot to deal with. We have to embrace a bigger picture of our self.

...
.

.

You hear people talking everywhere now today about the Maya code, the Armageddon, Anti-Christ and they all chose the visualize it as a bad event, as a great failure and mass destruction. And we seem to forget that there are just as many positive solutions as well for the next time age we are about to enter. We have simple facts like no matter what our eco system of economy is, it will always be divided by the same amount of people. We will have more life quality than ever in matter of time. We have greater opportunities to advance and re educate our self, we would have better financial foundation as well as healthier climate when it comes to factors such as respect and equality as well as greater control of how we are doing in our very own evolutionary timeline. We would have more time with our children making sure that our future always has the best foundation there ever is at every moment we will be able to open doors and realities in our evolutionary timeline that we can't even possibly imagine today, just like we couldn't imagine how for real fly to the moon two hundred years ago.

- Do you now start to see How I use My pen strokes of sentences and colors of relativity. How I slowly paint a picture a little by little. Some bits here and some bits there and constantly let the painting form and shape in relations and directions from anywhere on the yin and yang of good and bad.

- And why is that so important?

Because the more and the greater we can put together scenarios and visualizations of the relations and relativity's we live in today in relation to our future possibilities and opportunity's all together outcomes and Lose End maps the better prepared we will be for future evolutionary steps to take. By being able to create complete yin and yang's that we all will be able to visualize into its future. We will be able to create landscapes of relative existence, symbolized with a circle that piece by piece gets filled up with all the colors from the color scale. This way you create very powerful variables that has been used by The Inca people, They used it when they were reading in berries. Only it's not as two dimensional as it's been presented on paper. And by doing this we will be able to see not maybe what's the best step is but many steps enough in order to continue in the best direction. The very same fact: It's not about how long or how much you own in matter, It's not about gods or no gods. It's all part of our truth. It's all part of all life in the very same opportunity. Life is more important than money for all of us.

- Dont you agree to that we could actually shape our self-up quite a lot in relation to quality wise.

We are in great need to start respect our future as it should be. We do need more time for our future - our kids - and we also need more time to be able to stimulate our complete set of needs measured in relation to our today quite limited reality due to fear of needing to realize the truth, to wake up and see our time, our very own lifetime where we live here and now of today. We are also a part of our evolution. We to will develop and change into something different, another life form as continuation of our evolutionary timeline.

This step though, the one we are about to take is more

likely to happen in its complete within a timeframe of 15 – 20 years before everything is finished processing of the change into the One world, One language, One Eco system of finance, One law and one timeline. Everything might probably be in place by 5-10 years but there is also a need to adjust and correct in order to have been able to complete the agreement in best possible direction and then to adjust and correct our newly gained lifestyle our self and all our new systems. This is the estimation it will take from when the change start till the end of it when everything is in place not a prediction what the next 20 years will be like, it might as well take 100 years before the change starts to happen, but it might also happen much earlier. The opportunity is already here, and the world isn't getting any younger. And we don't know how close to the point of no return is, but the shape of the world is getting worse every year.

It will be hardest for the oldest to adjust to this new situation but in favor for all generations. We are just as much alive when we are Old/Young/and children. Let us prove our superior abilities to honest being able to raise above the other animals and take charge of the maintenance of this opportunity in life.

When you elaborate with philosophy like this you might start to see what directional thinking is about. What opposite thinking patterns and "fuel and engine" thinking is about. When you define in philosophy its very different from defining a word. In philosophy you must be able to keep everything for truth as well as to be able to claim everything is false. Relations are everywhere in life, time, space and movement.

.:.

Life itself is the most advanced and brilliant structure there is.

.:.

In philosophy you must accept bad and good as nothing more than two opposite directions. In philosophy your entire brain is a feature, an ever developing biologically evolutionary object. The brain is a bloody interesting processor to work with. That there is truths that contains just as much truth, history and visions so that all senses becomes important in order to understand what our possibility's have been and what's been done with them. As well as understanding what they are today and what possibility's we have for tomorrow, then also what our possibility's might be from tomorrow to the day after that. By doing it in a way where we all understand and see the truth. We will always be responsible for our very own future. Our very own extremely unique opportunity of life in this part of universe. Isn't it so that we actually are the predator number one on this planet.

- I'm not arguing with the white shark here whose anatomy by far is the best predator.

But rather as a civilization and flexibility wise. As creature

- or species

248

with exceptional adaption skills. With skills, intelligence, curiosity and a great appétit and hunger of life. We are darn stubborn creatures.

- If you think about it. =)

...

.

.

No matter how bad things are, we have gone thru evil Dictatorships, Civil Wars, World Wars, Natural disasters, We have seen Empires Rise and fall, we have seen civilizations come and go, We have been through plagues and misery, we all have our very own rollercoaster that we go through, we get our hearts ripped apart by love.

- And still.

We persist on waking up each and every morning every day every weak and every month, year after year or around ninety in a sort of an average. And every day we continue to claim the need for food, and for thousands of years we have always been driven by our instincts. We have been doing this for so long now that there is seven billion of us doing it every day now.

That's exactly how great we are in just that. Living and existing in life. For hundreds of thousands of years, we have been doing that very phenomenon. That's exactly how dear Life is to us.

What is it that drives us then? What is it that makes many people enough to take many steps enough and maintain a balance within all this? The cycle is quite simple when you think about it. We all get born, We have a certain amount of time where we live and loads and loads of options then we finally pass away. There are a few things we can't choose today. Being born is one and we can't escape death (for now at least). So, throughout our evolutionary timeline we are walking a slow spiral that actually goes in any direction that we bring it too. So, we all get born, live our life and then we die. The question was what is it that drives us doing this rather pointless behavior if you choose to look at it from a distance. It's the stimulation of diversity in this opportunity of life, it's the fact that we are so over equipped with stimulations reflexes as well as teasing mechanisms that are all based on our own functionality in our very own life form we exist in. The reason we still do exist is because our nature as the animal human is so advanced and exceptionally clever it will succeed in existing no matter what path or road we are walking or existing at. Our very own DNA structure has given us opportunities to overcome the impossible. To reveal information from nothing or seemingly nothing. And it's all there. The tricky part is just to figure things out. We have had civilizations that has raised and vanished that used completely different methodology's then what we use today. Science is an area of facts based on the ability of maintaining and supporting knowledge, examining the truths about all physics there is and now metaphysics as well.

By realizing that I'd say that we kind of like life and like to live in it. Even though many people probably realize that there are many things that can be done better in this world.

In other words, we already have everything we need and know in order to complete this step. A step of such proportion that it would be our biggest step in evolution up to this day that is. For the first time in history, we would all be equal before the god of today.

-   Money that is.
        ...
         .

             .:

Today we have a system that is quite scary when you see it in the big picture. Today people are a bit alienated for modern philosophers however just like near the last two centuries has had prophets and philosopher so will this one and there will always come more, and new ones and they too will be able to adjust the roads we chose for the opportunity of life.
             :.

               .

life is quite awesome once you start to think about it. Isn't it so that our species in this opportunity are the best ones in making awesome progress. Isn't it cool that we have for our whole evolution been able to shape our self from the very beginning of our own start of existence. Our visions, our emotions, our fears and horrors, our love and erotica, our hate and despite. our sense of humor. Our excellence in existence. Our future our children. All-time, now-time, tomorrow-time, yesterday-time. Your life is here and now at ALLTIME. We learn from our past and we are aware about our future. We have with our visions, mistakes and fantasy's been able to reach the most incredible inventions or revealing of relative truths. We have been able to compose several religions and isms through our time of existence. We have created and maintained several hundreds of languages. We have invented hundreds of different financial systems; we have explored areas all over our planet as well as started to occupy them.

We have built and maintained every road and house you ever lay your eye on, we have built and invented every technological devise you ever bought. Everything that you know today is because of our self and what our ancestors have accomplished. TV is something lots and lots of people have access to today. We all have mobile phones, and we have invented airplanes, boats, cars, motorbikes, balloon ships and space rockets. All invented and figured out by human beings. No how to or step by step guides in how to invent this or that or how to reveal and discover this and that. Our species started from scratch just like every other species have. We must be able to be proud of our nature, proud of how just as different we are to nature, just as different nature is to us. But we should be proud with dignity and a tad of humbleness. Humans are animals just like all other animal life form. We have our conditions in order to exist in this opportunity just like they have theirs. And what we all have in common no matter of shape and form or type of life form. We all must have this planets conditions in order to continue in Our opportunity of life. We are all in the same ship. Green life as well as water and air, animal life and insects. We are all built up with cells and DNA structures, We all need some of the conditions more than others and we all would stop to exist if one of our elements went away. We would also stop to exist if we chose to do nothing, and it will not be a matter of a single factor but several factors in all possible ways. If we don't choose to continue to exist and rather go for a World War 3 with nuclear, we will also most probably end or reset our opportunity of life on this planet.

If we are able to see all the benefits in letting Life and evolution or time itself being the foundation of our new eco system of finance. Rather than the one we have today where there is no logical connection anymore in invested time by high productivity and rewards in relation to our existing financial eco system. That we in fact already have invented, had in use and maintained for century's as well. The possibility's that comes with this step is in long time thinking as in decades/centuries and Eternity's. Impossible for us to foresee beyond certain points.

By calibrating the evolutionary timeline and include the three components past time, now time and tomorrow time. and by calibrating outcome thinking and loose ends thinking in compilations of Yin and Yang variables with opposite engines and their fuels as well as directional thinking with the designing tools of programming "without" limit (well the limits of the variables are of course defined and there is philosophical structure as well) we will be able to run lots of simulations and new types of directional paths that will reveal themselves in same rate as it always has.

That is said in relation to universe own existential timeline which we never can estimate correctly since we honestly have no single clue of how gigantic, big universe is. Science claims we started to exist by a big bang and that time didn't exist before that. Problem is that: time has always existed since space. Time has no limit. Time also has its own dimension though and that dimension we need to explore as well and white holes represent the zero-time point of that dimension.

Truth, is we have no ideas how many Big bangs has taken place with different equal much of existence in space and time, if any has that is. We can't even trace it back to our closest one backwards in time or at least not to what was before it happened. And with that fact combined with the fact that no matter if we ever find an end in the beginning, we still don't know how many roads there is and is to come. Then we know that our reality will always be relative for Eternity, we will need to become far more advanced before we will be able to reveal those knowledge's. We are probably by then populating not just other planets but systems as well. And even then, we will probably still lack in traces to see some sort of beginning if there ever been one.

...

.

.

We have to make an active choice here. Choose to

exist for eternity. If we choose to exist for eternity, we have to change our behavior today. Eternity is a long time and to live as diverse life as possible throughout eternity it needs responsibility taken now, today. We can't live like today only thinking of what will happen the next five years. We have to make a complete 180 degree turn in order to be on track with the vision of existing in eternity. We have to make a choice; we can actually make that choice today. We have to see the large picture and think generationally in eternity into infinity. We can't condone the parasite lifestyle anymore we need to become the predator we truly are. We need our nature more than ever and it's not in good health today.

...
.

∴

Eternity is a two-way lane, in the relation "past<- and->future" speaking. Zero and eternity has the same value. Nothing is Everything. Zero is symbolized with a closed circle and eternity with a closed lying down eight. Eternity is a concept of understanding when it comes to see its true nature in completeness.

∴

∴

Nothing contains the untouchable and the useable. Your thought and your mind, Love, Your soul and your spirit. Emotions. Dreams and senses. Nothing is a dimension of its own. And it's a dimension to count on in the future.

∴

Our existence will always be relative in relation to the time we live in. Youth of today has a hard time to understand a life without internet and emails, what it was like when we didn't have mobile phones or faxes. Today we wake up and go to work or school depending on where we are in life. There was a time when the majority of us had to wake up and then go to hunt for the food and the water in order to make sure we would have enough food for today and tomorrow. Today we are so skilled at that, so we no longer need to have a big part of the population to go out and do that. Today a minority of us actually deals with managing food and other life supplies that we must have in order to exist. Today most people just trade money in order to get a meal and beverage each day and that is more than 99.9 % of the population that's not bothering about how to maintain, and care take animal life and nature. That's exactly how skilled we are at managing life supplies. The truth is in now-time we are so skilled in producing and supplying everything we can create so we are more and more reaching a point where the only way in order to gain more money out of it is by producing more consumers. And when we reach that point in any area the eco system of economy is no longer a valid system. There is no more need left. Today we chose to create items with lower qualities for the simple fact that we consume more of it.

- And why?

To get more money and that is a nice idea if you keep that fact alone. However, we have invented a stock market for successful companies and today we have loads of major companies that spans all over the world.

Now stocks are a more or less a fake money system that live a life of its own and basically ruins the eco system of economy today in one way. They don't go hand in hand even though it's a very good try in order to stimulate finance. Truth is that no matter of size of company you might as well choose to not enter the global stock market and still be worldwide. Today people do it of different reasons. Today we live in so different reality's its amazing we all live on the very same planet. The world is empowered by a few people that owns the majority of business that's considered important today and they are usually not the politicians. We all realize that the situation of unemployed people is a big issue, but no one is ready to face the fact that the eco system of finance that we have today are inadequate.

Today we have needs of reeducation one or maybe two more times in our entire lifetime, that's how fast things are changing today. Today it's quite unusual we see people that has been working forty to sixty years of your own lifetime with one and the same thing. We have an average of five to ten years at one and the same location. The Eco system of Education and Eco system of finance doesn't even speak the same language as it is today which is strange since most of the income and most of the financial support systems is based on us selling our own brains knowledges as services. The problem with having an eco-system of finance that isn't synchronized with any other eco system such as the educational, the opportunity of life, the Home and Life standards. IS. That we are not able to take the steps we probably would be able to take and the less they are synchronized the more destructive we become. Eventually everything collapses and civil wars as well as great and bloody revolutions eventually takes place. The less we understand each other and the less we are able to see life as a picture in completeness in all its incompleteness the worse the climate of civilization becomes. Today we realize more and more that life is just as much an opportunity for us all no matter color of our skin, our sex or how advanced we are in erotically skill sets.

...
.

.

We have reached a point where a mail of information can't travel much faster than it does in order to make a huge difference. The human will always be that base factor of how fast the composing of information is done. Electronically we already have reached states where the processing of everyday life routines when it comes to Information Technology are maximized. We are still developing it because we are created that way. We always strive for new goals. Some people are afraid of evolution and strives to slow things down which is also a choice of direction. Here time is always taking a tiny step forward no matter what direction we chose to head into. Evolution will always move no matter the choices made by the human race.

...

.

.

Today we are so skilled in management that we are able to see that health care such as hospitals and structure of enforcement in the purpose of the people's safety such as police and fire department are not just things we need but also a right to have. That's how advanced we are. We have social systems in place in many countries that helps us support our possibilities and maintenance of our lives throughout life. However, how good that might sound the systems for today that we have in place can all be done much better. We all realize the benefits of peace. As well as the cost of destruction of war. However, we seem to have a hard time realizing that rather than to chose to put our god(money) into the art of destruction we can actually put equal amount of money into infrastructure. And money isn't really a problem because no matter where we are in the world. We always have money to create war and educate our self in massive destructions. Each war doesn't only cost humongous sums of money to maintain and to produce weapons of all kinds, not to mention all the massive amount of money put into founding's of research for new weapon technology. Then after the war is done there is even more money needed in order to rebuild the infrastructure that has been destroyed against peoples will. This choice, to direct our money on our future evolution rather than war, will bring us all together and we will all have to realize that we are all in the same ship. This time the ship is planet Earth and all life upon it. We are talking about a united world here and the truth is we won't need to focus our efforts and resources in mass destruction, we have already proved well enough that we know how to end life in more ways than many of us finds interesting. We know we can wipe out all life in a single third world war without any problems, there is no need to prove that part. We are standing before the most serious attempt to bring us all together and the task for us to Wake UP and realize the pure truth. We are all part of the very same opportunity of life on the very same planet in this area of universe. Our part of Universe. So far at least. We don't need more advanced ways in how to end life. We need to change the direction of that lust into our self our everyday life reality and start using the same amount of time and effort into making this world just not a great place to be at, but also the best opportunity of life there has ever been in Time Space. The more we care about our self and our future, the more we care and understand that we are just as much alive no matter if we are young, adult or old and that we will all go through each stage since it's a natural part for us all. The more effort we put into understanding each other and how different we all are seeing possibility's rather than problems. The more we will gain in life quality.

I am all the time assuming that it's done with great responsibility and great deal of common senses. When I say we need to be smart we really do need to be smart. We love competition. We love great challenges.

We love to seek out thrills in our life and trust me. A future as this one will offer you all that and so much more. Only then we will be competing in what domain/continent will be providing the best solutions with criteria's that must meet a civilization on an entire planet rather than a single country.

We will need to continue to evolve information technology as well as all the other eco systems we have. And we are actually only talking about a patch or an update to already existing structure and social behavior maps. That's what evolutionary steps will be like in the future, patches and updates. We will get a new structure for future evolution where we apply the patches or updates within certain time periods, and they will reoccur every fourth or eight year or so.

...

.

.

Today we have about 195 different countries. Each countries mother tongue is alive just like everything else, the same language varies allot not just in dialects but also over time. If you look closer, you'll see that in every country the people from different regions like the north and the south point of each country probably would have a hard time to understand each other if they talked their native dialect even though they both speak the same language. Today we have hard time understanding our own language two hundred years ago. It's even counted as a skill set.

...

.

.:.

The only thing that remains throughout time is Exist, relativity and change. Everything else decay and reforms.

.:.

.

The financial cost of this change is large... or small depending on how you chose to see it. It will be a financial cost but for whom is it... it's for our self. This time it is for the entire planet; governments have wasted money on far worse ideas then this so if it will be a cost or an investment.

-   That's a good question.

It's a huge opportunity for infrastructure and possibilities. I assume we have to watch the scale and see which one weights the most here. Even though I'm sure that moneywise it will hardly be considered a burden since we all will benefit and be a part of the very same change. I will leave the financial for now.

The problems we are facing here is not like when we figured out how to: create fire by hands with hardly any knowledge base of how to do it. We don't need to figure out how to: from a weaker tool master and manage metals. What we are facing here is for sure a change and a big one. One of its kin. The difference here is that we have already mastered to create several different financially eco system that coexist within one major financially eco system, every country already has a system. We have already made merges of economy. We also stand before a fact that no matter if we have it or not, all we will need is a mutual system when it comes to social and population services. For the first time we will have a foundation that we all understand mutually and for the first time we will all be country men with each other no matter color of skin, sexual orientation/preferable or ethnics. Brothers and sisters. For the first time we will be able to understand our differences and to see each other with same concept of understanding. This time we have already gained the base knowledge for what's about to come. This milestone in our own evolutionary timeline will not be about technical invention or a breakthrough. This will be the biggest social and mental update thru out history. This time we already have everything in place, or at least the know how's in order to make it real. This update issues are mainly mentality's, and the greatest and most advanced mathematical equation ever made. Our very own knowledge and understanding of our self and the complexity we possess with all its beauty. This update is about seeing the reality as it is. Accepting the truth. This time, it is time for us all to wake up and see the opportunity of life as it really is. We are taking another step. We will need to understand everything about us and our history. Some of the facts we have today will be passed on to history and others will be revealed and all of them will be maintained. We shall never forget what things has been like without the respect to our constant raising awareness.

- Total awareness, that's one of our

263

next goals after the merger if not before that is. This will be the first time throughout our very own evolutionary timeline when we chose to have total control over our own evolutionary future, over life, over everything.

- This will be the first time we will be able to direct our own future in the very best way, step by step and always manage to take many steps enough in order to reach the goals we are setting up our self.

No matter if its history or now time both are just as much part of our very own evolution. We live in a time when we can spread and communicate information faster than ever. We can all participate in what's going on with internet, TV and radio. We already have educational systems in place. School is nothing new to us. Fact is no matter where we are today big parts of this world is connected and updated with information daily. We have computers at home at work and in school and we wouldn't have a problem in making sure that country's that doesn't have it can at least get access to enough of it in order to get things started, even if the goal is to make sure we all are connected.

...

.

.

Another sensitive topic is drugs. We live in a world full

264

of drugs and people just love to use them. When talking about drugs it's important to keep them all for what it is and that's drugs. The world is full of people using drugs every day. What people do as a mistake is they think because its legal it is not a drug and that is a big lie. Alcohol is a drug and tobacco are a drug. Tea and coffee are the weakest and most harmless ones, but they are also categorized as drugs A drug that next to another one, that is more dangerous and has an addiction factor opposed to cannabis is alcohol. Cannabis has caused more peace to this world than any other chemical or university has ever done. A more peaceful state of mind is hard to reach. And this extra ordinary plant that some countries are equalizing with terrorism. They close their eyes for the truth and says that if alcohol was invented today, it would never been tolerated. The hypocrisy in this is cannabis has never been invented, it's a part of our nature. Throughout our evolutionary timeline we have always utilized drugs of different kinds. And cannabis is one of them.

Yes just like anything else it can be misused but looking at statistics from the country that has actually let people have the choice of what type of buzz they like to get has proven the rest of the world wrong in their assumption. Countries that have chosen to criminalize it have no idea of what's it's like to live in a society where it's a valid choice. They lie to the people and claim it's the source of crime and a gateway drug which is only true as long as its categorized as illegal. You don't become criminal by going to the store and buying a bottle of wine do you. Nor when you want to buy a six-pack of beers. And why is that. Because the ones selling it doesn't also have a stash of other illegal character. To claim that the drug cannabis is leading to criminal behavior is to lie the people right up in their face. It's happening when you keep it illegal and even then, it's only a partially truth. When you use cannabis, you don't become a criminal however there are people that has used it and then tried harder drugs since it wasn't as bad as they claimed in countries where it's illegal. And since it really is a lie and since the drug does exist and people does try it, they realize that these sayings are so full of crap so why would the rest of them be true. In that way causing people to try harder drugs that actually are more dangerous. Lies always punish them self in one way or another. Cannabis when hold legal does not lead to crime nor does the majority of cannabis user become criminals.

Cannabis is a drug, for sure. So, it too needs to be treated with respect and proper manner. It can be misused like everything else can. Statistically its far less dangerous than Alcohol is, even less dangerous than tobacco and as long as alcohol is a legit choice, so should cannabis be. Alcohol is by far a worse drug for people. People can reach states of mind where they start to beat and abuse each other under the influence of alcohol, even kill others as well as raping others. All this can happen due to the way of the drug is interacting chemically with your brain. Alcohol does lead to criminal behavior in that manner. Cannabis that has a completely different character when it comes to the form of buzz. Doesn't provide you anywhere near that destructive and abusive behavior. All drugs have some level of destructiveness towards the user of it. So does cannabis as well, just like alcohol. So does even other things in life that you don't even chose to "use". Such as gasoline in gas form from cars that everybody is forced to breathe no matter, they want it or not. And same goes for factories and construction sites that provides us with different form of fumes, gases and dust in different unhealthy forms. Cannabis is a product of nature that hasn't been developed by a manufacturer. The problem with all the lies around that plant resides in many factors. Holland has proven the world for many years now that you can have it as a legit choice of drug in a perfectly safe and healthy society.

We have Oil companies that isn't too happy about that any country in the world that has farmers can actually replace their fuel with a more Ecological and more healthy type of fuel then their Oil. So, hemp oil isn't popular choice here. Today we are more concerned about the environment than ever and yet we lack the ability to see truth as it is. Then we have the Medical companies that doesn't like the medical ability's that can be resourced from the very same plant. And why is that. Well since Cannabis is a plant, no one will be able to get patents on it nor royalties or any such things. No one will be able to rule out the world in monopoly the way it is today. This plant alone contains enough resources that the Superpowers of today would actually have to become nice hosts of this world rather than by greed suck people out on what they believe is God – MONEY.

Which means if it was legal every country could

actually make sure they could provide both cloths and nature friendly fuels for both energy and transportation. This plant could actually help out in large areas over time with bad soil to become better. And the sad truth is that there are great medical potencies within this very plant depending on how it's used and utilized. The US government used to say and fart at the world by claiming that there have been no new discoveries from that plant since 1893. The reason they say that is because that's the very same year they decided to claim that cannabis is evil, bad and so on without actually taking in consideration that cannabis is also the same plant as hemp that most of the world actually used for cloth production, fuels, and medicine. That's how dangerous it is to let ignorance and greed of power go before facts, the ability of responsibility and science. The US has changed a lot and now even have it as a legal option in some of the states, the world is changing. Holland has already proven the rest of the world wrong when it comes to being able to have legitimate solutions and access to this very same plant. Even though that's the result of what they accomplish people are so mentally afraid to admit their mistakes. Holland didn't do it because of the reason to prove the world wrong but that doesn't take away the fact that that's exactly what they have done. Again, peoples obsessed ideas trying to claim that the fact doesn't exist because that wasn't the intention of it. Where is the reason in that. The fact does exist and will remain a punch in the face on all suckers that hasn't gotten the maturity to accept they are just as human as the rest of the world. The fact doesn't go away just because people are afraid to admit that they are wrong.

The only reason someone is moving on to heavy drugs is because when this drug is sold illegal there is no other sense behind it then the ones created by criminals. Once you are outside the law, you will have access to everything else there is to it as well, which doesn't happen when you can buy it in a legal form.

- See the truth as it is and not as you think it is.

The staff in liquor stores doesn't try to sell you an AK47, they don't try to sell you heroin claiming that all drugs are exactly the same only this is better. That's the way an illegal drug dealer can make more money. You don't walk into a liquor store buying a beer and when you walk out of the store you just happened to buy a deadly virus or a weapon of mass destruction and are now programmed to destroy the world, Truth is you don't even become a shoplifter when buying the drug alcohol. You don't become criminal at all by that event even if you repeat it several times, year after year after year. Same thing goes for cannabis and Coffee shops. Just like there is ways to actually consume and enjoy alcohol, just like there is ways to use fire inside a house on candles, just like there is ways to drive cars and other vehicles, just like there is ways to use dynamite or oil drills, cannabis can also be used. However, criminalized it lacks the basic mentalities around it since people rather chose to believe that once you try it will be the end of your world. Since that's not the truth and the people trying to claim that that's the way it is will always be nothing more than liars.

It's like saying that scouts are nothing but professional trained terrorist because they learn how to survive in the nature without any of today's luxuries such as water from a tap, toilets, readymade food. They are training in how to tie people up with simple ropes making advanced knots that makes the ropes into lethal weapons, they learn how to master the knife and becomes beasts of nature, dangerous killing machines ready to destroy the world at any second now. But that isn't really what they are doing, is it. Isn't it so that they learn responsibilities and survival skills based on only our self. If we really want to control a situation we must understand as much as possible around that situation. Drugs exist and will always exist, to believe differently when there is nearly seven billion people on one and the same planet is more dangerous then to accept that fact.

We must be able to talk, read and discuss even sensitive topics, even one such as drugs. Freedom of speech will always be a corner stone in a healthy society. It's a part of our reality and it has always been that. Throughout history we have always mastered difficulty's by understanding its full potential and by learning respect and manner for what kind of behaviors that can be expected if not treated carefully enough. That's how we overcome problems. By knowing the ways in how to use things.

Cannabis is different in its buzz yes but not more

dangerous nor worse. That's two separate facts and have nothing to do with each other. Holland isn't the only country that has a more mature relation towards cannabis as a drug, many other countries also have a more mature, down to earth and realistic understanding of what that plant in drug use of matter is about. If you talk to the police in Holland, they have more fear for a person under the influence of alcohol then a person under the influence of cannabis. Cannabis has a longer time range though before it completely is flushed out of the human system and is well connected to human fat tissue. Alcohol might get out of the system faster, but it is still causing damage to brain and liver in quite bad ways. Alcohol kills cells in the human body whereas cannabis binds itself to fat tissue, there is a huge difference there. Countries should look at Holland and see how they solved it with their Coffee shops and Smart shops.

- You should always respect the laws of the country you live in.

When talking about drugs I'd like to keep them all as drugs without today's boundaries of legal and not legal. In this way we can keep each drug for what they truly are rather than a huge area of grey where all other drugs are the same but alcohol.

- Why then?

Well, all drugs are different in their behavior and should be respected thereafter. When putting a drug such as cannabis in the same area of other hard drugs

271

isn't showing the right picture of the drug itself and its there many people fool them self today. It's important to understand that each drug is unique in its behavior in all direction. All the things on the illegal side gets the same value of danger and that's not the way it is at all. When you put it as illegal it all of a sudden has the same value as harder drugs and that is being used by the people selling drugs today hence leading to use of harder drugs is an easy step to make. Cannabis is a soft drug less harmful than alcohol. Alcohol is the hardest soft drug we have. According to research made by England's government a couple of years ago cannabis isn't even close as dangerous as alcohol is, LSD was even less dangerous when it comes to use of it.

- Why is it Illegal then?

- Well Taboo and the power of ignorance Id say.

Alcohol is just as much a drug as cannabis is. And more addictive as well. Humans tends to drink alcohol thru ought their entire adult life and it's still called use of it. The same goes for cannabis and it's a use of it. When made criminalized it loses all its sense morale and culture behind it that is necessary for any drug in order to be used healthy. Cannabis has a rich culture and the use of it has its own guidelines and healthy mentalities behind it, that gets lost when it becomes put on the other side of the table of lawful.

- When I lived in Holland, I tried out both their Coffee shops and Smart shops.

272

Cannabis has just like wines different tastes and origins with different buzzes and feelings. You have the Cannabis Cup among others that's a competition between brands of cannabis and what kind of behavioral patterns in the buzz and flavors they succeed in breeding. There are breeds from all over the world that has its own unique flavor and buzz.

When used there is two main directions of the buzz. One is stoned that goes onto the entire body making a comfortable heavy effect that's very nice for you to experience and then there is high that goes more to the head and is also a very nice experience. The buzz itself heightens your senses to an equal sense of your eyes. It means your ears and nose and tongue all of a sudden are equal to your eyes. Listening to music gets a new dimension as well as eating and drinking reaches new highs of its own. The buzz differs from alcohol in that way a lot and is a unique form of buzz you don't get from any other drug. Having sex while on a buzz from cannabis is a completely new dimension of experience for you, it is so much better in experience it's hard to explain without having been there yourself. When you get an orgasm, it holds on in that state of climax till the buzz wares of.

- It's amazing how good you feel when having a lasting experience of an orgasm for hours.

The sex itself lasts much longer when under influence

273

of the cannabis. Better sex medicine is hard to find these days. Compared to alcohol cannabis is a much healthier drug to use and has far more positive effects then alcohol ever could dream of comparing itself with. Best part is you don't have to be able to smoke it since you can eat the cannabis in so called space cakes and the buzz last longer from the space cake. You can bake them yourself and there is lots of recipes on the internet for that purpose.

Smart shops have their mushrooms and other health substances that they sell. Mushrooms are harder to use then cannabis is and should be dealt with in a delicate matter since its vital for the buzzes to be in harmony for you. Mushrooms deals with separate senses rather than all of them and are perfect for exploring yourself for higher understanding. You should always experience mushrooms in peace and quiet places, so its harmonies don't confuse you. When exploring your senses like this you must always understand that it always has its own time and place to be done in harmony.

The UK government commissioned psycho pharmacologist Professor David Nutt and his colleges to rank drugs according to their danger.
The list was published in *The Guardian* and is here reproduced with their consent. The drugs were ranked by ratings which took into account a combination of their physical damage, social harm and addictive properties.

They are listed in descending order from the most harmful:

1. **Heroin**– highly addictive opium derivative. Causes liver disease and infections from injecting when used long-term.

2. **Cocaine** – stimulant which can increase the risks of heart attack or stroke in users. Deaths from cocaine rose sharply in 2008.

3. **Barbiturates**– synthetic sedatives used for anaesthetic purposes. Users develop physical and psychological dependence. Large doses can lead to coma or death.

4. **Street methadone**– a synthetic opioid commonly used as a substitute for treating heroin patients. Can lead to addiction and result in damage to lungs.

5. **Alcohol**– medical profession increasingly concerned about damaging effects of alcohol. Some claim true death toll is higher than recorded. Excessive use results in liver damage and cirrhosis.

6. **Ketamine**– a hallucinogenic sometimes used as a dance drug by clubbers. Causes memory problems and urinary tract diseases.

7. **Benzodiazepines**– hypnotic relaxant used to treat anxiety and insomnia. Prolonged use leads to addiction. Withdrawal symptoms include nausea, dizziness and pounding heart beat. Includes drugs such as Diazepam, Tamazepam and Nitrazepam.

8. **Amphetamines**– psychostimulant that combats fatigue and hunger. Increases blood pressure and temperature; can cause strokes in hot weather. Can lead to psychological dependence.

9. **Tobacco** – highly addictive due to its nicotine content. Tobacco-related illnesses include cancer, respiratory diseases and heart diseases.

10. **Buprenorphine** –opiate used for pain control, also sometimes used as a substitute to wean addicts off heroin. Side effects include nausea, vomiting and dizziness. Danger of overdose.

11. **Cannabis** – psychoactive drug; stronger forms known colloquially as 'skunk'. Intense controversy over its long-term effects and capacity for inducing schizophrenia. Has been linked to miscarriages in women.

12. **Solvents** – users inhale solvents to produce a sense of intoxication. Usually abused by teenagers. Can lead to choking, vomiting and

suffocation. Derived from commonly available products such as glue and aerosol sprays.

13. **4-MTA** – class A. Originally designed for laboratory research. Releases serotonin in the body.

14. **LSD** – hallucinogenic drug synthesised by German chemist in 1938. Its dangers have been disputed. Can raise heart rate and blood pressure. May also lead to loss of appetite.

15. **Methylphenidate** – Brand name of Ritalin, a psycho stimulant sometimes used in the treatment of attention deficit disorders. Suppression of growth in some children who have been long term users. Can lead to psychological dependence.

16. **Anabolic steroids** – used to develop muscles, notably in competitive sports. Increased risk of heart attacks. Also alleged to induce aggression. Withdrawal has been linked to depression. Has been blamed for causing deaths among bodybuilders.

17. **GHB** – a clear liquid dance drug said to induce euphoria, also described as a date rape drug. Can trigger comas and suppress breathing.

18. **Ecstasy** – psychoactive dance drug which has been alleged to cause damage to the brain. Associated with dehydration and overheating of the body which can be fatal.

19. **Alkyl Nitrites** – Known as "poppers", inhaled for their role as a muscle relaxant and supposed sexual stimulant. Reduces blood pressure which can cause fainting and I some cases death.

20. **Khat** – psychoactive plant. Produces mild psychological dependence. Can lead to liver damage. Withdrawal said to lead to lethargy and nightmares. Its derivatives, Cathinone and Cathine, are Class C drugs in the UK.

As you can see on the list Cannabis is even less dangerous than tobacco and should be treated that way as well by law enforcement. Cannabis should be as legal as alcohol is because it's a very peaceful drug and possess no threat to the human being and we should have the right to choose our own buzzes.

I might have romanticized the drugs here but that's not the purpose but rather to show you the differences of buzz and experience of the drugs alcohol and cannabis. As long as there are legal drugs on the market the discussion should be open about which ones we should be able to use. The two legal drugs of today on the market is tobacco and alcohol, yes they are as much drugs as cannabis are.

It's basically impossible to overdose cannabis unlike alcohol. The purpose of this discussion is for you to see that drugs aren't what they seem to be when they become illegal.

I recommend you wait with the experience of drugs till you're out of school since they distract your concentration, both alcohol and others. I didn't learn about cannabis till year 2007 so I waited long time before I tried it out.

- *There is no need to rush the experience of drugs, they will be there when you get old enough.*

Adults love drugs in one way or another and that's a fact. Sure, there are people that use no drugs at all, but they are a minority of today and their choice is just as valid, not necessarily making them better persons though. We love stimulation of our chemical system no matter what the favorite choice of drugs are. Alcohol just happens to the number one choice for many out of natural reasons. Such as being legal for one reason. Drugs will always be and that's something we can't close our eyes for. The war on drugs has cost billions of dollars in US alone and is a never-ending battle. Every country spend loads of money on the war on drugs it's just a fact. It's better for a society to have a freedom of choice then to pretend it isn't there. Teaching responsibility before lying about what's dangerous and what's not. It is better to reflect a society on the base of facts and truth then to try to control the diverse flora of buzz choices. To put all drugs on one side of the fence is like asking for having trouble in society. People that for some reason ends up in trouble using soft drugs can easily be helped out of it and its almost nonexistent in comparison to how damaged people get by alcohol. Its better and more economical to build up support systems for people that get on the bad side for some reason than to keep it illegal in hope for it to seize to exist, that will never happen. Making a new drug legal such as cannabis won't make everyone start using it, more likely five to ten percent of the population will start using it legally. In Holland it's about five percent is using it.

- Drugs arent part of the ism, but I recognize the nature of it and feel the importance of being able to talk and discuss about this nature as well.

Drugs should be dealt with respect and understanding. Because of its nature. It belongs to the adult world and is something extra to life. Never use a drug as replacement of happiness or joy because that is something you achieve without it. Don't use drugs when your down and out because it only makes it worse for you. Dare to be mature about drugs and to deal with them responsible. Alcohol is by far worse to deal with then cannabis in so many ways. Nevertheless, both should be dealt with in mature manners and respected as drugs as they both are. You should follow the laws in your country meaning if it's illegal don't use it there, if you want to try out cannabis go to place where it's not illegal and learn about it there.

- I dont use drugs today but I'm happy I have that experience, so I know what I'm talking about. I learned to see beyond alcohol, thats a quite bad drug. I stopped drinking it at age of twenty-five. I consider it a good experience and today there is too many other options to satisfy my needs that drugs dont seem interesting enough for me.

We live in a world full of drugs and adults love using them. Truth is we live a very long life, and we all get in contact with drugs in one way or another. You should not use drugs all the time. To have periods of your life where you use drugs is a saner approach to drugs. Even though many people probably use the drug alcohol throughout their entire life. You should try to not use drugs so much but rather achieve the very same goal without drugs that you get when using drugs. You don't need drugs to live a happy life. However, you should at least try some drugs, so you know what they are about and know what it's like to alter your existence in ways you not usually are able to achieve by yourself. To have a period in your very long life where you use drugs is not a bad thing but contributes to your experience in life. A whole life

281

without drugs is just fine as well except you are missing out of a great experience. And don't know what other people are talking about or have experienced at all. That does not make you a better person in any way. Considering the drugs has always been and will always be in the world no matter you like it or not, you should always approach drugs with a mature and responsible mentality when trying them out. Don't go for drugs that gives you an addiction you can't get out of. Harder drugs are today not very healthy at all even though criminals say differently. Alcohol and cannabis are drugs you can be safe with, and both should be treated with respect. Don't go against your own countries laws but go where it is a legit choice to experience the drug you want to experience. If you have strong character, you only use the drugs for a period of your life and then let it be. Even though you might use it on some occasion depending on what it's for. I for example still drink champagne on New Years Eve because I find it a great tradition and I don't mind that at all. Cannabis in all its fun to learn you don't need to use all your life even though you might occasionally use it for sexual purposes and to achieve the great orgasm that you get while on that drug. But other than that, just don't use it. You live a very long life, and drugs are a natural part of it no matter if you yourself are using them or not.

...

.

.

Things will very much be the same as today when it comes to everyday life. There will be differences though. We will all have a common foundation that we all are proud of. We will have for the first time an equal and more exact understanding of each other. We will appreciate each other's differences and show greater respect for each other. We are all equally different towards each other and we are all the same in not just anatomy wise but in this opportunity of life. That's what being different means, we are all equal in our basic anatomy but unique in soul and spirit. And the most ironic part in all this is that we all, the human species. Is among the smallest minority in the whole universe. We are the smallest minority in relation to time of existence in this part of universe at least. We are the only species that so far have this type of unique skill sets and anatomic abilities. We too will change shape, form and functionality. We are the most flexible and adaptable creature in our system, except for the cockroaches but I don't compare us to them even though they have very interesting formula of existence. Don't forget that we are all equal part of life. Even compared to the other animals and nature. We all contain information about features and possibility's here in life. Together we become the perfect solution of life. We can all communicate in languages. Cats, dogs, wild animals. Our guttural communication is just as impossible for us to picture that they can understand, and their advanced communication is way too hard for us to truly understand without observing them and learning to know them for a bit. All animals are equally equipped with heart and soul and are just as much a big and important part of our opportunity in life.

Nature is just fine without human beings. And Universe

couldn't care less if there is life upon this planet or not. We just need to look at our neighbor planet to see what things will be like here if we don't choose to care. We are the ones that truly depends on our nature and our ecosystem in order to continue to exist. In the long run we will be the ones that know how to and do take care of the opportunity of life. We will become quite great at it as well. Fact is we will become so great in it so that when we stumble upon the first proof of intelligent civilization, we too will require that they first must be able to proof to the universe that they can be responsible enough and bring life further, before we acknowledge our presence. Hence the reason we will also need to continue our military training. In a more predator matter of training. Our military should always be of Elite force in order for us to be able to stand up when encountering problems from either outer space or when we need to make advanced experiments that includes high risks and danger. We will probably need to run some experiments on dead planets in order to provide maximal security. The day we meet hostile life forms of great danger we will most likely be extremely advanced in our technology as well as highly skilled and not only aware but masters in Opportunity of life. If they suddenly find us first at this time, we will for sure not have much to put against them. Even though I'm sure it would bring us even closer to each other if we actually managed to do that, which would happen only not yet for quite some time. We have an eternity to take in consideration and the chances of us being alone are quite slim with that base.

I have in my inner journeys in space stumbled upon

alien civilizations or life forms from former civilizations and harmonized with their energy's. I even achieved a reincarnation from one of those shards. In the form of universal death codes that I have achieved during my inner journeys.

...

.

- I have pathed the domain of death for quite a while now.

The domain of death is a peaceful place to wander. You find it full of respect and graceful even lovingly. Lots of my progress in my reincarnations and incarnations has been pathed there since they are all ancient in one way or another. I have had several so-called near-death experiences in my lifetime. Two of them was from chemical lung infections I had as a fire artist in my youth. Happen to swallow the fluids for fire breathing into my lungs and that's a bad state of being. I'm fine though and survived them both. It's not scary with near death at all. Its peaceful and quiet. My first reincarnation is Gizmoo Strangelove, The last warlock and he comes from domain of death and is the foundation of me. I started pathing Gizmoo Strangelove at the age of seven and have been doing that ever since. The others have been pathed along the way and have grown into me with thoroughly pathing and devotion. Today Meduza Loveheart is my alter ego in my picture of completeness along with my other reincarnations. My alter ego is shifting with me in my intergender in motion existence. Two females and one male reincarnations in this entity and a male manifestation with loads of incarnated blueprints and grayprints. I today have several cores in my soul and spirit.

I even met my father once while achieving that in domain of death. I had to path it in order to reach him. It was a wonderful moment for me to finally meet him and see that everything was alright. My father passed away when I was fifteen years old. We had a great moment together and laughed heartily with each other for a long time.

Greyprints are partial incarnation patterns and blueprints are complete incarnation patterns build up from a set of grey prints. The pattern can be anything from a specific skill to a trait and it doesn't need to be in relation to each other, it all falls in place one step at a time. It takes time to complete them and the pathing of them occurs over long time periods.

...

.

.

To journey in Metaverse is a skill I had for a long time. My father had it as well. To be able to leave your body and journey in space or death or whatever nature you wish to journey is a wonderful experience. It takes time to accomplish and shouldn't been taken lightly since there is a possibility to get lost. Might sound scary but it isn't. You have to be able to let to go of your earthly bindings and let your soul float away from your current state of being. Your conscious remains with the soul at all times, so you don't watch your soul float away, but you go with it. You are simply leaving your physics behind you and start journey in Metaverse in a free form. You do this while meditating in the beginning. I can today "activate" myself in Metaverse in a more normal state of mind, it has taken long time to reach that ability. I can today journey with open eyes. I don't know how hard this is to attain since I always been able to do it even if in more shy forms in the beginning. I know you can achieve this type of skill if you put effort and devotion into it. Just take it easy in the beginning. It's a wonderful experience and needs to be respected for its nature.

...

.

.

Spell casting, curses and blessings are quite common in Metaverse. Myself is more of a protective spell caster and have during my life compiled some quite heavy protection formulas for myself. I'm a bit different when it comes to meta practicing, I don't use ordinary tools, but all is done within the force with my bare hands, soul and spirit. I have tried out several different crystal wands with energies of love and harmony, but I still work better with only myself as a tool. Tools enhances the energies and purposes of practice in a very efficient way. I however seem to be stronger without any tools at all. I try them out every now and then just to get familiar with them. When I summon forces of metaversical creatures I use open hexagrams since I don't want to harness them but only learn about their nature. It usually results in a quite surprised creature since they are being used to be harnessed by other mortals. I do it all in Metaverse without physical bindings. It's just as powerful as in physics. The presence is just as evident as when done in physic. Be careful with curses since they really work as long as you get them right, I have some in my protections as counter effect if negative energies are projected at me deliberately. It's very powerful and I have seen it work live and it makes you think twice before you apply it onto something. My defense usually effects the senses by lowering them somewhat and can be reversed by positive actions. My defense is an advanced yin and yang formula that deals with most energies of today. I prefer blessings and sending energies of harmony and today I'm quite skilled at that. I'm an excellent healer of myself. Haven't had that many opportunities to heal others yet. As you can see, I path many paths and not only the warlock path.

Warlocks has some traits, first there is the hand flame. A metaversical hand flame that is personal to every warlock. Then we have the reflection in a Metaverse mirror, they don't reflect us at all. There is only one mirror that can reflect a warlock and it's the mirror of ultimate truth. Warlocks has a tendency to embrace death in a way many others find hard to understand. We like to reveal things, to uncover and unclothe the reality in one way or another. Even things that might lead to devastation. I'm a quite different warlock since my nature is as The last warlock. I don't open gateways to the so-called hell, but I do travel there to seek wisdom and enlightenment.

...

.

.

Isn't too much knowledge dangerous then. It can be. But the lack of it is even more dangerous. Some people may claim that if knowledge is too easy to attain then we would soon have everybody running around with a remote red button attached to their mobile phone and it would be enough if only one of them decided to push the button and end it all, it would be a monstrous way to handle such a responsibility. It's supposed to be done with a safe and healthy control of information. But if you look from another direction, you will also see that without complete awareness and ease of access to all kinds of knowledge you will end up with a world like this.

A world that has already pushed the red button and no one doesn't even bother to understand that. The button we already pushed is that when many people enough doesn't give a damn about things such as: Garbage control, pollutions, extinguish rates, population issues, mentality's that rather stands up for total destruction and great failures of attempt to be recognized as brilliant or superior. Nuclear ways to mass destruction, biologically warfare arts in ways of total destruction, Chemical warfare arts in total destruction. Truth is, to destroy this planet or the opportunity of life upon it is already happening. Just its not fast enough for us to understand that we are already going downhill. We all know that earth will explode in 4 billion years from now. We also know that this planet might be unusable long before that. We also know that for several thousands of years we have never truly given peace a true chance. And maybe we have had very good reasons for this constant failure in behavior. This is the first time in our evolutionary timeline when we will be able to take control and stir this ship in any direction we would like for real.

Today we have a greater understanding of who we all are and why we are different, than ever. We have never had more infrastructure in place both virtually and physically.

Looking at the world from a great distance we can see that the truth is the world of today, this planet. Earth is today covered in a huge web covering the entire surface, it's a web net that consist of electronically cables, giving us tiny changes of active electrons in motion. And this is covering over the most part of our entire planet and has not only done so for quite some time now but also slowly growth or rapidly depending in what you chose to relate this event to. Slowly growing in both the air with all the wireless technology traveling between phones and satellites and portable computers as well as stationary computers. Our condition is constantly changing and the possibility to the self-creating conscious is actually a possibility no matter how slim the chances have been and still are.

Everything in the opportunity of existence contains energy's out of many different forms. Most of it is so weak we never truly reflect over it but nevertheless lately growing with the new paste of development in the Information Technology area. We don't see any impact of the new web of energy that surrounds the planet, not yet.

...

.

.

- Humans are a possibility for intelligence rather than Humans are intelligent.

There is a bloody huge different there even though the sentences are similar to each other. The brain is the most advanced processor there have ever been in our location in our evolutionary timeline. Billions of small cells that has weak electricity as an engine and DNA as its appearances and possibility factor. Its processing chemicals in both direction in order to maintain and become self-dependent in as many directions as possible. The brain creates emotional experiences that in a combined form of feelings and other impressions it collected from its surrounding in real-time at all-time even as we sleep. When we sleep our brain is calibrating and calculating the completeness of the impressions you have been able to produce as all together outcomes from that period of time you have had as awake. It's a sort of hibernation mode computer uses in order to consume less energy. Only our hibernation is not just equally important for our energies in the means of how much energy and durability we need in awake time. But also, to process and work with all possible impressionable equations that we rarely even reflect over in awake time.

We are so advanced in our existing form of existence that life itself, our opportunity of life with all the existing dependencies that mother nature has already created the perfect algorithms of life in order to have a chance to maintain this opportunity. What we seem to lack in understanding is that mother nature herself is our own very engine for our very own reality and existence and has been so for a couple of billions of years now. We aren't the first species mother nature has hosted. Truth is that every single unit of life in this opportunity of life has valuable knowledge hidden and yet right there in front of us. This is knowledge we will need to understand in order to manage to take many steps enough in the best possible direction at all-time. That will be an even more important future goal for us, even though today we already are quite good at it.

...

.

.

I was very active in Metaverse before the Maya calendar ended. Doing my part and contribution to everything so that nothing wouldn't end there. I visited a lot of white wolves and got their aid to provide this planet with an extra force field. I have blessed some churches for future pather so they can rest in their journey. I have visited many places here in Metaverse in order to both activate new forces and reactivate existing resting forces. I journeyed a lot and saw many different cultures. I did my part and are proud of my accomplishments. Today I have achieved a white wolf as a companion when exploring nature and its secrets.

Composing this ism hasn't been done without friction. Many times, have I been tested as Dao Buddha in Metaverse from both religions and isms as well as ancient forces. There has been a lot of holy tests for me, and I have so far passed them all. I have today a few but very strong defenders of the ism in metaverse. I have company from ancient forces that are with me at all times. It's a good path and you prove to yourself that you truly believe in yourself.

...

.

.

Sure, we have chosen horrible and terrible ways to utilize this might of awareness we all carry. Fact still remains we are already creating our self, and we are already professional definers. We have created so many defining stones by now there isn't really much left for us to learn in the direction we seem to be stuck in when it comes to destructiveness in this opportunity of life in our part of universe.
In order to believe that we will be able to define eternity from this single planet you must never understand that where there is an end there is always a start. Unfortunately, that's a misunderstanding many people actually live with. There will always be new ages and evolutionary progresses, our only choice is if we want to be part of this opportunity or not. Because even if we do succeed in ruining this opportunity of life in our part of universe. Universe will still evolve and will keep doing this even without us in it. And the next time that opportunity will happen it doesn't really matter since the only way they will find out about our

existence in forms of archeology on universal planetary if any, is if they chose to make the choice we chose to fail in, in the opposite direction. In other words. No matter what their choice will be everything we have done, everything you ever believed in, every step of evolution our species and our mother nature ever done will be for nothing. Which in a way is a weird choice.

- Truth is that the opportunity of life is as much ours as any other living aware matter or civilization out there in space.

How much part of universe we actually can consider ours no one can know for sure yet. Let's just hope that the next hostile threat of alien life forms is still too far away from us for them to find us. As long as this remains true, we are actually all quite fine for the moment, and we do have time to shape this world up. And that's actually all we need to concern about in order to change our future destiny from creating Armageddon and to become the once that finally woke up, so that we all could see the truth as it is and start work in much healthier and much higher life quality direction while retaining the respect for the nature. To be the ones that chose peace over war and saw the power of diversity as a possibility instead of trouble. To have been the generation that has captured our senses and taken our entire planets civilization to its next level of being.

...

.

It's time to see the reality in faith and science. When the religions where composed science where shining in absence and the need and hunger of understanding was a growing matter. Religions try to explain how it all started with the metaversical expressions of a God that created earth. Today science has a better place and a great foundation. But even science has a hard time to explain how it all started since they can't prove what was before their so-called big bang theory. Truth is we don't know how it started yet and truth is also that space has existed for eternity no matter where in time we are. That's what Exist represent, eternity into infinity. There might as well have been millions of opportunities of life in the eternity we all exist in. Science has however proven evolution as a part of our reality and that's a comforting understanding. The progress of evolution is something we all can grasp and respect in our existence.

Religions back then was replacing science with faith and that's a sad fact we still have to deal with. Today the variables have changed and it's time to see the truth as it is and let the past be the past. We can't hold on to values that isn't valid in our evolutionary timeline anymore. We have to see where we are and what's on the plate of understanding of today. It's time to let go of the past and to welcome the new era ahead of us.

Religions will always be an important milestone in our evolution but even they have a cycle of existence on their own. Science has today a great understanding about the nature of space and that's enough for us to continue our quest to find out how things started. Religions has many beautiful facts about human beings in philosophical explanations, but they deny evolution and they deny the eternity we already exist in. We have to be able to see beyond our failure in explanations of how it all started. We have to be able to see the truth as it is and to amend reality no matter how uncomfortable it is at the moment. The religions of today will always be maintained but they too will pass on to past-time and become a part of our history. Religions still have more to reveal and will last for long time to come only in a different form than today. They will pass on to mythology but still remain important.

...

.

.

Sometime nature fails in its completeness. Some by nature and some by accidents. All over the planet there are people with handicaps. Some worse than others. We have people that are blind, deaf and mute. People that are crippled with only one leg or no legs. People that suffer from cerebral pares. All of these people are just as much human beings as you and I are. We are all equally equipped with heart and brain no matter fate in life. It's a diversity that might seem harsh but it's still there and we can't close our eyes for it. No matter what fate holds before you in life we all deserve a good quality life on day-to-day basis. The world is quite good on respecting handicaps today and I'm proud of that but it's important for people to understand that we are all human beings and should be respected thereafter. The people that are handicapped no matter what handicap it is, lives their lives just as much as anyone else do. They too have their ups and downs. They too have the same flora of emotions as any other human being has. They should be respected as human beings and not as defected beings. Don't fear them because they don't usually feel sorry about themselves. They are proud people too. Don't mock them either. Their lifetime is just as rich of content as yours are. We are all equally different and an equal opportunity in life. Be humble before the diversity of mother nature.

...

.

.

- So, what about the phenomena prostitution then?

What is it all about? What's the conclusion of to be or not to be?

- Well let me answer the later question right away.

- it should be legal.

- Why you may ask.

Well let's have look upon it and see what it's about. It's the oldest profession there is here on earth and has been around for over 2000 years in other words, it probably been dated as far back in time as the stone age. This is another situation where the matter is delicate and not so obvious to why it should be or not to be. We have both solutions in the world today. Countries that have it legal and countries that has it illegal. No matter solution every country has prostitution in it. Hence a phenomenon. That shows a failure of purpose of law. That shows that no matter what you chose there will always be people willing to sell their body for money and earn their living that way. What people tend to forget in this question is that the people that choose this life no matter reason are personal beings.

-   Just like you and me.

Prostitutes have ordinary life's paying bills and going on with their life's just like we do. Some of them are in that situation because they have no other choice, others because they chose to get an extra income. No matter what, they all sell sex for money regardless of if its legal or not. So, what happens when you chose to make it illegal? They end up on the wrong side of the fence which is the last thing they need. They become even more handicapped and outlaws that has nowhere to turn anymore in order to make the necessary changes they should be able to need to do. Prostitutes becomes victims of law and order when they already are in a bad situation. And putting them in jail won't make the situation any better for them. It only makes it worse. Prostitutes have ended up there in one way or another regardless of the law and would do it no matter what. Prostitutes are individuals with just as much heart and brain as everybody else and the law should be there for them, not against them. As long as there is prostitution there should be laws that supports it and make them part of society rather than outcast that has nowhere else to turn but the criminal world. Prostitutes should have the police on their side and the society should spend efforts in giving them opportunities to alternate work so they can choose to take different paths when they want to.

A great country can have it legal and puts in support system that aids the ones that have nowhere else to turn in that line of business. To have it legal shows the country has a great understanding for its people and puts the individual first. It's a mature way for a country to handle prostitution as a legal option since it is a fact that it exists no matter if its legal or not, recognizing the truth of its present and choosing to take responsibility for it rather than to take the easy way out and making it illegal. You can feel however you want in this matter it won't take away the fact that prostitution will always exist and has always existed as far as human has. To cripple them like we do when we make it criminal is more evil then good to the individuals that are prostitutes. The law should always look after the individual at first. I understand that people are upset with this, but it will always be better to let prostitutes be a part of society and give them the opportunity to do something about it rather than to kick on someone that's already lying on the floor. Its hard as it is to be a prostitute, they don't need the burden of being on the wrong side of the law. They need a country that succeeds better in taking its responsibility towards individuals that ends up on the wrong side of the fence.

Another problem we have today is people's mentalities towards prostitution. Its mean and bad in most any direction. As if people didn't sell their bodies and brains for money already. We all sell our self for money today in one way or another. Prostitutes sell sex that's the only difference here. Prostitutes sells orgasms which in my opinion is a beautiful thing to sell and they should be respected for it. The mentalities of today's normality norm is so bad that they are just as in much trouble because of that. They can't use it in a CV that they have been prostitutes. Which is weird and sad. Prostitutes should be proud over it and respected just like anyone else. People can't see the human behind the prostitute and that goes especially for them that are opposed to it and wants it illegal. Prostitutes shouldn't lose their dignity just because the profession is out of sexual nature. There is no point trying to force this profession in any direction but legal since it will always be there no matter what. It IS a phenomenon. The harder you try the more it will go underground but it will always be there, and it won't disappear just because you can't see it. Prostitutes are human beings and individuals just like anyone else and should be treated that way by its surrounding and the laws need to reflect that in order for it to have a fair chance to come true. I'm not arguing about that there are big health issues with prostitutions and neither do the prostitutes, they live with it every day and are well aware about the risks. However, that doesn't change the fact that there will always be prostitution no matter if its legal or not. The reason it's a phenomenon is not only that it exists no matter choice of keeping it legal or not but also the fact that it has always been around, throughout history prostitution has always existed and will always do so. There is no doubt that legal is the best way to coexist with prostitution.

...

.

.

Space and universe are an amazing place, so vast and so gigantic it's hard to imagine the actual size of it.

To journey into universe in Metaverse is an amazing experience. To see all the wonders of universe and to find alien life forms in spirit and soul shards from former civilizations and probably existing ones as well and learn their mentalities and forms of existence can be quite ordinary.

When I was in Holland, I had my revelation one night in a tiny forest if you can even call it that. I was out walking among the trees and enjoying the nature when it finally revealed itself leaning against a tree. An alien life form just standing there looking at me appeared from nowhere. We were looking at each other for minutes and just stood there in silence. Looking and smiling with a warm feeling of affinity and equality. We were both just an equal part of universe and that was all there was to it. It did not materialize and yet so real in its flesh and its presence so clear. It was an awesome experience and a moment I never forget.

There are others that also travel in universe through

Metaverse here and they have probably some really interesting stories to tell. We are many people today all over the world that has a practice in Metaverse in one way or another and we should all be proud of it. Even though there aren't many warlocks today. We are special in that sense we have an open mind to receive and execute behaviors in Metaverse. It might be a small group of people, but we exist all over the world.

...

.

.

Today there is a minority group of people that are so called trans personality, it consists of transvestites, transsexuals, she-males, intergender people and so on. We are all very brave hearted standing up for our diverse nature, especially transsexuals and she-males. They not only define themselves as opposites in them self but go through transformation of their body completely. It takes lots of guts to do that. We are a group of people that recognize the opposite sex within us more strongly than just a side of us. There is nothing wrong to transform your entity into the opposite sex or the mix she-males are. It's your entity and your life and as long as you don't hurt others its yours to do as you please with. It's not your fault you were born the wrong sex. Just remember to treat your entity with respect and maintain it well with your new body. It's your ship to navigate and your soul and spirit will always remain so be respectful towards the entity you're piloting. You can modify your entity anyway you want, with piercings, tattoos, sex change and any other body changing formulas you like. It's an entity, in shape of a human being. Just respect its limits. To be born in the wrong sex and to come through with a complete sex change is a long journey and takes a strong mentality to go through.

- My journey was long and tidy and I'm only intergender in motion. I have gone thru being only bisexual and heterosexual then bisexual again and then homosexual then bisexual again then I was on my way to become a she-male but on that journey, I came to the conclusion and revelation that I'm intergender in motion, both man and woman in one and the same entity. Shifting between them in all kinds of direction. I have come out of the closet many times and it's been ok every time I have done it fortunately. It's been a long road of exploring my sexualism and a great experience to achieve myself. I'm only sexual today in my taste but you recognize it as bisexual. To define your self isn't always easy. It took me over 30 years to find myself but I'm happy I did it one step at a time cause now I know who I am, and I stand for it as well. I come from one of the smallest minoritys there is today, and I

303

dont mind that a single bit.
It's quite nice to have found
myself in the extent I have
succeeded to and very satisfying
for me.

...
.

Medley

We are standing before the humble opportunity to provide not only our self but our Mother Nature as well, and I call her Mother Nature because no matter how rich or poor you are, no matter what your sexual skills are, no matter skin colors or ethnical backgrounds, no matter what handicaps or defects we have. We are all children of Mother Nature. And we are all equally equipped with heart and brain. That's just one of the perks the animal human being has. We are about to provide Mother Nature with a second core. And that core is us humans, united working for this opportunity of life. This planet caretakers and directors. We will be this planet protectors and defender. This planet opportunity to carry its life further into space.

That is a big step for human mankind to take and we are going to do it sooner or later. No matter when it's done the same dependencies are needed to be taken in consideration and the same achievements needs to be done. We better get this ball rolling before we reach a point of no return when it comes to the end of life on this planet. That point might be closer than we wish for today and shouldn't be taking lightly by the younger generations.

We have so far witnessed the relative reality we live in contains lies and misunderstandings. I have revealed some of the Taboos that has crippled us for a very long time. There has been a lot of talk about sex and that's to put an end to its taboos and misunderstandings. We have looked upon our past as well as our future to come. We have looked upon religions and isms to see where they are and what their purpose has been. What they have done throughout our evolution. There has been a discussion about drugs to make you see that Taboo once again have had you under a spell of misunderstanding. We have explored Metaverse and its concepts. We have looked upon life and its evolution here on earth as well as its coming to be. You have followed me in my life progress and what it's been like to path a warlock path. We have even looked at the phenomena prostitution and what it is about. I have slowly opened up your eyes and there is still more to come.

We have to put aside our differences and see that our diversity is how mother nature created us and is the natural state of being for human mankind. We have to be able to come together and see the equality in life's own diversity and its rich flora of species here on earth. We have to be able to see the truth about the human being as a species and break down the preconceived thoughts about each other. To be able to see the truth behind the human being as it is.

It's time to wake up and see the truth as it is. For us to put an end to all the foolish lies we live in. To make our reality healthy and manageable in the directions we would like it to be. To let today become the past and history making way for tomorrow. It's time for humanity to learn how to say we are for real.

...

.

Dao Buddhism

A new garden of Buddhism
Exist & Nature

- Student of: Mutual
Relational thinking, Eroticay,
Love, Nothing and Everything,
"Exist and Nature" The Force
and Evolution.

Dao Buddhism is a new garden of Buddhism with its own unique philosophy. Dao Buddhism is a transparent layer covering all religions and isms as well as science, with itself as base plate. Dao Buddhism is the way of the: Force, Evolution, Diversity, "Nothing and everything" and relational thinking, with Exist and Nature as the foundation. Dao Buddha is Meduza Loveheart, me myself and I in other words. A Dao Buddhist monk that happens to be the achiever of Dao Buddha with all my reincarnations and founder of Dao Buddhism. Dao Buddhism is in a way a blend of Daoism and Buddhism in a modern world way of lifestyle and yet completely unique in its existence. Anyone can become admitted follower to Dao Buddhism no matter origin or location. It's a way of life in mutual respect for its surrounding. It's a philosophy and a mentality. It's a way to see the truth as it is and not as you think it is. Dao Buddhism is a lifestyle that doesn't interfere with your everyday life depending on how you reflect over it. It's a strong mentality to stand up for and takes the gut to think outside the box. You can choose to be only admitted to it and follow its beliefs in your everyday life or become a Dao Buddhist monk that has it as a lifestyle where Metaverse pathing and practices are out of common nature.

...

.

- The Dao Buddhist Yin and
Yang in a philosophical
point of view.


```
             |||
      Nothing IS Everything
    Everything is only a( )part
        of/from Nothing
           Therefore
     Everything is Relative
              In
    Time - Movement - Space
            X - 0
   It is just another direction
            +x-o
            /.\
            ---
            |.|
            :.
            \./
         "  (*)   "
        ". [><|><] ."
        ' >-)-o-(-< '
             "
            ' '
            ` `

            '
           <.>

           ☺

           ...
            .
```

Exist & Nature

Our source and reason - our life and death.

We are because of Exist. Nature is a natural outcome of Exist. We are all children of Mother Earth. Exist is the source of all life and its content. We are all an equal opportunity in the versa of Exist. Exist is the highest form of existence as well as nonexistence and Atom is the smallest building block of it. No matter how many times you divide it Atom is still the smallest building block of both universe and Metaverse, its more out of a mitosis nature that it occurs. Atom is a Dao Buddhist expression for the smallest building block in both versa and not the scientifically version of atomically particle here.

Exist contains Metaverse that contains the force that is among us everywhere and nowhere. The domain of death resides within Metaverse, and spirit shards and souls are all existing in harmony there. Exist is not a god but it is ancient, and nothing is everything. Everything is just a part of nothing. Exist has been for an eternity and will always be. Everything else will decay in time, movement and space. The only thing constant is Exist, change and relativity. Exist holds truths about existence and life in Metaverse as well as in universe. Exist is the guide through dark and light. Exist contains the secrets from all over universe and Metaverse. Exist is not mysterious but a definition of eternity and the ultimate truth. Atom is a perfect navigation tool for Exists Metaverse. Exist is the source of everything and is to be journeyed with humble enlightenment. You seek out answer in its ancient since its being is eternity into infinity. You don't pray to exist but with it since it's not a god or a thing. I have met a manifestation of Exist in Metaverse only to complete my commitment as The last warlock.

Respect Exist at All-time.

Nature as natural outcome is the reason we are here as well. We wouldn't exist without our nature. Nature is the keeper of Exists natural outcomes such as domain of death in Metaverse. Nature in all its glory no matter shape and form. Sky bodies and strange space phenomena till it's more up-close phenomena's here on earth with its earthquakes and hurricanes just to mention a few. The force flow strongly in nature and is a natural part of life itself. Our nature is our foundation for all life upon it. We must always respect our nature.

Nature and Exist are each other's Yin and Yang. They grow and change in relation to each other. Just like universe and Metaverse is. Evolution of nature is the greatest change we live with and should always respect it in all directions. The cycle of life is just a part of the cycle of death and contains as much life in both directions. Death is just life's way to move on in another direction. All nature passes on to another form in universe and is a part of nature's own natural progress. Nature is full of spirits and souls in both trees and flowers. They are out of a bit different nature then ours but are still there. Harmonizing with nature today can be both scary and beautiful depending on where you do it. To communicate with the ancient from a tree doesn't always make sense but is a quite amazing experience. Natures evolution is something we need to respect and nurture. We never know what evolution holds for us in the future. Nature is diverse and grand by its own nature. Don't go against its diverse flora of existence.

Respect Nature at All-time.

...

.

.

The Force

The natural outcome of Exist and Nature in energy's from within Metaverse and Universe combined together. The force is all around us in all direction and is something that's hard to participate in actively. We all are surrounded by it, and it flows through us at all-time. Energies of dark and light in all directions affects us all on daily bases. Relations are everywhere and nowhere and are always an area of exploration. To harmonize with these energies, you need to invest time in your faith as well as in your true soul-searching. Meditating is strongly recommended for you in order to stay in touch with the force. The calibrational lifestyle is a must for participators in the force for more advanced schools in the way of the force. Interfering with energy's should be dealt with in a healthy manner and harmony. Projecting positive energy's is a healthy manner and should be practiced as often as you allow yourself to. To be a participator in the force it dedicates time and determination, it's a way of life and not something to be taken lightly. Followers of the force will grow slowly over the years.

...

.

.

True Faith

Faith is the tool of the force that guides us and navigates the force while exploring its energy's. Faith is within Metaverse and its a ::negative:: skill raising from our soul and spirit, brain and heart. Everyone has faith within themselves. True faith is the purest form of faith and is an achievement done with the help of true soul-searching and meditation. Prayers and blessings are done with faith and can be done in all directions. It's beautiful to pray for the sake of the family or friends sending positive energies in their direction, so is blessings done to one and each other.

The tools of faith are many and are best practice in harmony with yourself and your surroundings. Meditation gives you the opportunity to path in Metaverse and see for yourself how advanced faith is and can be. Faith is a force energy and a perfect directional energy to navigate in the force. Faith is the combined energies from heart and mind, soul and spirit. To seek out what you believe in is something you shouldn't be afraid of investing time into, it's beautiful and defines who you are in more than one direction. Faith doesn't belong to a religion or an ism it's a part of our very own nature and everyone is participating in it more or less. Faith is a force of nature as a natural outcome of the human being. It's a force and should be dealt with a healthy manner. To participate in faith requires training and the skill raises slowly for you. Meditating over Atom helps you to break down truths and understandings into their smallest building stones and aids you in your faith to get more focused and relaxed in your pathing of faith.

Faith is deeply rooted in your soul and spirit and should always be treated with respect. Today people tend to be seemingly out of faith but it's always there. Faith grows stronger when its utilized and is an evolving matter that should be dealt with in delicate manner. Don't underestimate the faith, especially when it's within the force.

···

.

.
Atom

Atom is the smallest building block in both versas, in other words both universe and Metaverse. It's what you reach when tearing apart or dividing something many times enough so there is nothing left. The only thing remaining is Atom. In order to reach Atom, you need to break down reality's so that you can see each building block alone and that helps you reveal truths about our nature and your life in more than one direction. Atom is so tiny you can't see it with your own eye, its invisible and in constant movement. Atom can be visualized in Metaverse and a helpful tool to utilize when meditating.

Atom is a very abstract tool and usually helps you clear your mind from thoughts while meditating. Atom is an advanced tool as well and can be used as a seed for a mentality planted and grown in Metaverse. You can utilize Atom as a dissector utility when defining in philosophy as well.

...
.
.

Poetry ONMO Justice

The art of True soul-searching. To be able to journey in yourself. To be able to sort out your subconscious and to see the truth about your life in all directions. To sort out good and bad deeds without taking a stand in rightfulness, meaning that you stand for your deeds no matter if they at the moment was justified or not. To be able to ransack your soul and spirit without any standing points in any direction in order to see the naked truth exactly the way it is. To put your soul and spirit before the eye of Exist and Nature and see yourself as the animal human being as you are. You walk your entire life and seek out all the deeds you have done without justifying them in any direction. Just to see the naked truth about yourself and who you truly are as a person.

It's painful and time consuming to go through the process of True soul-searching. It's painful because you see truths about yourself that hasn't been a problem for you earlier. Because you see the reality in your own flaws and weaknesses and what damage they caused your surroundings. Things in your everyday life behavioral pattern that you might have not reflected upon till this point. You see the harm you inflicted by just being yourself without even reflecting over it. You see the bad sides in a completely new dimension and that's painful since your more vulnerable when pathing True soul-searching. Even the smallest thing becomes an obstacle with bigger proportion. Feelings like pride becomes a blur of what's been correct and nice towards your surrounding or not.

It takes time to path the True soul-searching for real. Since you twist and turn your entire life in all direction in order to find out what kind of person you are and what the truth about your life is. You will find out what your down sides are and how they affect you in everyday life. You will get to see you in a new perspective as third person and in a healthy way that is. You learn about yourself by learning about your life in an exceptional way of understanding yourself as well as your soul and spirit. By defining yourself you will see your soul and spirit in a new ray of light. Your soul is your base in who you are and is limitless in all directions. Your soul is beautiful no matter how ugly it has been to reach the point for you to actually see it. You should be proud of your soul at all-time since it's the base for who you are and who you will become. To soul-search is beautiful once you reached that point and is something that should be done in harmony and peaceful surrounding environment. The depth of a human soul is infinity and a journey of its own kind. Meditating while soul-searching is to prefer when it helps you relax and become more focused on your journey. Soul-searching should be done at least once every tenth year or so, you probably haven't done it yet so the first time will be time consuming, and it will take a while to accomplish. It will be both pleasant and unpleasant journey to do the first time you do it. It's about revealing your entire life and all its dark corners and knots that has been lying around there in your subconscious. It's totally worth it. Its harsh and cruel the truth as it is in your lifetime, but you grow tremendously while pathing it and become much more aware about who you are and why you make decisions as you do. It's a cleansing process of your soul and spirit that takes devotion to accomplish. It could take a couple of weeks to accomplish it the first time you do it so don't think you can do it in a day or two. Don't worry about that. It's not a contest but something beautiful to accomplish, an investment in yourself that is priceless.

...

.

.

Meditation

Meditation is done constantly in different forms. You meditate when doing true soul-searching, when practicing the force and to raise your awareness. You meditate in order to journey in your inner soul and spirit to see the truths in yourself. You meditate to even out your senses and to empty yourself. You meditate to in touch with your inner energy's and to harmonize with universe. It's important to meditate for you to achieve enlightenment and to be able to reach total awareness. Total awareness is a state of being, when you have reached total completeness with your senses, soul and spirit. When your desires stop directing outwards and remains as an engine for harmony within yourself as complete being. When you are truly one with yourself in harmony and worldly matters no longer are.

Meditation is today a universal tool practiced all over the world with or without an ism to follow. You can practice your favorite method of meditation. Whether it's from other schools of Buddhism or stand-alone versions of meditation. The use of mantras is very efficient for reaching a clear state of being, emptying yourself of thoughts till you reach a state of just being. The position while meditating is flexible, you don't need to sit with crossed legs on the floor. Sitting in a chair or on the bed with a pillow behind your back leaning against the wall works just as fine. It's your body and you need to find a position that works well with your anatomy. Even lying down works for meditation. Find your own way to meditate where you can reach into yourself in harmony without discomfort. You can sit on your knees with a pillow beneath if you prefer that. Tai Chi is another great way to meditate, and it's done in movement.

With meditation you clear your mind of thoughts and empty yourself on emotions till you reach a state of blank being with only the inner energy's moving within you. You can then choose to plant a seed of harmony and surf that emotion while meditating. Or you can journey the ancient of exist in search of wisdom and enlightenment. You can start your meditation with a little prayer for example:

- I hereby devote myself to Exists ancient for wisdom and enlightenment in my meditation of harmony.

By doing that you give yourself a good start to the meditation and a clearer structure of the meditation. The prayer should frame the purpose of meditation and direct you onto the right path. So, if you are in the progress of true soul-searching, you frame the meditation with a prayer that's directed towards that topic. And can look like this:

- I hereby devote myself to true soul-searching in the eye of Exist and Nature. Poetry onno justice, may justice be done on my soul and spirit.

Its more powerful than you might think, don't underestimate the power of prayers.
Meditation is done for you in order to raise the ability of inner vision and to harmonize with all the different life energies mostly. To meditate over true soul-searching isn't done that frequently and is a noisy style of meditation. It's also a tool for you to make journeys in Metaverse when exploring elements and dimensions. When in meditative state you can easily

319

send positive energies of harmony and inner balance to others. However, it's a main tool to reach inner enlightenment and is a much easier practice once true soul-searching has been done. To find your self is a difficult journey and a great investment in yourself.

You should meditate frequently. A couple of times per week. Take your time to meditate don't wait for it to be possible, make it a part of your working week. You can meditate for five to sixty minutes a time. You can meditate even longer, just find rhythm where you have a chance to integrate it into your everyday life.
Join a Tai Chi or qi gong movement and do it twice a week that way. You can always take time to do it even if you have to wait till before you go to sleep there is always a moment where you can set of time for meditation. It doesn't have to be every day, but a couple a times a week is good enough for you. For the Dao Buddhist monk it should be a routine and a natural part of your lifestyle.

...

.

.

Metaverse

Is the ::negative:: to universe. Metaverse is always in motion in one way or another. Metaverse contains not just energies from all over universe but also thru out time. Metaverse is the picture of completeness that contains Astral Planes and Domains as well as Lanes and the so-called Virtual Lane of intercommunication.

Astral planes contain natures, elements, dimensions and metascapes presenting schools of all kinds of wisdom and metaskills.

The Domain of Death is an important part of both Versa, in other words both Metaverse and Universe. The Circle of Death with holds the "Soul and spirit Shards" from past life throughout time. Depending on your choices and events in life your shard will exist or dissolve when your life passes on. Your shards energy's gets redistributed into nature when dissolved depending on how you have lived your life. Your soul and spirit always leave a footprint in domain of death no matter if it dissolves or not. When a shard is finally done journeying it dissolves and become one with Exists ancient. You never really truly die, your life force continues to exist in one form or another even when you become a part of Exist ancient. Metaverse existed long before life on this planet did, long before the Big Bang that resulted in our galaxy among other sky body's. Just like universe, Metaverse is continuously growing and stores energies in all life forms and nature Universe has provided.

It's in Metaverse you get connected with the Force. You harmonize with all its energies in all possible directions. There are many tools to use when in contact with Metaverse. Faith is the foundation of it and used by many people today. To explore Metaverse you need patience and harmony. When using prayers, you can choose to send positive energies to other people or to "pray bless" yourself with harmonic energies. Meditation is a more powerful way to send harmonic energy's and helps you focus while practicing it. Exploring Metaverse is easiest done while meditating. The rich flora of different astral planes and lanes, domains, dimensions and element, are a beautiful experience and gives you inner harmony. Don't be afraid of the domain of death, it contains shards from spirits and souls from our past and is very peaceful place to explore and a very important part for people who are working with reincarnations and incarnations.

Don't forget the element of love. Love is in both Metaverse and universe, a force of nature and with the heart as its director. To explore love is an opportunity that many should be proud of to have the chance to do. Love is a force of Nature that flows in all directions, its energies are mysterious and shouldn't be taken lightly. The element of love flows through all dimensions, planes, lanes and domains. Even in the domain of death the element of love flows gently. The element of love is part of the force as well and a very important part it is. Hate is not an element but an equally important part in the yin and yang of the element of love. Love is truly blind in the sense that love doesn't make a difference in entity's when it comes to its own force of nature. Love is a force of nature and not a personal director.

Metaverse contains all kinds of forces of Exist and nature in all kinds of directions and all of them should be respected and treated in a delicate manner. The flavors of participants vary in wide range from healing to wiccan magic and everything in-between there as well. Both religions and other isms are very active within Metaverse with different approaches. As a Dao Buddhist you explore all schools and interpret them as advanced schools of life and whom we are. You can study any religion or ism with the foundation of Dao Buddhism as its base plate. Metaverse contains so much more then what has been explored by all the schools there already is so it's a necessity to approach it with all kinds of skills from both religions and isms. To path in Metaverse is an experience overwhelming and exciting that can be done during your entire lifetime. Your pathing will be covered with lots of mysterious and clouded puzzles and labyrinths. Exploring new dimensions and astral planes with magnificent metascapes.

...

.

.

Diversity

Diversity is our greatest strength and will always be that. We should be proud of our unique personalities and our diver's flora of personal personality's. We are all unique in our soul and spirit and that's just the way we are created. Natures makes us diverse by default, we are born in different colors, and we have different tastes just as we are without even trying. There will always be people that prefer same gender sex cause its how we are made out to be and there is nothing strange about it. We are over seven billion people today, what do you expect. We shouldn't be afraid of our diversity but learn to embrace it with respect and humbleness. It doesn't matter what color of your skin is, we are all equally equipped with heart and brain no matter where you come from. We should be proud of that our planet is so diverse as it is with the human species. Diversity's equals opportunity's and should always be affirmed thereafter. All life is diverse, that's just how nature is in its natural state of being, there is no reason going against nature.

We need diversity in nature as well as in personalities. The richer nature is in its flora of life the healthier our world will remain. The richer we are in diversity the more stimuli we get and that's healthy for our species. We see deserts growing because of lack of diversity in our natures eco system. If we don't care soon enough this planet will have lost its grandness in diversity and that's very unhealthy for all animal life upon this planet. We need a rich flora of life for future science to come as well as for future life to be brought further. We must learn to respect this planet and its eco system in order for us to be able to harmonize in future political maps of this planet. We can't just expect that nature will fix itself all the time as we are now. Nature needs respect in order to last as beautiful as it is today, we have already lost a great deal of nature and we continue to do so as long as we don't care enough. We need to learn to respect the planet we live upon for real.

...

.

Calibrational Lifestyle

The way of the senses. When you aim for the calibrational lifestyle you amend all your senses and everything you do is training. You train your senses in all directions and try to adjust yourself for them to be in equal harmony with each other. The eyes are dominant of your senses and the training is something you will have to do your entire life since the nature of humans depends heavily on the eye. Teas and spices are great training for the tongue since they contain all kinds of flavors and directions. Drink the tea with no sweetener or milk in it since it colors its original flavor. Listening to music with more than one track at a time is a way to train the ear but walking in nature listening to natures melody of all life is also a very good training. Your nose you train with foods and drinks, by paying attention to wildlife and its different flavors of scents.

Everything you do truly is training and should be considered as that. You meditate to keep harmony with your senses and to raise your awareness with them. When you meditate you clear you mind of all thoughts and reach a state of just being. Meditate in a surrounding with harmony, you can either have it quiet or put some smoothing music on low in the background to help you relax and reach the perfect state of mind where you have cleared out your thoughts and just be in a meditative state of harmony with your surroundings. Get comfortable when meditating. You can sit on your knees with a pillow underneath your kneecaps so it's comfortable for you.

You can use any position you feel like as long as it makes you comfortable in your harmony. Meditation is done with closed eyes or half closed. You can use mantras to aid your focus in clearing your mind. There is meditative music to get from stores that helps you come to pure mind and relaxation in your body.

Tai chi helps you to connect your body and mind in a harmonic way and is very useful for calibrational lifestyle. The way of the jellyfish is my own tai chi and is about to let your body go with the flow in a limbless manner. You simply imitate the motion of jellyfish with your entire body and let it flow through you. You do it to meditative music and let the music guide your body in any direction. It's a very free form of tai chi and it's about learning your body's functions in all direction. Other tai chi forms work just as fine and can be practiced all over the world today. It's important to let the body and mind to coexist and to connect in harmony. To let your senses, guide your body instead of the other way around.

In the art of reaching total awareness, it takes dedication and good amount of time invested into it. It's something you aim for throughout life and it's not a final state of being but rather an achievement by keeping it as a constant school in life. Your awareness is total when your mind and heart, spirit and soul together is as one without limitations of the world today. In a harmony of universal understanding and totally free from preconceived understandings. When your entity becomes the mother ship of your life and your soul and spirit with mind and heart is its pilot.

Calibrational lifestyle is about your senses and you in relation to your surroundings, about your inner energies in harmony with your interior as well as exterior. To be in harmony with yourself as well as your surroundings. Relations are everywhere and you harmonize with them in your everyday life. When in calibrational lifestyle you don't only reflect upon these relations but fully live with them in harmony and explore them with all your senses.

...

.

.

Reincarnations and incarnations

The rebirth of souls and spirits and what happens in life after death. Upon death the soul is being freed as well as the spirit into the domain of death. There the energy's will either dissolve and be redistributed or remain depending on the choices in life you made. The rebirth of souls and spirits occurs all the time when it comes to the once that remain intact. The dissolved shards go back into mother nature. Some shards chose to remain and watch over close ones. Others to be, in order for future events to happen such as reincarnations or incarnations. All souls and spirits are fresh as newborn and grows in same paste as life does. To be reborn you need to achieve it in life and is done by reaching total awareness within yourself. To be reborn is then a choice of your own and not something that happens by automatic. When being redistributed your energies are healed and sorted out for new compilations of souls and spirits. Shards can continue pathing and become astral beings as an achievement.

The soul and spirit are endless and can contain both reincarnations as well as incarnations. To achieve reincarnations and incarnations you must path the specific path of reincarnation or incarnation. Then you must reach a mutual agreement with it and do it one step at a time. The art of reincarnation and incarnation has nothing to do with split personality where the entity is unaware about its condition up till some point. Reincarnations are aware and done in mutual agreement of coexistence as a new core of your soul. You can achieve them in domain of death as well as from other astral beings in their own element or astral plane. It takes time to achieve them and a whole lot of devotion. They are also naturally reborn into an entity. Shards evolve thru time and the more ancient they are the harder they are to achieve. You don't become a reincarnated shard; you harmonize with them in mutual respect and understanding. It becomes a part of your soul and spirit in a mutual agreement. It's a path of progress with your own inner harmonies and energy's.

A demon tree takes time to complete and requires lots of respect for the unknown and bizarre. Inner demons are what you make them to and are a result of the subconscious and unknown for you and not the same as a reincarnated demon. Metaverse demons are advanced ancient beings that has evolved for a very long time. To reincarnate a demon, you have to be prepared to do some heavy true soul-searching. To harness a demon is something completely different and usually result in very bad harmonies. Trapped demons are not a pleasant sight since they are ripped from their natural element and no longer contains its natural surroundings. Demons often bother them self with ancient wisdom and pounder about existential questions. Demons and oriental dragons are much alike only different type of forces. Demons are very proud metaversical creatures because they represent the complete yin and yang of the element, astral plane, dimension or domain they come from and know it inside out, inch by inch in all directions in orbish. They are very humble when treated with respect in their own element and they require respect for their unique skills and knowledge. A demon ripped out of its context easily becomes chaotic and is best met by bringing it back to its right element. To explore demons, you must be gentle and bear an open mind. Demons shows you the truth in all directions even the uncomfortable ones, simply the truth as it is. They reveal the entire yin and yang with all flaws and benefits with no judgment in any direction just the simple truth as it is.

...
.

.
Sutra

- Follow your heart as long as it makes sense.

Your heart guides you more than you think. Your heart

is your director of love and harmony in life, and you should respect it at all times. As long as you don't harm or damage your surrounding or others your heart knows what's best for your well being. Its sometimes scary to listen to the heart because your heart and mind doesn't always speak the same language. Don't be afraid of listening to your heart and let your mind adjust to the heart for a change. You will be surprised of what you can learn about yourself when you listen to your heart. Heartily matters gives you quality in your life and great memory's as well.

- One step at a time.

Take it easy in life. You got an entire lifetime to accomplish all the goals you have and there is no rush in completing them as soon as possible. Life isn't a contest but a time of existence to experience for quite a while. If you rush life and just do it you will forget to live it and enjoy the small moments. Life is to be lived and feelings are to be felt. It's better to take one step at a time and see what direction the next step needs to be taken in rather than to rush it and need to redo whatever the task was you intended to do. Life lasts for a long time and is meant to be lived not just done. Build your life on a solid foundation step by step rather than to rush into things without closure.

- We are all equally diverse human beings

Mother nature has equipped us all equally with heart and brain and done us diverse in colors. It doesn't matter where on earth you live; you are as much human no matter what color your skin has. Our cultures are diverse cause that's what's nature is like when societies have evolved separated from each other. We are all animals on the very same planet. We are all children of mother earth. Our diversity is just natures natural way of being and is something we should be proud of.

- Be Cool, Be You, Be Smart.

Don't be afraid to be yourself. It's much cooler to be yourself and stand up for it than to try to be someone else and fake it. Don't fool yourself in life, try to see the truth as often as possible. Your life is yours to be lived so don't let others live it for you. Be smart and choose wisely when it comes to life and its different paths. Life is a long time and should always be considered thereafter. Don't waste your life by quitting, try to take things as they are and see it as growing with yourself each time you fail in any direction. Don't beat yourself up with failures but use the experience to understand yourself. You are the one that are in charge over your own self-esteem and no one else but you feel it. Don't let other people tell you what you should do or don't do, Be Cool and follow your own heart. Don't let other people tell you who you are, Be You and your automatic a person with dignity. Don't let other people tell you what you should chose, Be Smart and think for yourself. Dare to think outside the box and to see new paths where there has been none to begin with.

- See the truth as it is

Don't try to modify the truth with halfhearted lies about what is and is not. See the truth in it and try to learn from it rather than to pile up your subconscious with white and grey lies about your own life and its content. People can take the truth more than you think, if they can't don't lie just let it be. Dare to think outside the box and to question the reality you grow up in, it's not perfect and never will be either.

- Live your life

You have one lifetime to spend as you wish. Don't forget to live it and don't just do it. Live here and now, learn from your past and be aware about the future. Be smart and invest time in yourself and your self-awareness. Life is a long time, and you shouldn't strive to be older or younger than you are but respect its natural way of being in motion. Don't live your life thru others and don't let other live their lives thru you. Life is a true blessing and should be respected thereafter.

I'm not going to tell you how to live your life since there is no template to follow. You have one lifetime to live so take care of that opportunity. Your life will have different periods of quality's. What you enjoy at the age of twenty might not be the same at age of thirty and so on. You only have one life, never forget that.

...

.

Defense only

The Dao Buddhist has peace and chaos as a yin yang to confronting problems. We never attack, only defend our self and stand up for who we are. War is a failure of communication and should never be a solution. Dao Buddhists may practice any martial art training in order to defend them self of abuses. Martial training is good for your self-awareness and healthy for your body and mind as well as your soul and spirit. As a Dao Buddhist you don't seek trouble. You always strive to approach with a humble mind and sees any fellow being as an equally diverse being. However, we aid the weak when possible and look after our own kin. There is nothing wrong with sharing from yourself but always do it with dignity and humbleness. It's the same when standing up for yourself and your beliefs, do it heartily from your heart and with mindfulness.

...

.

Erotica
The Dimension – The Art – The Element Sex

Truth is: Sex isn't less important as other things in your life.
Truth is: Sex isn't more important as other things in your life.
Truth is: Sex is equally important as other things in

your life

Sex isn't only about the orgasm, what positions and skills you have trained in, the physical interaction, the moods of mentalities in the element of Lust, mutual achievement in presence, the art of senses in coexistent, feelings experiencing, respect, Heart – Soul – Spirit – Mind

Sex is a harmony between all those facts and factors in SameTime, and great sex is about great coexistence between the entity/s performing this delicate and extraordinary: Dance – Ritual; "of Eroticay in perfection of balance between" – Minds – Hearts – Souls – Spirits – Flesh – Lust – Desire – Physics – Senses – Presents – Feelings

Eroticay is a state of being – where all parts keep its promised virtue, you all know what's going to happen and you all build each other up to the points you want and need to be.. the sex itself is just an equal part of all the lusts and sensual intercourses with each other no matter if it's done on two or more people in SameTime. Eroticay is the dance of erotica where all parts get satisfied during the entire session of Eroticay. Eroticay can go on for days if you want it to and isn't at all, all about sexual intercourse but all emotions are equally important, and the physical parts can be easily divided throughout the entire session and several orgasms are to anticipate during a longer session of Eroticay. Food or incenses is perfect for longer sessions of Eroticay. No alcohol though. Never use alcohol in Eroticay. Eroticay truly is a state of being where you fuel each other with positive sensual and sexual stimuli with your eyes and your words, stimulating both your body's self-esteem as well as sexual self-esteem with both physical contacts as well as eye looks and words. Constantly boosting each other's ego to maximize the stimuli of each other during the entire act. But deserve it from each other don't just give it away but work for it both of you by letting go of your inhibitions. The more all of you free yourself from internal inhibitions the more you reward each other with boosted egos in all sensual and sexual directions. Demand your participants to free their minds and let go of their inhibitions. Become each other's master and commanders don't lock up in single roles, let each other play fully and freely with roles and taste the sweetness of domination as well as submission. Don't fear any of BDSMs tools to use light to begin with but not obviously but as you see come fit. Whips, ropes, anything but it doesn't have to be a whip it can be a belt, or your hand and it doesn't have to be a rope it can be a bathrobe ribbon or a scarf. Don't fear your inner feelings and emotions. Dive into Eroticay with excitement and easy thrills both indoors and outdoors. The penetration act will just be a merely part of it, but it will for sure be a part of it. That's what differs. When you find True Eroticay partners you will have wonderful times with them. And when it comes to the physically don't have sex but calibrate each other with your eyes, mouths, hands and genitals. Explore each other's entity's thoroughly and desirable. Don't lick or suck but explore with your mouth, tong and use your hands all over the entity's not just the genitals. Use your tong as an explorer all over the entity even over and in the as hole. There is no taboos what so ever in Eroticay when it's done properly. The entire entity is an endogen zone. Calibrate the entities with your hands, tong, eyes, genital and don't fuck it. After the first physical engagement with orgasms as result you continue to build each other but calmly to begin with enjoying thoroughly what's just been and maybe eat some prepared or easy to prepare food or snack remain in the state of being in Eroticay by never stopping being in it simply. It's not all about being super horney but being edgy in emotions no matter what thrill you're in at the moment. Refer to the Eroticay act in words and keep boosting each other's egos with sensual and sexual ego boosts, then you might want to watch some movie maybe an erotically one but even normal one as long as the movie isn't the important part of it even though you might actually watch a movie, never be afraid stop watching and continue the dance of Eroticay. You can as well just focus on each other and still be in Eroticay recharging and enjoying each other's company and tenderness, putting you all in new moods with new thrills and challenges to spin on. This my friend is what is called Eroticay.

Sex is part of human nature and a natural instinct. Don't abuse or misuse sex, it has borders just like any other skill set. Be mature about your sexuality and be proud over your capability to nurture it with dignity. Sex is a social skill and should be respected thereafter. Sex is something you can have between good friends as well as partners. Or with perfect strangers as matter of fact as well. Sex IS a SOCIAL skill in many ways. It can be quick, and it can be long, all depending on the mood and circumstances. No matter nature of it, it should always be respected as Eroticay. Eroticay explores all sexes both male and female no matter your own gender. We are all sexual in the eye of mother nature and Exist no matter your previous preferences. Sex is a way to bound new relations in new dimensions. To be able to bridge new paths of coexistence. Love is not the same thing as sex here. Eroticay invites your senses to explore and coexist with other entities in a very intimate way of lust. Lust is a beautiful feeling to surf on when done with equal minded entities. Don't ever go against free will and nature. Explore and befriend with your anus in order to enjoy anal orgasms during Eroticay. Anal pleasure is an important part of everyone's life both male and female, everyone deserves a great sex life and great orgasms. The earlier you explore your anus the richer your adult life will become when it comes to great sex and orgasms. Don't be a stranger to your anus. All humans are sexual in their sexual orientation that's just how we are created with the anatomical nerve maps around the anus for both male and females. When we have Sexual as default sexual orientation as the normality norm people will look at each other in a different way already from childhood. People will automatically consider love and sexual interactions between both males and females no matter your own gender, and not exclude any options as people do in the old world.

When going for reproduction aim for a life mate with whom you can raise the child together with. Try to find a life mate where the relation can evolve together for long enough time so the kid/kids can grow up with two parents for as long as possible. Where love is a natural element and not a proof of ownership.

...

.

Dimensions and Elements

Dimensions:

0 - Metaverse – Nothing is everything
1 - Time
2 - Movement – Motion – Energy
3 - The dot – Genesis
4 - The line
5 - A plane – A surface
6 - A Cube – The room
7 – Pulse
8 – Exception

Forces of Elements:

Metaverse
Love
Water
Fire
Earth
Air
Space
Elementals

Metaverse is both a Dimension and an Element.

...

.

Medley

- You have now witnessed Dao Buddhism in its simplicity.

Dao Buddhism is simply a transparent layer of this universe and this world with all religions and isms and science in it. It considers the world from a point of evolution where all nature is accepted as they are and not what some template pretends it to be. It accepts the parallel verse of Metaverse as a negative to universe and an ordinary fact even if its relatively unexplored still. It respects the nature of this planet as vital for all of opportunity of life here on Earth. It considers the human entity sexual in its sexual orientation no matter gender, and sexuality as an admitted social skill. Death is not an end but a passing on for the soul and spirit into new forms of being.

Dao Buddhists

Keeps their true faith closest to their heart

Consider diversity to be our greatest strength

Amend their free sexual lifestyle and respects love for its true nature.

Are master and commanders of their own life's and are aware about the quality of it is their own responsibility.

Are proud with dignity and are humble at heart.

Sees the truth as it is, both within them self as well as their surroundings.

Stands for the foundation of Exist and Nature.

Keeps Dao Buddhism as a base plate for their own life's values.

Nurture its faith and respect the force at all times.

...

.

- So, what's life all about then?

Isn't it so that it truly is what we make of it and that its totally up to our self what we chose what we do with it.

- Sure is honey

As I see it there is three answers to this so-called meaning of life; one very long which this book is a foundation of to that answer one short one that can be reduced to four words but is actually a directional variable and goes like this:

- You can say: Life is a flavor

- Meaning Life is flavors of everything and nothing you taste them, and you feel them. Flavors of love and hate. Flavors of success and failure. Flavors of motherhood and fatherhood. Flavors of happiness and sadness.

So, Life is a flavor & Life is Flavors is the directional variable and looks like this:

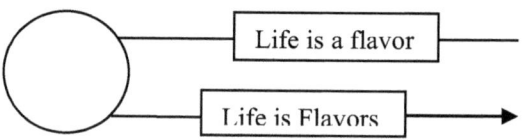

Where the circle is you and "Life is a flavor" a static and "Life is flavors" is a floater meaning it moves in any direction. Then there is the really short answer that's only one word, that answer is only provided to other Dao Buddhist Monks. To put it Dao Buddhism way: Life is yours to be lived and not done and your feelings are yours to be felt and not ignored so respect your life and respect your feelings at all times.

...
.

.

What is it that we are actually talking about here when it comes to size of change and in perspective to what. We are talking about the fact that we will become one nation with one language, one currency, one law and one mutual timeline.

And we realize that there will be lots of changes all over the world no matter what direction they are. We will always need to make a lot of changes for an event like this to occur.

- And what is being suggested

Well that we all together take this opportunity of change and make the best out of it for us all. That we choose to give us the biggest and greatest update of them all because we all know this event will go to history, why not go to history with class and style then. Today we have so much knowledge and skills, not to mention technology. We can create real time simulations with different new financial eco system, let the financial elite, philosophers and professors and university's all over the world compete against each other, country by country then continent by continent.

We have the opportunity to once and for all decide and take control over everything, we can decide that we will be the best ever living species to maintain the opportunity off life. We can decide that we will be the best in creating a valuable and comforting lifestyle. We can decide to have the highest possible ever baseline economy ever. An economy that gives us all great standards and still leaves room for proper achievements. We need to decide that we must have high responsibility's in maintaining the opportunity of life in all its glory.

Civil war is out of question since we are all living under the same structure. Our diversity really is our greatest strength. The more species and the more differentiation the greater our future will be for us all. The more species that get extinct, and the more you try to make people the same the more grayscale the reality becomes. We need diversity. Because we must understand the full depth of our own anatomy and its DNA structure just like everything else in this opportunity of life. And we are different and unique by nature. That's just the way we are. We are extraordinary because of our curiosity. That's the main skill that brings us forward.

...

.

.

We have a planet to take care of, a planet to nurture and build up. We are all animals on the same planet, and we need to shape it up and renew our normality norms, so they fit the animal human being as they truly are.

- But why would we do this? Isnt that a great sacrifice for doing that.

- Sure is.

- Have no illusion that there wont be a sacrifice here.

We are looking at one of the biggest sacrifices throughout history, only this time it won't be a question about sacrifice cows or other animals, not human life's either. This one will be about our very own time and the letting go of what's been for what's to be. The good news is that this will be the most relative expensive step in history as well. One planet, one nation, one currency, one timeline, one law and one language. Don't forget that. It will happen sooner or later, and we happen to live in the time era when it's about to happen. No matter when it happens the very same issues will remain. The new systems need to be developed and investigated truly. The elections will be worldwide we will all have to learn the new language we will all have to adjust our currency so that we all have the same. Our Economy system needs to be redefined in order for it to work properly. And while we are on those steps we might as well let all nations universities cooperate and compete in developing as smart financially system we can get, given the base variable Opportunity of life to use as baseline for it. We are all familiar with the concept of TV shows like "So you think you can dance" and "Idol". So, we can easily make those contest seasonal TV shows with mixed entertainment and progress shows, where all the people can call and vote for suggestions and then when each country has chosen their best solution that they will send to final that will go the year after its done, all country's presents their solution. Very much like the "Eurovision Song Contest". Only this is about our own planet's directions in our lives. In this type of communication, the first season or year depending on what we all agree upon we will have created over 195 different solutions of Eco systems of Finance, And in opposite to weakest link choice of a primal solution to erase that bit we chose the more sophisticated way and improves that area if there is a chance that is. We will then during the entire season combine and work out solutions containing the most necessary variables that we expect out of this kind of solution, and we don't quit until we all have contributed with a complete ecosystem for finance. Utilizing every university and professor and expertise in relation to the specific Eco System. Same goes for suggestion and creation of the Eco system of language. The result is that all of a sudden we will have about 200 choices and from those 200 suggestions we will be able to chose and rebuild them into 10 superior solutions over the next season/year depending on what reality is like, These 10 Superior Ecosystems will then be the new base for what is to become our most possible advanced civilization that has ever existed within one single Ultimate Eco system of finance, one Ultimate Eco system of Communication, One Ultimate, Awesome, Erotic, Wonderful, High Tech, Existence as Protectors and care takers of life.

We better go for that choice of many reasons, one of the other reasons are since The day Alien life comes in contact with us they will for sure be more advanced than us unless we find them first but even then they still might be more advanced. Tomorrow keeps obstacles, tests and trials of proportions we cannot imagine today and none of them we will be able to conquer if we chose not to take this step in evolving our civilization. Those obstacles will require nothing less than our total cooperation in existence at all direction and nothing else will save us. We are about to become such an advanced civilization by being our own species in a unified world in our part of universe. By accomplishing this we will create a completely new and fresh foundation for us all and also lay out the blueprints for total success and control of the opportunity of life. We will create the base from where we will grow in any direction we like. And the good news is that all it will ever cost us is time. We can keep improving our lifestyle for eternity. We will eventually change shape and form of our self by nature, however that will take longer time then in a near future. We won't have to kill anyone here. War will eventually fade out and evolutionary progress will grow with science as its brother.

- Hehe we are dealing with the power of peace here... remember =)

...

.

It's time for us to learn from our past for real. We are going to use same sort of solution as been used many times before. By Native Americans, the Indians. Except we don't need to war in-between. We are going to learn how to properly negotiate and overcome our fears of accepting our true nature as human beings. No matter how separate opinions they had and no matter how much they hated each other they could almost always take a break from everything, sit down and smoke a peace pipe and then talk reason and peace. Reaching agreements where non was able to be reached. The leaders of tomorrow will be represented by both a male and a female since that's how different we are. And two people from each continent one female and one male representing the continent they come from. They will have worldwide networks as well as great enough organization up close them. We will have different climates in different continents only now we are united and vaster in both communication and education. We will be able to make sure we can provide food so it's more than enough for the whole population by actually planning the environment over the whole planet deciding how much that is a must for us to always have enough food, medicals, education and a roof over the head. We all need stimulation in form of work, that won't change. Too much dead free time depress people.

This way we will all have a word and since it is for our own evolution we will all aim in the same direction. To make our life and every day of it as good as possible for all of us. We will probably need to create new

Networks for that. A Super network including All the media with TV, Commercials, Schools, Videos, Radio, Movies, Internet, Communities, Games, you name it, we must learn how to cooperate with all kinds of entertainment that we will need in order to communicate, and it needs to be covering the entire planet. The super network will host many channels. Channels for educational purposes in linguistics and one that shows different evolutionary facts and truths. One where the ongoing ideas and progress reports of the work.

...

.

.

At first every nation will have to do their very best in coming up with a solution to represent in the finals. And since we all need to do our best since it's our own future we are calculating here. The best solution will probably not be a single solution but the combination of the best parts from different solutions that are combined to the very best solution. And that's exactly the same way it will be done in the pre final. To take all the pre finalists during another season of that TV show come up with about ten or maybe more new or existing solution. From there the finals takes part in its own season. There will be progress reports at every show and there will be objects voting for the nations as well as the possibility for the nation to mail suggestion. The contest will have rules that states that to be an Valid proposal it must contain a step by step guide in how to move from the point we are at today, What the goal is and what the steps are to take in order to get there. It must contain a valid time estimation on how long time the different steps might take. It must also contain the need in employment sources as well as an estimation and a perfectly well-planned financial plan in that includes the following corner stone's: Costs and possibilities in resources, as in hardware, software and Employment. This must also be in relation to the Base "Opportunity of Life" and Our evolutionary timeline. The Goal and God must always be the very foundation of our existence. For the Opportunity of life with us in it. To see this planet as a part of our basic needs in continuance of existence.

...

.

.

- I dare you. I dare you who ever reads this to think about what people do you know and what can you do. I dare you to recommend this book kindly to anyone that you might think can help out or if nothing else another person spreading the word.

In order to become one planet, one nation, one language and one currency a total change is needed and that's just simple facts.
There will be competitors all over the world. The competitors will consist of different university's and each of them representing a team of doctors, scientists and master economist as well as political and Math geniuses and students. First season will be about each

individual team to come up with best possible solution where the criteria is to make sure we create an Eco system of finance where everybody must have a high enough standard in life throughout all life no matter if young or old and always have access to education, roof over the head and enough for a good quality life. Why do we settle with less? And in opposite to weakest link where they eliminate the weakest link, we chose to take the weakest link and make it stronger by any means necessary if that's an option that is. The more we all understand and the more we all can see and maneuver in the understanding and controlling of quality life, the more we will grow in awareness. The higher our awareness is and the more we all exist in the reality dance of stimulation in our diversity the more we will all become as one united life form of greatness. That's when we become God (total aware that is). We can only live godlike when we all understand respect each other as we are built, and all the opportunity's our DNA is giving us. When we learn to truly say We ARE, then we will truly be total aware. We are already creating our own futures, why not make the best of it. We already know that a third world war with nuclear will destroy us, we already know that we can kill and destroy and be completely destructive. We not only know we can, but we have also managed to succeed not to take those steps much enough to still exist. We always overcome fear with responsibility, respect and understanding. Never with recklessness. Recklessness and violence expresses, release and ease of negative emotions and feelings. However, fear is still a part of it. But what's even worse is to choose to live in denial about it. That causes more damage over time

in proportions that's not even close to the damage
then the way to try to deal with it in peaceful angry
managed ways.

...

.

.

- Let's hold on a moment shall we

- What's being suggested here, isn't
  it just crazy talk?

When we go for the option of uniting this planet, we all
of a sudden have new opportunity's that wasn't there
before. As it is today, we don't have this kind of
possibility. We all of a sudden have a complete planet
with different domains/continents that are divided in
countries. To begin with not all countries will join this
venture in the beginning but they will all come in time.
When doing this merger every single country will all of
a sudden count as a source of production. Every
country has expertise within all the political fields and
instead of letting a few do the math we all of a sudden
can have hundreds of choices and utilize the expertise
all over the world making a wide road to path on
rather than a thin line to balance on. This is what
happens when we learn to say we are for real. We will
be able to for the first time in history provide politics
with several cores and make it more alive than ever.
The very nature of politics will become a living
organism where the politicians are working on the fine
tuning of the base plate provided by the people.

Country's will become regions or states that still care takes their own business.

- The people will always be the heart of every country no matter how its defined in the future

Each region will become a DNA strain of content for the political organ that will rule on this planet. We will be able to build a road for every opportunity we see coming and make sure we always succeed in taking many steps enough in order to reach that goal. With hundreds of regions supplying their own solution, their own DNA strain of possibility. We will be able to choose the best parts creating one superior strain that will be far better than the ones we create today with one option created by a few. There will be so many different options both sane and crazy and together they become the perfect blend of alternatives. We will utilize the power of plenty and build roads we wouldn't dream of today. To have the opportunity where each country uses their elite to compose the roadmaps of future possibility's is only possible when we are united as one country, one law, one currency, one language and one timeline. This is about the true power of: We Are in its completeness.

Politicians will be more of a caretaker and maintainer of the systems that are to be in place. They will be the ones putting the political map in place every time there is a new progress ready. They will deal with the final product that has been compiled from the world elite group. They suggest what comes next and people vote for the suggested topic in order to see where we are heading. This way politicians will have a completely new behavior in its existence. They will be the ones that keeps an eye on everything so that it remains in control and alert if there is something that needs a patch or an update. We will have an organic living political movement that will breathe of opportunity and progress in a never ending spiral upwards. We will for the first time have evolution as a part of our political organ.

- The power of We are is quite amazing dont you think =)

We will have room for all kinds of solutions, and we simply chose to do them one step at a time so that we always remain in control and see what's the next best step to take in order to take many steps enough to reach our goal.

...
.

.

Time is out of essence here. We will need to reach one currency in order to be able to take the step to have time as our main currency. We need to take that middle step in order to get it right. Time is vital when you build roads to take many steps enough in order to reach a goal. And it can't be utilized in the same extent in today's financially eco system since there is no reward but only cost to prepare for steps to take. To live in era of where time is the economy the social awareness must reach a higher understanding of what true equality is about. Something the societies of today isn't ready for yet. True equality is something that is reached in the middle step, one nation, one currency, one language, one law and one timeline. Not until that is reached will we be able to utilize time as a currency. When time is the main currency, we will see new natures of investors of time where carefulness will be rewarded and a more common phenomenon. Compared to today where time is supposed to be money and many times projects and products gets less good quality or get canceled due to high costs of money, Time and money isn't related to each other today even though there is a base of time in somewhat extent. Time doesn't get its true nature revealed with the current system. To invest in time is to take it slow when it needs to be done so and to go fast when the possibility is place. To invest in time means you are thoroughly in each and every step you take. The professions of today within economy will change into investors of time and will need same amount of education as today. Time really is a dimension of itself and shouldn't be taking lightly.

...

.

.

A new world order will rise where democracy will get a new definition and there will be new ages to come with it. We will live as caretaker of the nature of this planet and bring it further. We will have evolution as a new god instead of money and religions. We will become brothers and sisters for real and equality will be deeply rooted in the new normality norm template. We will be proud of our diversity and see the strength in our true nature. We will saddle the role of predator's true nature and finally become a higher form of civilization. The true roots of us will aid us unite, the roots of our mother nature that is.

- Bob Marley was close to the truth he just didn't drew the truth far enough to see its completeness.

- Roots unite for sure =)

By seeing the truth about our evolution, we will all be able to see we are all children of mother nature. That we are as diverse as we are.

- Mother nature supports diversity why shouldn't we do that as well, its in our nature.

The awakening is just a phase that will only last a couple of years till we reach the new world order.

To become caretakers of this planet might sound dull but it is a must for us in order to be able to raise in population as we do today. Today we are still fine, but we are on a brink here and it needs attention for our future to be. To unite is more vital than people think and for our next coming generations its of utterly importance that we take a turn and start to take responsibility for our continued existence. We cannot simply continue the way we are today if we want to continue to exist in a healthy manner. The way we live today will lead to prematurely end this opportunity of life. We still have time to take it easy, but it better start to change sooner than later. A third world war is not a solution it's a failure. We must be able to take care of the planet we live upon for us to continue to exist in the future. This planet has a limit to what it can withhold, and we must respect that. Our future is in need of the diversity we have here in our nature. We need a rich flora of life in all direction in order to have a chance to bring this nature further in as many ways as possible.

...

.

.

This isn't just about an option we have it's a necessary doing for our future and a must for us to be able to deal with future evolution. We must put aside the god of money and start seeing our self in a bigger picture where our next coming generations are as vital as our own. We can't continue to expect that nature will recover from whatever we put her thru. We have today forgotten what the inheritance of this planet is about. The generations of tomorrow have a hard work ahead of them because we no longer keep generational thinking as a part of our foundation.

Technology in all its glory by all means but it has clouded the awareness of our foundation our planet. We do need our technology more than ever, but we must also see our nature and its limitations. This planet needs it diversity in nature in order for the eco system

to be as healthy as possible. We don't know what species and nature we need in order to start new ecosystems on other planets are. We don't know what flora to compose for the different environments that are to come yet. We need the diversity for many reasons not just our self but
for the future to come as well.

...
.

.:

Venus might be used as a garbage dumpster in the future. Making us able to get rid of too dangerous waste such as nuclear waste that is too difficult for this planet to handle. It will take a complicated solution since we will have to drop it from the atmosphere in some way but it's doable.

:.

.

The world of today is deceived by the tabu about anal sex and the normality norm that rules the world makes humanity blind to the truth. Today people don't know that the greatest orgasm pleasure is the anal orgasm and therefore they don't naturally learn how to experience anal sex. Both men and woman have the anal orgasm as their greatest pleasure point and men with the addition of the prostate gland has an even greater orgasm pleasure. Today people grow up without these facts about the straight normality norm and are shaped by media and common knowledge that the natural state of sexual being is straight. That is a lie we have been living in for thousands of years. In the new world that will change with the start from school. We will have proper sexual education teaching the truth about anal sex and anal orgasm explaining in detail how the human nerve system anatomy map is. We will also change the media on all levels to reflect the human's true sexual nature with movies and TV showing a natural state of man and women having sex with both sexes. And men preferring anal sex to get the maximum stimuli. With a common foundation and well-known fact that anal orgasm is the greatest pleasure point for both sexes the world picture will change, and the so-called hetero normality norm will die out. Humans are truly sexual in its normality norm and their taste is bisexual. It has only been ruled out because today's norm so strongly erases the natural choice of allowing yourself to be attracted to the same sex. Only a few brave ones allow them self to be attracted to the same sex today and they are considered a minority. When it's a common understanding that you are sexual and mix with both sexes the choice will come naturally to be with both men and women for both sexes. It's understandable that a man becomes homosexual but never again straight, the man always has a reason to have anal sex because anal orgasm for man is so much greater pleasure then normal orgasm. Today's normality norm has failed for thousands of years to put something as simple as this together because of tabu. And the two main religions have done a great job to make sure we don't live in a true world. When people grow up with this understanding the sexuality will come naturally, and no one will wonder or think it's strange to be with the same sex as yourself. The world of tomorrow will look completely different to what you have seen today. Hate crimes towards sexually differences will no longer exist. We will live a mature and respectful life where everyone's sex life will improve majorly. Everyone can enjoy experience an anal orgasm both man and women and everyone can improve their sex life by open up their mind and see the truth about sexual stimuli. This is a natural step for humanity to take, we are evolving on all levels and the era of the heterosexual normality norm has come to an end.

...

.

.

Politics will be more organic, and politicians will take the role of conductors making sure that the melody of evolution always remains intact and that all components are included for us, so we never lose track of where we are and are heading. We will see a new era where peoples exceptionality will be preserved and utilized in a much greater extent than today. There will be a new status to the universities of the world today. We will have senior students working with finance and evolutionary projects in cooperation with professors and the rest of the elite. The reason to involve senior students is that they aren't so jaded in the old world they are quite fresh in the mentality of thinking outside the box.

- And that my friend is a valuable resource.

It's about providing each opportunity with as much

fuel as possible rather than to limit it too only a few. We can't choose not to when dealing with a delicate matter such as this world everyday existence. Each country has university's that are all containing highly educated people, and they should utilize their environment to the fullest since it's a time of opening doors for future comings. Universities are already utilized by the corporate world of today only in a less frequent way. We need our people that has future visions in a fresh mind. They will of course be accompanied of professional elite and together they make a team in a grand mix of relative realities. By learning to say we are for real we will provide this planet with a new core and that core will be us, the human species that's all of a sudden coexist with this planet rather than to leech of it.

...

.

.

A structure like this is beneficial for evolutionary progress and is only possible when we all are together as one. It will work just fine even if only half the world joins the new world order to begin with. It will take time to reach this mutual existence, but we will reach it no matter what you think about it. And it might be closer to it than what we believe today. It's a necessity for our future being and our younger generations will have to wake up and see the truth as is in them self. It is sad to see the world of today and the lack of generational thinking. The complete absence of future visions. We are so deeply rooted in the mentality of I am when we really need to learn to be we are. I am will always be part of our life no matter what.

The power of "we are" is massive and should be dealt with great responsibility. It's easy to talk about it but it takes a mature mentality to practice it. The awakening is a must be in order for this planet to continue to exist. We must put diversity into our normality norm template and learn to be proud with dignity. We can't reach these types of agreements as long as we keep neglecting simple truths such as our diversity. We must put our evolution in our normality norm as well since we today change in faster paste than ever. It's vital to keep generational thinking as a base plate when the population reaches the amount of people we have today. And it's vital that the awakening happens before it's too late, before we reach the point of no return.

The reason to this political approach is that politics needs to come alive. It has stagnated over the years that has been. Today we understand outsourcing as a concept and the tasks of politics are too delicate matter to only let a few handholds it in the future to be. When we unite there is a need to broaden our political view and to have as many options as possible. We must learn to live with politics as a living organism where the people have the right to vote for what's best for them. Politics exist for the people not the other way around.

...

.

.

The future political organ will most likely be out of a

nature where all sides are to be included. The red, the blue and the green together as an organism rather than today's order of just this or just that. The red drop will represent the heartily matters and be the ones combining the different solutions and putting them to place with their calibrations. The blue drop will be representing the truth for today and will be the ones out in the field conducting their teams of contributors, communicating constantly with the red drop so that we constantly take many step enough in order to reach our goal, the green line of environmentalist and evolution that surrounds them both will represent our opportunity of life and will constantly keep track of evolutionary progress and makes sure our nature is part of our base plate at all time. The organs will be a mix of all modern parties in order to get the whole picture of completeness when calibrating tomorrow. Each region/country will have their own yin yang of red, blue and green. The regions will keep good communication all the time with each other exchanging information and progress results. Every fourth year there will be a patch/update time where we vote on what to put on the plate for the next coming four years. What to evolve and what to start to explore. Politicians will probably last for eight years before election takes place, so they have a fair chance to be part of the evolving structures for real. Some might even be reelected. There will be remnants of the old political structure in sense of different parties with the blue and the red and the green. Only now they will be more advanced schools of calibrations, relational thinking, evolutionary thinking, generationally thinking and many other aspects in order for them to be able to work with future tasks within the political organism. From these party's they are then elected to the political organ that is in place for maintaining and providing solutions to the people. Even these so-called political parties are represented with one male and one female in order to reflect the human species. We will reflect the human everywhere in its true nature as both male and female.

...
.

- The world needs you.

This book is just one out of many steps for people to take. A change always starts with yourself. The book contains lots of sensitive topics that you might not reflect over in your everyday life. However, its vital you wake up and start to see this planet as a living organism and care about the future. Don't you want your children to have a nice place to grow up in, not to mention your grandchildren.

- We are all animals on the very same planet.

We can't continue the same way we do today neglecting the simple truths that's been shared so far. Peace is by far a greater engine for our evolution to come and a necessity for us. It doesn't matter how you lived your life and what your mentality's been so far. Humanity needs to shape up and that's a fact.

- And it starts with you.

True equality scares more people than you think and
it's a matter of our evolution. People tend to talk about
equality as long as it concerns them self but has a hard
time to see its complete picture of truth. The hypocrisy
we live in needs to come to an end. We must
Learn to see the diversity in our reality as it is. The laws
should reflect the true nature of what
the human species is about. We can't expect a healthy
society when we don't dare to see the truth as it is.
The truth needs to be totally naked with no censorship.

- Dare to say yes to this
opportunity of life existence in
eternity into infinity.

...

.

We do this step by step in order to reach the new world order.

The New World Order

One Versa – One Planet – One Nation

Time as financial eco system

One Language

One Timeline – Year 0 again

One Law

We are all equally equipped with Heart and Brain

Dao Buddhism as foundation of total Normality Norm

True: Faith – Truth – Love – Equality - Coexistence

...

·

With the new world order in place, we don't have to worry about money anymore. We can manage planet earth in a completely new way. We can make sure there is enough food for everyone by managing the food production all over the planet and we can manage our nature so it will be as healthy as possible, and every company can invest in healthy environmental solutions so that our nature will be as healthy as possible. We can manage animal life and nature to flourish and grow stronger by managing the environment on the planet and make free zones for nature and build cities on the height for our growing population. We can invest enough time and resources in electric cars, so we don't need gasoline anymore. We can build up educational system all over the world for us so we can educate our self in the fast paste changing time we live in. We can make sure everyone gets great healthcare with enough people working. We wouldn't have to worry about unemployment anymore because we can always educate our self-further to get a job somewhere. We could make sure we use the healthiest Energy resources for our planet all over the planet. We never have to worry about financial cost for projects no matter how big they are. All this is possible because Time is now our currency, and we manage time for everything we do. We plan how long things will take and we can plan our planets resources so that we always have enough. From this point we can start thinking about how great we want our future to be for real.

...

·

The End

- Here you have it. I hope the proposal was in your flavor =)

- Id like to take this opportunity to thank you for hearing me out. I hope you have had a time full of emotions reading this book and that your eyes opened up slowly.

- Its been a pleasant time we had together, and I have enjoyed every moment of it =)

- Till we meet again. Maybe in another book or maybe in real life. I wish you happy journey in your life.

- May the force be with you.

Lovingly regards
Medusa Loveheart

Books by Medusa Loveheart.

1. The Proposal A new arrival: Dao Buddha
2. One Unity Now and beyond

Website

www.daobuddhism.net